ETHNOGRAPHIES OF WORK

RESEARCH IN THE SOCIOLOGY OF WORK

Editor-in-Chief: Rick Delbridge

Associate Editors: Andreas (Andi) Pekarek, Gretchen Purser and Markus Helfen

Recent Volumes:

Volume 1:	Class Consciousness
Volume 2:	Peripheral Workers
Volume 3:	Unemployment
Volume 4:	High Tech Work
Volume 5:	The Meaning of Work
Volume 6:	The Globalization of Work
Volume 7:	Work and Family
Volume 8:	Deviance in the Workplace
Volume 9:	Marginal Employment
Volume 10:	Transformation of Work
Volume 11:	Labor Revitalization: Global Perspectives and New Initiatives
Volume 12:	The Sociology of Job Training
Volume 13:	Globalism/Localism at Work
Volume 14:	Diversity in the Workforce
Volume 15:	Entrepreneurship
Volume 16:	Worker Participation: Current Research and Future Trends
Volume 17:	Work Place Temporalities
Volume 18:	Economic Sociology of Work
Volume 19:	Work and Organizations in China After Thirty Years of Transition
Volume 20:	Gender and Sexuality in the Workplace
Volume 21:	Institutions and Entrepreneurship
Volume 22:	Part 1: Comparing European Workers Part A Part 2: Comparing European Workers Part B: Policies and Institutions
Volume 23:	Religion, Work, and Inequality
Volume 24:	Networks, Work and Inequality
Volume 25:	Adolescent Experiences and Adult Work Outcomes: Connections and Causes
Volume 26:	Work and Family in the New Economy
Volume 27:	Immigration and Work
Volume 28:	A Gedenkschrift to Randy Hodson: Working with Dignity
Volume 29:	Research in the Sociology of Work
Volume 30:	Emerging Conceptions of Work, Management and the Labor Market
Volume 31:	Precarious Work
Volume 32:	Race, Identity and Work
Volume 33:	Work and Labor in the Digital Age
Volume 34:	Professional Work: Knowledge, Power and Social Inequalities

EDITORIAL ADVISORY BOARD

RESEARCH IN THE SOCIOLOGY OF WORK
VOLUME 35

ETHNOGRAPHIES OF WORK

EDITED BY

RICK DELBRIDGE
Cardiff University, UK

MARKUS HELFEN
Hertie School, Germany

ANDREAS PEKAREK
University of Melbourne, Australia

AND

GRETCHEN PURSER
Syracuse University, USA

emerald
PUBLISHING

United Kingdom – North America – Japan
India – Malaysia – China

Emerald Publishing Limited
Emerald Publishing, Floor 5, Northspring, 21-23 Wellington Street, Leeds LS1 4DL

First edition 2024

British Library Cataloguing in Publication Data
A catalogue record for this book is available from the British Library

ISBN: 978-1-83753-949-9 (Print)
ISBN: 978-1-83753-948-2 (Online)
ISBN: 978-1-83753-950-5 (Epub)

ISSN: 0277-2833 (Series)

Printed and bound by CPI Group (UK) Ltd, Croydon, CR0 4YY

INVESTOR IN PEOPLE

CONTENTS

ABOUT THE EDITORS

Rick Delbridge is Professor of Organizational Analysis at Cardiff Business School and Co-convenor of the Centre for Innovation Policy Research, Cardiff University. He has research interests across various aspects of work, management, organization, and innovation in both private and public sector organizations and has published widely on these aspects. He also has a long-standing interest in Japanese business and management and is currently undertaking work on traditional Japanese craft firms. He has been awarded best paper prizes by *Academy of Management Review* and *Organization Studies*. He has been elected to Fellowships of the Academy of Social Sciences, British Academy of Management, and the Learned Society of Wales.

Markus Helfen, Hertie School Berlin, Germany, is a Senior Research Fellow in the Hertie School as well as a Private Lecturer at Freie Universität, Berlin. He is a Member of the Advisory Boards of the *German Journal of Human Resource Management* and the journal *Industrielle Beziehungen – The German Journal of Industrial Relations*. He is a Regular Co-convenor at the European Group of Organization Studies (EGOS) annual colloquia and the international research group 'Organization Studies and Industrial Relations'. He publishes in leading management and industrial relations journals like *Organization Studies*, *Human Relations*, and the *British Journal of Industrial Relations*. He does research in the fields of organization theory and employment relations with a focus on collective action, institutional work, and sustainability. His current research focuses on the humanization of warehouse work in the digital transformation and on global labour standards in supply chains.

Andreas (Andi) Pekarek is a Senior Lecturer in the Department of Management and Marketing at the University of Melbourne, Australia. He is fascinated by how people work, and his research has focused on how collective action by workers and their allies can steer the world of work in a more sustainable direction, towards fairness and social justice. His recent projects have centred on gig work in the platform economy, unions and industrial relations institutions, the HRM occupation, and interdisciplinary approaches to the study of work. He has published in leading journals, such as *Industrial and Labor Relations Review*, *Human Resource Management Journal*, *British Journal of Industrial Relations*, and *New Technology, Work and Employment*. In addition to his role as Associate Editor for *Research in the Sociology of Work*, he serves on the Editorial Board of the *Journal of Industrial Relations* (Sage).

Gretchen Purser is Associate Professor of Sociology at the Maxwell School of Citizenship and Public Affairs at Syracuse University. She earned her PhD in Sociology from the University of California at Berkeley and has held postdocs at the University of California at Davis and the American Academy of Arts and Sciences. Her research predominantly focuses on the intersection of low-wage precarious work and urban poverty and, more specifically, the growing role and significance of labour market intermediaries in the United States. She is a committed ethnographer and has published in leading sociology and anthropologyjournals, such as *Ethnography*, *Journal of Contemporary Ethnography*, *Critical Sociology*, and *Anthropology of Work Review*. She is the recipient of numerous publication awards from both the American Sociological Association and the Working Class Studies Association. In addition to her role as Associate Editor for *Research in the Sociology of Work*, she serves as the Editor-in-Chief of the Marxist Sociology Blog and as commissioning editor for Work In Progress.

ABOUT THE CONTRIBUTORS

Alma Andino-Frydman is a Junior at Stanford University, studying the future of work from the disciplines of Labor Economics and Sociology. She is originally from Argentina but grew up in the San Francisco Bay Area. Following the onset of the COVID-19 pandemic, she began her informal investigation into digital nomadism by travelling through Mexico, Costa Rica, and Panama, teaching yoga in cowork hostels and sparking a deep interest in the changing nature of work. Having worked for a labour rights advocacy organization, she wanted to investigate these changes more formally and gained sponsorship through the Chappell Lougee Scholarship program to execute this investigation. She has previously written about digital nomad productivity and motivation for the Stanford Institute for Economic Policy Research. She hopes to continue her exploration of remote work by investigating its impact on gentrification, management practices, industrial organization, urban planning, and development opportunities.

Monica Bhatia is a PhD candidate in the Department of Sociology at the University of Texas at Austin. Her dissertation focuses on sustainability and inequality in ecological intentional communities. Her research and teaching interests include gender and sexuality, organizations, work, inequality, and environmental sociology. Her work has previously appeared in *Environmental Sociology*.

Michael Dunn is Faculty at Skidmore College's Department of Management and Business, Skidmore College, USA. His education began with an MBA, shifting to the study of work and employment, including studies of contingent work and platform work, during his doctorate (in sociology) at the University of North Carolina-Chapel Hill. His work is focused on issues at the confluence of technology and labour market outcomes with a specific emphasis on precarious and non-standard work arrangements. His work is theoretically informed by the sociology of work, and organizations and labour studies. In the previous decade, he has worked on five NIH-funded efforts focused on precarious and underserved worker populations (i.e. tribal workers, day labourers, and ex-offenders). From 2015 to 2017, he was a Visiting Researcher at the Bureau of Labour Statistics. His methodological orientation is primarily qualitative and has field-based research experience with rideshare/transportation, delivery/task, crowdwork, and online freelance platforms.

Hanna Goldberg is a doctoral student in the CUNY Graduate Center Program in Sociology and holds a master's in Food Studies from Syracuse University's Falk College. She studies work and labor across the many realms that constitute the 'American Century,' from shopping mall service work to missile production.

Her recent, principally ethnographic research examined tipped service work in a national chain restaurant and the emergence of the US tipped subminimum wage.

Felicity Heathcote-Marcz is the Head of Behavioural Insight at CDS, a Digital Agency that is part of the Bailie Group. Before joining CDS Felicity worked as a Research Consultant for public and private sector organizations while part of Atkins Intelligent Mobility Practice. This work enabled access to the wonderful world of the Traffic Officers. She completed her PhD at Alliance Manchester Business School and is interested in the critical praxis and dialogues between industry and academia. She has published a book chapter in 'The Science of Superheroes' for the *Royal Society of Chemistry*, and a book review of *Tim Ingold's Life of Lines*, also with Sideeq Mohammed, along with thought leadership articles at various media publications.

Krzysztof Z. Jankowski attained an M.Phil. in Sociology from The University of Hong Kong where he examined global-mobile society and identity. He is currently a PhD student at The University of Glasgow, Scotland, where he is researching at the intersection of precarious work, adulthood, and urban sociology.

Floris De Krijger is an Interdisciplinary PhD Researcher at Hasselt University (Belgium). He has a background in critical organization studies, colonial history, and political science. He specializes in qualitative research methods (discourse and affect analysis, participatory observations, etc.) and mostly draws on Marxist theory, queer theory, and psychoanalysis in his research. He is currently preparing a PhD dissertation on the politics of corporate activism tentatively called: 'Corporate activism and its discontents: Psychosocial essays on capital, activist affect and (un)desiring the political'.

Sideeq Mohammed is the Associate Dean of Education and Undergraduate Student Experience at Kent Business School. His work draws on the writings of philosophers Gilles Deleuze and Felix Guattari in order to critically reflect on the social, political, and ethical problems of 'organisation' in the contemporary milieu. He is the Author of 'Stories and Organization in the Anthropocene: A Critical Look at the Impossibility of Sustainability'.

Isabel Munoz is a PhD candidate at Syracuse University's School of Information Studies (iSchool), Syracuse University, USA. She received her Master's degree in Communication from the University of Wyoming. She is focused on human–computer interaction, namely, information systems design and technology-supported resilience research. Her specific interests are centred on supporting underrepresented populations and women in pursuing and succeeding in digital work.

Clea O'Neil is an Undergraduate Research Fellow with the Digital Work Group and a Sophomore at Skidmore College, USA, majoring in Business-Political Science and minoring in Anthropology. Broadly, Clea is interested in understanding career strategies and how they relate to non-standard work arrangements.

Most recently, Clea's focus has been on how the gig economy has changed over time and where online freelancing is headed in the future.

Lauren A. Rivera is Professor of Management & Organizations and Professor of Sociology (by courtesy) at Northwestern University's Kellogg School of Management. Her research analyzes gatekeeping and inequality in organizations and markets. She is the Author of the award-winning book *Pedigree: How Elite Students Get Elite Jobs* (Princeton University Press). She received her BA in Sociology and Psychology from Yale University and her PhD in Sociology from Harvard University.

Steve Sawyer is the Faculty of Syracuse University's School of Information Studies, Syracuse University, USA. His research focuses on the changing forms of work and organizing enabled through uses of information and communication technologies. This is done through detailed field-based studies of scientific collaborators, software developers, real estate agents, police officers, organizational technologists, freelance and nomadic workers, and other information-intensive work settings. He has also been active in advancing sociotechnical approaches to studying computing collectively known as social informatics and emphasizing the sociotechnical basis of digital technologies. Sawyer's work is published in a range of venues and supported by funds from the National Science Foundation, IBM, Corning, and a number of other public and private sponsors. Prior to returning to Syracuse, Steve was a Founding Faculty Member of the Pennsylvania State University's College of Information Sciences and Technology. He earned his Doctorate from Boston University in 1995.

Laurianne Terlinden holds a PhD in Economics and Management Sciences from Université catholique de Louvain, Belgium. Her research focuses on new ways of working and identity construction in organizations. To study these issues, she uses qualitative and, more recently, ethnographic research methods.

PREFACE

A Welcome from the New Editorial Team

We are very pleased to welcome you to Volume 35 in the Emerald Series *Research in the Sociology of Work*. This is the first volume edited by the new editorial team of Rick Delbridge, Markus Helfen, Andreas (Andi) Pekarek, and Gretchen Purser.

First, we would like to place on record our gratitude to Steve Vallas who has edited the series for a number of years. It was Steve's suggestion that we might like to take over the series and we are grateful to him for that and also to Katy Mathers of Emerald for the opportunity. Our primary reason for agreeing to take on the editorship of *RSW* was to ensure the continuation of a home for research which explores the realities of work, the dynamics of workplace relations and labour markets, as well as the wider societal contexts that shape the worlds of work. It would appear that researching work and workers has been given less priority in the last few decades. Or at least, such studies seem to appear less often in some of our most prominent journal outlets. There are notable exceptions, of course, and we are pleased to take our place alongside the colleagues who edit, for example, *Work, Employment & Society*, *Work & Occupations*, and *Work in the Global Economy*.

The study of work, workplaces, and labour markets is more important than ever. There are a series of developments, one might say a confluence of circumstances, which are threatening to make the day to day experiences of workers ever more challenging. To note just a few, there is the increasing prevalence of precarious and insecure work arrangements, developments in new technologies that are heralding major changes across occupations in many – new as well as mature – segments of the labour market, and the ongoing economic and social upheaval wrought by climate change and the COVID-19 pandemic. These developments are all shaping the contemporary workplace and the wider landscape for workers in various ways across the globe. Naturally, each of these individual elements has echoes of previous periods and it would be mistaken to assume that all of the current conditions facing workers are novel. Nonetheless, the current combination of challenges represents a particularly problematic context. It is one which we hope will be closely recorded and evaluated by researchers of work and labour markets.

It is our intention that forthcoming editions of *RSW* will provide a home for critical, rigorous, and interesting research, and we intend to offer a variety of ways in which researchers can communicate their findings to our readership. You will see in this first volume that we have contributions documenting a variety of different ethnographic studies of work and that these adopt a range of styles and formats from shorter reflective pieces through to extended presentations of empirical findings and analysis. With this series, we have some greater flexibility than is often found in more conventional journal outlets and we are keen to draw upon this greater breadth of form. This enables us to both respond to how authors feel is the most effective way of them communicating with their audiences and to make our volumes accessible and interesting for our readers.

We are also particularly pleased that this first volume of our editorship is based on ethnographic research as we are keen advocates of this method. Across our editorial team, we have had diverse and rewarding experiences conducting our own ethnographic research immersed as participant observers in diverse settings ranging from factories and union offices to the practice of day labour in a variety of dangerous, dirty, and degrading jobs. We remain keen to promote and support ethnographic research since it can offer the type of fine-grained and exploratory data that provide insights beyond other methods. What is particularly gratifying is that we have a number of doctoral studies represented in this volume. It is great to see the continuation of strong traditions of ethnographic research within the sociology of work. We anticipate that we will run further calls for ethnographic-based contributions in the future, and we hope that this will become one of the features of *RSW* during this editorial team's period of office.

There are further volumes in the pipeline, and we encourage readers to continue to monitor the series webpage for future calls for papers. We are currently working with calls for submissions to thematic volumes rather than having an open call for contributions but we welcome ideas both for volumes and individual papers and would be happy to discuss these with potential contributors. Finally, we want to thank all of the reviewers who read and constructively commented on the submitted manuscripts.

We hope you enjoy Volume 35.

Rick, Andi, Gretchen and Markus
Editors
Research in the Sociology of Work

CHAPTER 1

WHY ETHNOGRAPHIES OF WORK? AN INTRODUCTION

Rick Delbridge[a], Markus Helfen[b], Andreas Pekarek[c] and Gretchen Purser[d]

[a]*Cardiff University, Cardiff, UK*
[b]*Hertie School, Berlin, Germany*
[c]*University of Melbourne, Parkville, VIC, Australia*
[d]*Syracuse University, Syracuse, NY, USA*

ABSTRACT

In this chapter, we underscore the enduring importance of research on work, workers, labour markets, and the places and spaces of work. We then examine the particular and valuable contributions that come from ethnographic research in providing detailed studies of work, particularly when these are situated and interpreted in their wider socio-political contexts. We discuss the key dimensions of ethnography before overviewing the contributions to the volume. The volume presents cutting-edge ethnographic research on contemporary worlds of work and the experiences of workers from a range of contexts including an alternative community, working online, the gig economy, and the hospitality industry. Alongside novel empirical chapters, the collection includes the reflections of ethnographers with regards to, for example, the experience as a young female management researcher working amongst journalists in a media firm, personal feelings of precarity within and beyond the field, and how to navigate the challenges of researching inequalities ethnographically.

Keywords: Ethnography; sociology of work; qualitative research methods; doctoral research; social relations of work/places; contemporary work settings

Ethnographies of Work
Research in the Sociology of Work, Volume 35, 1–8

Published under exclusive licence by Emerald Publishing Limited
ISSN: 0277-2833/doi:10.1108/S0277-283320230000035001

> As the automated pace of our daily jobs wipes out name and face – and in many instances, feeling – there is a sacrilegious question being asked these days. To earn one's bread by the sweat of one's brow has always been the lot of mankind. At least, ever since Eden's slothful couple was served with an eviction notice. The scriptural precept was never doubted, not out loud. No matter how demeaning the task and no matter how it dulls the senses and breaks the spirit, one *must* work. Or else.
>
> Studs Terkel in his introduction to *Working* (1972, p. xiv)

Work is intrinsic to human existence and studying work remains essential to understanding contemporary society. Indeed, one might argue it has never been more important. Yet, developments in the academy have left research that is centred on work and workers somewhat isolated. Management studies and organization theory have burgeoned in business schools, but the research specifically focusing on work and employment in these fields has receded. Moreover, despite the study of work being central to the emergence of the discipline of sociology, sociology departments have tended to move away from a focus on work and fissure into increasingly diverse areas of specialization. More generally, the disciplinary silos and emphasis on 'novel contributions' of contemporary academia have produced a very fragmented body of literature that spans work, workers, labour markets, employment and industrial relations, and political economy but in ways that all too rarely set out to explore the relationships between these. Our aspirations with *Research in Sociology of Work* are that within and across volumes, readers will find interesting original research that is appropriately couched in the wider contexts that make it relevant. We are particularly keen to explore the potential of working across the academic silos and (re-)connecting these to shine light on the most important issues of today's world of work. We see great potential for scholars of the economy, management, organization, politics, and society in foregrounding the varieties of work and the diversity of workers in their analyses.

We are certainly not the first to argue for 'Bringing work back in'. Indeed, this was the title of a paper in *Organization Science* by Stephen Barley and Gideon Kunda back in 2001. In this, the authors reviewed the history of organization theory to show that past studies of work had provided an empirical basis for the founding theories of bureaucracy in the discipline, but that such research had become increasingly 'marginalized or ignored'. They made a strong argument for the value of 'detailed studies of work' in, for example, making sense of variety and diversity in post-bureaucratic organizing. Looking back at that paper now, it is particularly striking to see the authors suggest that 'For most of the twentieth century, the nature of work remained sufficiently stable for organizational scholars to assume that concepts and theories developed for bureaucratic settings were adequate for studying most organizational contexts' (p. 76). They note, however, the growing evidence at the turn of the millennium that 'work in industrial society has now changed sufficiently to render such an assumption suspect' (p. 76). The shifts in employment patterns and occupational structures, the fraying of employment contracts and declining stability of employment, the displacement and transforming effects of technology, and the changes in skill demands and work organization that Barley and Kunda note in this context have become ever more prevalent over the last 20 years. The desire to see detailed studies of work situated in their meaningful contexts has been a feature of our own work. For example, in picking up the baton of Barley and Kunda (2001), a special issue of

Organization Studies sought to put the study of work and workers back at the centre of organization studies. In the introduction, Delbridge and Sallaz (2015, p. 1449) 'advance four inter-related work-world metaphors or ways of seeing organizations: as physical worlds, as worlds of hierarchy, as spaces of innovation, and as fields of actors', arguing that '[r]esearch that puts work at the centre of organizational analysis, and places organization within its context of economy, politics and society, will provide important new insights into the experience of work and nature of contemporary organization'. Yet, Barley and Kunda's call for more focused scholarly attention to work was never fully heeded and much remains to be done.

THE VALUE OF ETHNOGRAPHIES OF WORK

The pressing need for detailed studies of work brings the value of ethnography into sharp relief.

Ethnography is 'designed to study actions, interactions, and the fine details of the here and now as these are articulated in the context of shared cultural meanings' (Zilber, 2020, p. 1). Within the qualitative research tradition, ethnography is typically celebrated as particularly suited to exploring new phenomena, developing social dynamics and processes.

Ethnographic scholarship encompasses a range of perspectives and approaches. For example, Decoteau (2016) distinguishes grounded theory (e.g. Corbin & Strauss, 1990), the extended case method (e.g. Burawoy, 1998), pragmatism (e.g. Abbott, 1997), and critical realism as distinct approaches to ethnographic studies. Decoteau, arguing from a critical realist perspective, proceeds to show how these approaches differ on a number of dimensions. These include whether they are inductive, deductive, or abductive in their explorative ambitions and how they establish the explanatory ground of their interpretations. Approaches include comparing cases with similar outcomes, by inspecting anomalies contradicting known theory, reinterpreting surprisingly inconsistent findings, or by generalizing single statements and re-applying them in different contexts. Without taking sides in long-standing debates about research process and practice, and instead opting explicitly for a pluralist view and the 'strength of difference' (Delbridge & Ezzamel, 2005), it is fair to say that, whatever their approach, ethnographies face potential limitations that may be summarized in three questions:

1. How is it possible to identify widely relevant insights by observing a (group of) unique case(s) in specific social contexts and situations? And what exactly indicates to us that a specific social aspect may become a mass phenomenon as the result of a peculiar, yet unnoticed, development or process?
2. How close and detailed must observations be in order to derive an adequate understanding of a phenomenon, given that its processes and practices are embedded in societal structures and contingencies?
3. How does the subjectivity of the ethnographic research process, that is, immersing oneself as a researcher in a different social reality, influence the findings, interpretations, and implications of the research?

The answers to these questions differ across the various camps using ethnographic methods. As for the first question, it is evident that ethnographies striving for theorization face the problem of generalizing from inductively generated findings. Seen from the deductive approach of conventional quantitative science, this is a cost of ethnography's advantage in the identification of new processes and practices for theorization. However, ethnographic interpretations assist in understanding and explaining quantitative findings that largely neglect or assume the very social mechanisms producing the data. Hence, ethnographic studies often justifiably aim for answering 'how' questions rather than testing 'if-then' hypotheses of the hypothetico-deductivist tradition. Burawoy's (1998) extended case method is one particularly prominent approach towards the goal of theoretical reconstruction.

The second question points towards the challenge of interpreting the detailed findings of ethnographic studies. Scholars of the labour process are all too familiar with this dilemma. Hyman (1987), for example, has cautioned that workplace studies provide only a partial window on capitalism:

> The inadequacy of reducing the whole system of capitalist production to the labour process has already been emphasized. Capital confronts labour not merely within the workplace but in commodity markets, in political life, in the sphere of culture and ideology. (Hyman, 1987, p. 47)

In other words, a narrow focus on the dynamics of a particular workplace may overlook the influence of other, exactly the same outcomes observed.

Nevertheless, and this is raised through the third question, the beginning of interpretation remains to be selected arbitrarily and can only be made intersubjectively plausible in reflecting upon the researcher's own standpoint *vis-á-vis* the 'object' of investigation. This reflection is not an easy task as it challenges the researcher in various ways. The researcher needs to be capable of combining expert knowledge of a field of inquiry with an openness to the novelty in situations in flexible ways that account for the vagueness in observing a messy social reality or 'real practice'. As Blumer comments, 'The observation necessary to sharpen and fill in this vague perspective in which everything combines in situ and in time must meet the two requirements of intimate familiarity and broad imaginative grasp' (Blumer 1947, p. 277).

Quality ethnographic research thus needs to be aware of the relationality of social practice taking place within contexts as well as the alteration of those very structures (including those imprinting on the researcher's agency). Ethnography hence aims for the thorough excavation of the action and meaning making in the social situations studied in connection to the wider societal contexts in which these happen in real life. Indeed, given such sensibilities, it should not come as a surprise that doing work ethnographies is often related to emancipatory projects, that is, aimed explicitly or implicitly at bettering the situation of those studied. The least an ethnographic approach can do in supporting such ambitions for emancipation is to bring to light those areas of darkness made invisible, forgotten, or neglected. Indeed, by studying social realities in context, ethnographic work helps identify where and how exactly wider structures impinge on the agency of the persons involved, and, by moving close to a given social situation, it assists in identifying those aspects that can or must be changed.

These dimensions and concerns of ethnography are amply and ably reflected in our collection.

AN OVERVIEW OF THE CHAPTERS

This volume presents a rich collection of cutting-edge ethnographic research on contemporary world of work and the experiences of workers. There is empirical work from a range of contexts and, alongside these novel empirical chapters, the volume also includes the reflections of ethnographers with regard to, for example, the experience as a young female management researcher working amongst journalists, personal feelings of precarity within and beyond the field, and how to navigate the challenges of researching inequalities ethnographically.

The first chapter by Hanna Goldberg presents a workplace ethnography of a restaurant to examine the experiences and views of food service workers which was undertaken for her master's thesis. The focus is the practice of tipping in the United States and Hanna explores the varying perspectives of servers, including why some workers apparently counter-intuitively oppose legislation that would increase their minimum wage. But, such change would also impact their ability to earn tips. This acts to divide workers with differing perspectives and also creates tensions around roles, shifts, or specific tables that offer better opportunities to earn tips. The result is a fragmented and individualistic set of workplace relations. Analytically, the study shows how tipping as a formal wage produces a 'two-employer problem' for workers with customers constituting a second, unregulated employer in the workplace. These dynamics divide and undermine workers negotiating positions relative to management and erode the possibilities of organizing.

Next comes a second empirically based chapter that draws on doctoral research by Floris De Krijger. Floris explores the forms of control experienced by gig workers, specifically those working for two food delivery platforms in Amsterdam. The study shows the technologically based controls that 'gamify' the labour process, wherein underpaid delivery workers employ game strategies themselves in seeking to maximize their income. By engaging in such activity, couriers inadvertently align their actions with the interests of employers and reproduce individualized and subordinated employment relations, somewhat akin to the experiences of servers under the US tipping system but created through very differing control 'technologies'. These findings are grounded and interpreted alongside previous shopfloor ethnographies to show both the continuity and intensification of control through a combination of task and shift allocation and piece wage games.

These opening two chapters exemplify very nicely the characteristics and importance of quality ethnographic research that we have outlined above, providing new and insightful empirical details that are situated, analyzed, and interpreted in wider contexts in order to produce new theoretical and practical knowledge with emancipatory potential. Our next two chapters provide new empirical insight into relatively novel and/or less well-understood social settings and relations. Again drawing on doctoral research, our two authors explore alternative 'work settings', respectively examining an income- and resource-sharing commune and the experiences and evolving identities of an emerging digital nomad workforce.

Monica Bhatia explores the implications for work and sustainability of an alternative, intentional community organizational form. The study examines the model of work at a long-established income-sharing and intergenerational community of over 80 people in the US state of Virginia. Analysis shows that certain key principles underpin the community, including how the values of sustainability and community well-being are brought into the work system, the importance and valorization of social reproductive labour such as cooking, cleaning, and care in the community, and how work is democratized in furthering the goals of sustainability. The study shows how a cohesive community has been conceived and sustained, demonstrating the potential well-being and environmental benefits of such alternative organization. Moreover, the prioritizing of community and the recognition of the importance of social reproductive labour carry implications for wider society, not least in reflecting on responses to the climate emergency.

Alma Andino-Frydman presents a study of an increasingly prominent category of worker, digital nomads who work remotely. Data gathered in interviews with 50 such workers across seven co-working spaces in Mexico are reported and interpreted through the analytical lens of identity. The research shows how digital nomads place much less emphasis on traditional social determinants of identity, such as nationality and religion, choosing rather to define their personal identities by their passions and by their personal interests in the professionalism and productivity necessary to sustain their lifestyles. While nomadic, the study also reveals the significance of work spaces and places in these evolving identities, developing a cyclical framing which links worker, socio-personal and relational aspects in their contexts.

In the following chapter, Michael Dunn, Isabel Munoz, Clea O'Neil, and Steve Sawyer continue the examination of digital workers with an ethnography of online freelancers working in the United States. The evidence questions common conceptualizations regarding online freelancing, suggesting that the flexibility of where to work, not when to work, is seen as most significant in such workers' choices. The chapter also presents some interesting comparisons on preferences for full-time or freelance work and assesses how these relate to workplace culture shifts and what this means for contemporary working arrangements, contributing to discussions of knowledge-based gig work.

The chapter by Felicity Heathcote-Marcz and Sideeq Mohammed is the most experimental of them all. It showcases the more expansive range of formats and styles we hope to continue to be able to publish in volumes to come. This chapter is based on ethnographic fieldwork amidst traffic officers along England's strategic road network. Rather than a typical ethnographic manuscript, this chapter is written in a series of disjointed voices and vignettes. The effect of reading it is jarring, but strikingly powerful. Refusing the pressure to 'make sense' of the piece, the authors deliberately lead readers on a 'journey that is durative and bumpy', all while raising questions about ethnographic methods of knowledge production and revealing some of the challenges faced by officers at the side of the road.

Our final three chapters turn attention to the conduct of ethnographic research and consider the subjective experience of the research process. These chapters speak to our three questions in various ways and each contributes to the situating of ethnography in meaningful personal, organizational, and societal settings. The first two are again the products of doctoral research and all three offer practical as well as theoretical insights.

In the first of these chapters, Krzysztof Z. Jankowski takes a reflexive look at the researcher's personal experiences of precarity both in undertaking the research and in their personal circumstances. The comparison reveals how the activity of being an ethnographer informed how the experience of precarious work was felt. The chapter is particularly revealing on the third question raised above, showing how the biography of the researcher informs field experiences. Furthermore, in presenting an ethnographically grounded assessment of precarious work, the chapter problematizes 'pure' or ideal typical characterizations of complex social phenomena.

Laurianne Terlinden continues the reflective theme with her personal commentary on her experiences of conducting ethnographic research. Using vulnerability as an analytical lens, she discusses how, as a young female doctoral researcher in management, her identity was challenged in the field when encountering mostly male journalists who were initially hostile to her presence and sceptical of the value of her research. Through a process of self-disclosure and a gradual displacement of a professional identity with a personal one, Laurianne revealed her vulnerabilities, built connections and trust, and ultimately successfully navigated her research setting.

In our final chapter, Lauren A. Rivera draws upon her own extensive fieldwork experiences to reflect on both the challenges ethnographers face in organizations when studying workplace inequalities but also effective strategies for overcoming these challenges. This chapter is, therefore, especially instructive for budding ethnographers planning to soon enter the field. The primary goal for work ethnographers is to figure out ways to push 'beyond the company line' to observe what actually happens in practice, including how opportunities are allocated, and how inequalities are reproduced. The chapter, thus, speaks directly to the emancipatory potential of ethnography.

CONCLUDING REMARKS

This volume showcases contemporary ethnographies of work, including several doctoral studies, that present rich and detailed data on work, workers, and the various places and spaces of work. The chapters address a number of key issues in understanding the nature and experience of work in the current socioeconomic circumstances. These include the individualizing and disempowering nature of service and gig work, the shifts in workplace and career heralded by digital technologies and exacerbated by the COVID pandemic, and the possibilities of alternative organization.

Each of these analyses of aspects of contemporary sociology of work is informed by the dynamic but increasingly concerning context for work and workers and how these are being impacted by current economic and political developments. We live in what some may label 'neo-liberal times' which are marked by the ways markets and their inequalities are taken for granted, the rise of precarity, and chronic disability, gender, and race inequalities. These developments reaffirm the increasing uncertainty anticipated by Barley and Kunda at the turn of the millennium and do so in spades. There are important and novel dynamics shaping contemporary labour processes and labour markets: the nature of disruption, work/career disjunctions, and impermanence of employment have grown significantly in the twenty-first century, while digital transformations and their implications for power and control give considerable cause for concern. All of these need to be researched, interpreted, and understood in the specific contexts of the social relations of 'work/places' and wider societal dynamics. This collection shows the central and enduring importance of ethnography in these research endeavours.

REFERENCES

Abbott, A. (1997). Of time and space: The contemporary relevance of the Chicago School. *Social Forces*, *75*(4), 1149–1182. doi:10.2307/2580667

Barley, S., & Kunda, G. (2001). Bringing work back in. *Organization Science*, *12*(1), 76–95. doi:10.1287/orsc.12.1.76.10122

Blumer, H. (1947). Sociological theory in Industrial Relations. *American Sociological Review*, *12*(1), 271–278. Retrieved from http://www.jstor.org/stable/2086516

Burawoy, M. (1998). The extended case method. *Sociological Theory*, *16*(1), 4–33.

Corbin, J., & Strauss, A. (1990). Grounded theory research: Procedures, canons, and evaluative criteria. *Zeitschrift für Soziologie*, *19*(6), 418–427. Retrieved from https://www.jstor.org/stable/23845563

Decoteau, C. L. (2016). The AART of ethnography: A critical realist explanatory research model. *Journal for the Theory of Social Behaviour*, *47*(1), 58–82. doi:10.1111/jtsb.12107

Delbridge, R., & Ezzamel, M. (2005). The strength of difference: Contemporary conceptions of control. *Organization*, *12*(5), 603–618. doi:10.1177/1350508405055937

Delbridge, R., & Sallaz, J. J. (2015). Work: Four worlds and ways of seeing. *Organization Studies*, *36*(11), 1449–1462. doi:10.1177/0170840615612021

Hyman, R. (1987). Strategy or structure? Capital, labour, and control. *Work, Employment & Society*, *1*, 25–55. https://doi.org/10.1177/0950017087001001004

Terkel, S. (1972). *Working: People talk about what they do all day and how they feel about what they do*. New York, NY: Pantheon Books.

Zilber, T. B. (2020). The methodology/theory interface: Ethnography and the microfoundations of institutions. *Organization Theory*, *1*, 1–27. doi:10.1177/2631787720919439

CHAPTER 2

DIVIDED WAGES AND DIVIDED WORKERS: TIPS AND THE TWO-EMPLOYER PROBLEM

Hanna Goldberg

CUNY Graduate Center, New York City, NY, USA

ABSTRACT

The extra-low minimum wage for US restaurant workers has remained unchanged for over 30 years. Periodic campaigns have brought this wage, and its connection to the perpetuation of inequality and exploitative work, to public attention, but these campaigns have met resistance from both employers and *restaurant workers. This article draws on a workplace ethnography in a restaurant front-of-house, and in-depth interviews with tipped food service workers, to examine the tipped labour process and begin to answer a central question: why would any workers oppose a wage increase? It argues that the constituting of tips as a formal wage created for workers a two-employer problem, wherein customers assume the role of secondary, unregulated, employers in the workplace. Ultimately, the tipped wage poses a longer-term strategic obstacle for workers in their position relative to management and ability to organize to shape the terms and conditions of their work.*

Keywords: Service work; tipping; labour process; restaurants; ethnography; labour organizing

Ethnographies of Work
Research in the Sociology of Work, Volume 35, 9–33

Published under exclusive licence by Emerald Publishing Limited
ISSN: 0277-2833/doi:10.1108/S0277-283320230000035002

> To the restaurant owners out here who think that their business model is dependent on paying people less than minimum wage, I would say they don't deserve to be in business. They should be ashamed of themselves to think that they can pay someone less than minimum wage for their hard work. And to the workers out here who are applauding people who want to pay them less than minimum wage, I think that you have really been tricked through fear into thinking that you won't have a job unless you get paid less than minimum wage.
>
> *Bartender from Ithaca, New York*
>
> I work hard for my money. I rely on my tips ... I receive no aid from New York. I have never received food stamps, I have never received any kind of help, anything. I have a beautiful home. I have supported my children. I have a mortgage, cars ... These people claiming that they can't make it, and they are getting harassed, and they are not making enough? You filled out an application to get that job. Fill out another one. A lot of us make it. If you know what you are doing, you know what you are doing.
>
> *Diner server from Syracuse, New York*[1]

The above accounts are taken from the testimonies of Central New Yorkers at a 2018 public hearing to weigh the possible abolition of the state's tipped subminimum wage. The hearing drew restaurant and other tipped workers from around the region, and these excerpts epitomize two sides of an ongoing debate over the future of the widespread use and legality of the US' lower-than-minimum wage for tipped workers. Many labour advocates across the country advocate a stance articulated by the first worker: subminimum wages are super-exploitative and should be abolished. Yet, the second worker is not alone in their defence of this wage structure, and in their message to those who 'can't make it' in the industry: 'fill out another [job application]'. It may seem counterintuitive that any worker would object to mandated minimum wage increases from their employers. In what follows, drawing upon an ethnographic study of work on the floor of a US-based chain restaurant, I suggest that the strange circumstances surrounding the political status of the US subminimum wage are traceable to the formalization of the two-tier wage system itself. This is because the tipped wage structure creates the customer as a secondary – and, importantly, *unregulated* – employer. It shapes relations-in-production wherein an entrepreneurial, hyper-individualist ethos pervades, and where workers look not to their bosses for increased wages but to their own ingenuity. While management fades into the background, the labour process *appears* to unfold only between the worker and the customer in each individuated service transaction, over which workers are often in direct competition.

Many diners, and those who have escaped employment in one of the US' tipped service occupations, may not realize that workers in 43 states around the country may be paid below the minimum wage by their employers. While the 1938 Fair Labor Standards Act (FLSA) set a minimum wage for most of the country's workers, a few select categories of workers were, and remain, excluded from that modest guarantee. Tipped workers, those who earn at least $30 a month in tips and spend at least 80 per cent of their time in tip-earning activities, are among those workers. Critics of the tipped wage link it to disproportionate rates of poverty among food service workers (Allegretto & Cooper, 2014), who account for over half of the nation's tipped workforce (Conlin, Lynn, & O'Donoghue, 2003).

Tips are, after all, a fundamentally uncertain source of income, and this wage structure compounds the overwhelmingly precarious position of food service workers, a condition only more glaring in the harsh light of the COVID-19 pandemic.

Opponents of the tipped wage have also argued that workers' reliance on informal tipped income creates unduly coercive working conditions, wherein workers are obliged to tolerate ill treatment to earn a decent living (Restaurant Opportunities Center (ROC) United, 2012, 2020; Ross & Welsh, 2021). Studies have found that tipped work encourages self-exploitation in the workplace and, thus, functions as a mechanism for increasing managerial control (Sallaz, 2002, 2009; Sherman, 2007; Ogbonna & Harris, 2002; and see Azar, 2003 for a managerial perspective), where the enticement of the tip elicits workers' unwitting consent (Burawoy, 1979). Others have challenged, or at least tempered, such critiques to assert that workers derive meaning from, and experience agency through, tipped work (Brewster & Wills, 2013; Erickson, 2004a, 2009; Gatta, 2002, 2009a; Paules, 1991).

Missing from both the emphases on managerial techniques and individual agency, however, is consideration of what the tipped wage and tipped work mean for workers collectively, united by shared material interests but also, in the workplace, through their engagement in a cooperative labour process. As organized workers recognized a century ago, it is to workers as a collective body that the two-tier wage system poses the greatest threat and has done the most significant damage. This distinction between workers as individuals, rather than a collective, helps explain the counterintuitive circumstance of workers publicly opposing a wage increase.

In what follows, I draw on an ethnography of the restaurant dining room and in-depth interviews with tipped restaurant workers to shed light on an under-theorized aspect of the tipped wage conundrum, which in these pages I refer to as *the two-employer problem*. In part, it is a basic unfairness identified by workers in the early years of the 20th twentieth century: waiters working for tips under an informal and unregulated system complained that they worked for 'two bosses', and felt 'at the mercy of the customer all the time' (Josephson, 1956, pp. 89–90). The subsumption of the customer into the traditional worker-employer dyad is a fundamental feature of interactive service work but, as I will argue, the institution of a *formal* tipped wage goes even further, and the customer assumes the role of a secondary, and entirely unregulated, employer and disburser of a legal wage, wittingly or no. Employers – that is, the *real* employers – obscured behind the screen of their ephemeral doubles, the customers, can shed ordinary obligations to workers. The two-employer problem framework, thus, helps theorize the many conflicting features of tipped work, as well as the seeming paradoxes of the contemporary political context. Notably, it creates the appearance that workers are engaged in a subdivided labour process, involving multiple distinct employers, in the tipped service interaction.

In the following section, I briefly contextualize this study and the contemporary debate over tipped wages in an abbreviated account of the emergence of the US tipped wage system. This history sheds light on the struggle between workers and capital out of which this tipped wage emerged and throws into stark relief both the peculiarity of the US system and the condition of tipped workers today. I then review the literature on tipped work, and especially tipped restaurant work, highlighting the various ways in which scholars have understood the tipped labour process. After a discussion of research methods, I turn to the world of the contemporary restaurant's front-of-house. Ultimately, I argue that, while this and other studies of tipped work demonstrate many ways in which working for tips can be a boon, materially or experientially, for certain individual tipped workers, the tipped wage has created a longer-term strategic problem for workers in their position relative to capital and in their ability to organize to shape the conditions of their work.

WORKING FOR 'TWO BOSSES': RESTAURANT WORK IN THE US CONTEXT

Tipping in US service occupations was once an informal practice, as it remains in many other parts of the world. Today, it is a firmly entrenched and structural feature in many US industries, the food service industry foremost among them. At the federal level and in most US, tips, in fact, constitute not a gift or gratuity but a legal form of wage – as the Supreme Court ruled in 1942 (*Williams* v. *Jacksonville Terminal Co.* 1942). Where tipping is normalized, employers have recourse to a special, lower-than-minimum wage category, codified in a 1966 amendment to the FLSA. This allows employers to subsidize state and federal wage requirements with the tips workers receive directly from customers.

This peculiar system evolved out of the particular context of US capitalist work and labour relations in the late 19th and early 20th centuries. The development of tipping practices and tip work became bound up in the legacy of slavery and thc insinuation of formerly enslaved workers into wage work. In the decades immediately following the Civil War, the Pullman Company was one of the country's earliest adopters, at scale, of a de facto tipped wage. Pullman cut labour costs by targeting formerly enslaved black men in the US South for their extremely low-wage and customarily tipped porter positions (Bates, 2001; Santino, 1989). Limited employment options made these workers more likely to accept substandard wages, and work in the sleeper cars – and the requirements of tip earning – invoked the very recent memory of racialized servitude.[2]

The Brotherhood of Sleeping Car Porters, in their struggle for recognition for their union and improved working conditions, linked tip earning to slavery and sought to ban the practice of tipping altogether (Bates, 2001). In contrast, the positions of the plethora of craft unions representing tipped service workers in the first decades of the 20th century were heterogeneous. Some workers clung to a system they found lucrative or that provided them a modicum of autonomy in work. More commonly, at the level of leadership, unions opposed tipping and the low hourly wages that became customary in many tipped occupations.[3] They recognized the challenge posed to the unions' growth and success, as tip earning encouraged individualism in the workplace rather than collective organizing. Tipped work lost some of the very socializing qualities from which would develop class solidarity (Segrave, 1998; U.S. Bureau of Labor Statistics, 1927). When service industry employers made the first large-scale push to cement those wages in a low, tipped wage and special exemptions for restaurant employers under the 1933 National Industrial Recovery Act, they were met with worker protests and the threat of strikes (Needleman, 1937).

The final push towards the institutionalization of tips as wages came, for the first time, from workers themselves. Throughout the 1950s, the IRS had become more aggressive in pursuing cases of tax evasion on tip income, but there remained a disconnect: tips were considered part of the wage for the purposes of tax collection but did not count as income in the calculation of workers' Social Security benefits (Segrave, 1998). Through a multi-year effort, and facing the opposition of service industry employers, unions successfully lobbied congress and the Social Security Administration to add a tip income provision to the Social Security Act in 1966 (Arlen, 1964; Segrave, 1998).[4] Later that same year, a formal tip credit was established in an amendment to the FLSA, allowing employers to subsidize up to 50 per cent of hourly wages with workers' earned tips.[5]

Thus, the pattern of back and forth out of which emerged the contemporary tipped wage was one in which unions did have significant influence, but employer power predominated. While service worker (and especially restaurant worker) unions' presence declined, restaurant industry efforts have not abated. In the mid-1990s, the National Restaurant Association's lobbying efforts froze the federal tipped wage at $2.13 per hour, and they have been further instrumental in blocking or overturning recent state-level efforts to eliminate the lower wage (Allegretto & Filion, 2011; Thielman, 2018). In what follows, we will see how, on a micro-level, the formalization of this wage system structures the tipped labour process and confirms the analyses of those early unionized service workers, creating and amplifying the two-employer problem. The institution and erosion of the value of the tipped wage had the effect of constituting the customer as a second, unregulated, employer in the workplace, and over time workers have become increasingly reliant on the generosity of that informal employer.

UNDERSTANDING THE TIPPED LABOUR PROCESS

While the tipped wage can apply to workers in a number of service occupations – including car wash workers, delivery drivers, and nail salon technicians – tipped food service workers, who comprise more than half of US tipped workers (Conlin et al., 2003), are the primary focus in these pages. Nationally and at the state level, much of the debate over the tipped wage has unfolded in policy-focused literature advocating either the elimination (Allegretto, 2018; Allegretto & Cooper, 2014; Haley-Lock & Ewert, 2011; Specker, 2016; and see the Restaurant Opportunities Center (ROC) United's various publications) or maintenance (Glans, 2018; Zahringer, 2014) of state or federal tipped wages. Detractors of the two-tier wage system connect the tipped wage and super-exploitative working conditions, arguing that its elimination could help diminish the problems of tipped service work (Glans, 2018; Zahringer, 2014; and see ROC United policy reports), in keeping with other studies that link tipped food service work to precarity, vulnerability, and material inequality (e.g., see, Ehrenreich, 2001; Paules, 1991).

Unlike in a more typical employment relation, tipped workers are faced with the constant onus of having to weigh the costs of inappropriate treatment – whether from customers or management – against the risks of lost income. Women working in service occupations are especially likely to experience, and be compelled to tolerate, workplace sexual harassment or abuse (Restaurant Opportunities Center (ROC) United, 2012, 2020; Ross & Welsh, 2021; Specker, 2016). Studies of restaurant work have also demonstrated the connection between tipped work and the demands of gendered emotional labour (Erickson, 2004a, 2004b, 2009) and gender disparity in earnings (Restaurant Opportunities Center (ROC) United, 2012, 2020).

Other studies have highlighted the perpetuation of racial inequality both in the amount of tip earnings (Brewster & Wills, 2013; Lynn, 2006; Lynn et al., 2008) and the question of which workers, in workplaces that are spatially stratified by race and class, are likely to access (or, alternately, be subjected to) tip-earning front-of-house occupations (Sachs, Allen, Terman, Hayden, & Hatcher, 2014; Wilson, 2018). More recently, publications from anti-tipped wage advocates and the popular press have made the explicit connection between the early implementation of tipped wages and legacy of US enslavement, linking the predatory conditions of tipped work in the late 19th century and today (see, e.g., Alexander, 2021; Barber, 2019). Lastly, the tipped wage is unevenly implemented across the restaurant industry and the country, so outcomes vary greatly depending upon where and how workers are employed (Haley-Lock & Ewert, 2011).

Tips have also been described as a lucrative means for employers to organize work to meet the constraints of interactive service work and elicit effort from workers. The tipped wage in effect provides a subsidy to the food service industry, but tipped work also functions to orchestrate workplace consent (Burawoy, 1979). Tip earning redirects workers' attention away from management and their objective relation to their employers (Sallaz, 2002, 2009; Sherman, 2007), obscuring relations of production and ultimately reifying managerial control (Ogbonna & Harris, 2002). Tips cultivate a sense of personal responsibility, of autonomy and self-management, but in the end, this autonomy is bounded by the persistent, if veiled, authority of managers. Perhaps most significantly, tip earning elicits the work of service – and not just service, but *good service* (Sallaz, 2002). These observations are in keeping with Marx's (1867/1990) description of another 'non-standard' wage structure, that of the piece wage, which similarly compels workers' effort and structures their labour process. I discuss the resemblance between these wage structures, and where they diverge, below.

A tradition of restaurant ethnographies also draws attention to the experience of tipped work. William Foote Whyte (1946, p. 129) warned that 'the emotional hazards of tipping [were] an evil that the server [was] helpless to combat', compelled as they were to extend the 'itching palm' (Scott, 1916). Others have contested this vision of tipped work, arguing that workers strategically navigate those 'emotional hazards' of restaurant service work to both maximize their earnings and preserve their wellbeing (Erickson, 2004a). So too have scholars studying the restaurant argued that tipped workers exert control over the labour process and customer interactions (Erickson, 2009; Mars & Nicod, 1984; Paules, 1991) and through the very informality of tipped work exert agency in the workplace (Brewster & Wills, 2013;

Gatta, 2002, 2009a). Gatta (2009a) explicitly argues for the preservation of tipping systems for this reason. Brewster and Wills (2013, p. 198) call 'the institution of tipping … the most salient source of servers' experiences of empowerment at work', writing that 'the institution of tipping … gives [servers] the ability to manipulate their presentation of self and influence the emotions of their customers'.

Notable in these accounts is an emphasis on the worker at the individual level, their sense of self and individuated customer encounters. Tipped work has also been construed as an important avenue through which workers can demonstrate resistance in the workplace (Gatta, 2009a; Paules, 1991), but these acts of resistance are likewise constrained by their individualized nature, and workers' efforts to resist – whether by circumventing ordinary rules of the workplace or refusing the tip altogether – typically redound on their coworkers or are bounded by a singular act of wage forfeiture.

A few studies have begun to shed light on the way tipping structures translate to relationships between workers and emphasize the way tip earning can function to divide workers in the workplace. Tips can heighten extant class and race inequalities (in one restaurant tips 'brightened the boundaries' between tipped and non-tipped workers; Wilson, 2018) and spur competition between tipped workers, fostering certain strategic alliances and antagonisms (Gatta, 2009b). In the pooled house, where tips are shared, the effects are markedly different. Workers may experience more cooperation in the labour process (Sallaz, 2002) but also a mutual pressure to perform (Wilson, 2019). Workers may also see tip pooling as a strategy by which they can exert some measure of control over their earnings, making them more consistent and less unpredictable (Mulinari, 2019).

These studies begin to illuminate the relationship between the tipped wage and the labour process and highlight the relations-in-production that span the workplace. From these accounts of tipped work, workers emerge as individuals – who suffer, cope with, and make meaning from tipped work – while managerial control is reified. Missing from this picture is a collective view of workers – whether and how workers can shape the terms of their work and increase their earnings in a way that is both more inclusive and more lasting than what can be accomplished in the individual service interaction. This individualizing is perhaps unsurprising under the circumstances, as today only 1.4 per cent of workers in the food service and drinking sector are unionized (U.S. Bureau of Labor Statistics, 2020a). This was not always the case, and the brief survey of the history of tipped work above reveals how organized service workers struggled to shape the laws and norms of their industry. It is this missing perspective of the tipped wage on which I will try to shed light over these pages, through the framework of the two-employer problem.

RESEARCH METHODS

This article draws upon ethnographic field notes, interview transcripts, news articles, and transcripts and video from the 2018 New York State hearings on the subminimum wage, gathered as part of a broader project on contemporary restaurant work and the history and political status of tipped wage systems in the

United States. Supplementing these data are ninety-five surveys with New York State restaurant workers collected by undergraduate student researchers from Syracuse University in a separate, 2019 project in partnership with ROC United.[6] These provided background on the Syracuse-area restaurant workforce as I formulated my own research plan and, where relevant, I also draw in this article on specific statistics gleaned from the worker surveys.

This research takes as a case study a large US-based chain restaurant, which I call 'Tastee Co.', located in a shopping mall in Syracuse, New York. There I undertook three-and-a-half months of participant observation, working two to three shifts per week as a host in the restaurant's front-of-house. I also conducted 10 in-depth interviews with area tipped restaurant workers. These conversations provided an opportunity to discuss my observations and early theorizing with my coworkers and to compare that experience with those of several workers in other Syracuse-area food service establishments.

While ultimately my field site was determined the moment the Tastee Co. general manager offered me a position, I had concluded early on that employment in the family-style chain restaurant offered several advantages to this project. The Tastee Co. front-of-house provided access to a larger and more diverse workforce than would many smaller establishments. Its design and labour process – in many ways indistinguishable from those of the other, similarly cavernous restaurants within a stone's throw of the entrance – was one that had been worked out in distant corporate offices and replicated across the country's suburban landscapes. Such restaurants share with those in the fast-food segment a degree of industrialization[7] but retain the labour-intensive production process characteristic of independent restaurants and the fine dining segment.

The confluence of my own project and the ROC United collaboration also pointed me towards this restaurant segment. Worker surveys had revealed that tipped wages were in widespread used in the relatively low-priced chain restaurants in local malls. I was surprised to find, as well, watching videos and reading transcripts from the New York State hearings that it was not only workers in the fine dining sector (where high menu prices translate to high tips) who defended the maintenance of their wage system. Many workers who turned out in favour of the continuation of tip credits worked for comparatively low-priced local chain restaurants such as Applebee's and TGI Friday's (Subminimum, 2018).

My first foray into the field was a job seeker, and in this process, I made clear my willingness to accept any front-of-house position available, a tactic which had both practical and investigatory purposes. Flexibility gained me access to the field as speedily as possible, but it also gave me insight into the managerial sorting mechanisms and the 'logic of aesthetic labor' through which prospective workers are shuffled into particular service positions (Williams & Connell, 2010). My own sorting was unsurprising. I had in common with most other Tastee Co. hosts that I was a woman and that I had minimal prior restaurant experience. It also proved fortuitous. The host stand was the place where servers, bartenders, bussers, runners, and managers congregated throughout the shift to discuss customers, tips, and anything else of note and positioned me at a way station from which I could observe the entire drama of the dining room.

Accessing the workplace, I would study in this manner was not without its drawbacks and hurdles. Entering the field without managerial approval required that I first obtain a waiver of the informed consent requirement from my university's Institutional Review Board (IRB). This approach left me with limited access to managerial decision making or the conflicts that arise between multiple layers of management. While I was open with my coworkers about my project and research interests, any notetaking I was able to do in the field was surreptitious or confined to the restroom when I was sent to perform 'checks' (clean), out of sight of the cameras through which our general manager observed us at the host stand. I recorded quick voice memos on my phone when it was more convenient and often began recording a narration of the night's events the moment I stepped out of the mall. That said, I had little confidence that I would be hired if I revealed my project, and I feared that managerial approval would come with managerial surveillance – or, worse still, might imply some expectation that I participate in surveilling my coworkers. Immediately following each shift, and into the small hours of the morning, I cobbled together those notes and voice recordings I had amassed while on the floor and wrote up lengthy field notes recounting the day's events.

Tastee Co. had a large floating workforce. Frequent turnover meant that the size of the front-of-house staff was in a state of perpetual flux, but the number hovered at around 100 workers during my months of employment. Many of these workers never appeared on the schedule, and a typical shift was comprised of just six to eight servers, two or three hosts, two bartenders, a take-out person, and managers. Overseeing our location's front-of-house operations were a general manager, assistant manager, front-of-house manager, and bar manager, and on any given shift two or three of their cohort would preside over the floor. The front-of-house staff was racially diverse and skewed young, a large proportion of college age, and many were students working part time. Save for one male worker, the host stand was made up entirely of young women, while the staff of bartenders and servers was fairly evenly split between women and men.

Servers and bartenders were compensated in the same manner. They were paid the New York State food service tipped wage[8] from the restaurant and earned tips directly from customers, as did the worker running the restaurant's take-out operation, who earned tips on top of the regular state minimum wage. Support staff – runners and bussers – was also paid the tipped wage and was expected to receive a 'tip out' from servers at the end of the shift, the total amount of which was left to the server's discretion, while hosts were paid the state minimum. Each wage structure adhered to the constraints and managerial objectives attending the various front-of-house positions. As I explore in what follows, these different wage structures corresponded also to distinct labour processes and the form of relations between workers, and between workers and customers, on the floor.

In this ethnographic research, I loosely followed the extended case method (Burawoy, 1998, p. 6), the 'reconstruction of existing theory', which has a lengthy history in ethnographic studies of the labour process (see, e.g., Burawoy, 1979; Sallaz, 2009; Sherman, 2007). Seeing in worker support for the tipped wage an unexpected expression of workers' *interests,* I sought to trace these back to the point of production and understandings of the orchestration of workplace consent and control. Field notes and interview transcripts were uploaded into the program Atlas.ti and then read, reread, and coded throughout the research process, using a semi-open coding system that mirrored the 'iterative' approach that I took as the project unfolded (Luker, 2008). While I began the project with a set of key codes drawn from prior studies of restaurant work and consent in the labour process, others emerged through this back and forth, in turn, bolstering and challenging the theoretical framework I brought to the field.

FINDINGS

While tipped service workers in the first half of the 20th century leveraged their collective power to pressure employers or entire industries to increase their wages, today, tipped workers primarily turn to customers for their pay. In this reliance on tipped income, the terrain of struggle has shifted from that between workers and capital to that between the individual worker and customer. But, workers are owed a wage by their employers and can make no such demands of the customer. Instead, they individually strategize, cajole, and attempt to demonstrate the value of their labour. In what follows, I examine the consequences of the two-employer problem for workers, as well as the way that this particular wage structure shapes the tipped labour process.

The Customer as Employer

Like many states, New York mandates a tipped wage above the federal tipped wage, but one is still low enough that many tipped restaurant workers dismiss their 'hourly' as something merely pro forma, and not their *real* wage. 'My hourly rate stays the same no matter what, but I'm not working off my hourly', Vanessa,[9] a Tastee Co. server, told me. 'I'm working off tips'. This was something I heard from servers time and again. Jack, a career server at a downtown restaurant, described his base wages as essentially pocket money: 'You would spend that as soon as you left', he told me. 'Stop at a gas station for a Gatorade and, you know ... I've never even budgeted that into anything I do. It's just extra money'. Workers' lack of attention to, and even ignorance of, the value of base wages was also reflected in surveys with New York State restaurant workers. While all respondents were paid the tipped subminimum wage, a majority (56 per cent) either incorrectly reported the amount of that wage or said they simply had no idea what it was. As Jack put it,

> I get it direct deposited and I don't ever see it. I don't ever notice it, open it up. It just goes into my bank account ... If you're worried about your paycheck, then you shouldn't be in the restaurant business, because you're just working on tips.

The significance of the tipped portion of the wage, over and above that provided by the employer, is part and parcel of a system in which workers are not only encouraged, but in fact compelled, to perform the work of tip earning. The very existence of a tipped wage category assumes, and functionally requires, that workers earn tips. Employers are legally required to ensure that workers earn at least the hourly full minimum wage, but it is questionable to what extent tipped workers can really count on this modest guarantee. Wage theft cases are rampant in the food service industry (U.S. Department of Labor, 2019), and in New York City alone, restaurant wage theft lawsuits made up 23 per cent of FLSA cases in 2018 (Allegretto, 2018). The FLSA also, as Ross and Welsh (2021) point out, only secures back pay for workers up to the regular state or federal minimum wage, and so does not address circumstances in which wage theft might include earned tips.

Even at Tastee Co., a moderately priced chain restaurant, servers expected to earn well above the minimum wage of $7.50 in combined income and servers commonly told me that they considered $150 for a 5- to 6-hour shift a 'good night'. One of the higher earners told me, just after preparing her taxes, that she had calculated her earnings averaged about $30 per hour, a not-uncommon wage for tipped restaurant servers (Haley-Lock & Ewert, 2011). Many tipped workers remain in service jobs for just this reason because they are unable to earn as much in their alternative or preferred modes of employment. Such was the case for Alex, who had returned to waiting tables after working as an adjunct instructor. Of course, restaurant service jobs are not, on the whole, extremely lucrative – in 2018, the median hourly income for tipped workers in New York was just $11.16 (Allegretto, 2018). But that so many workers rely on the customer for such a disproportionate amount of their earnings suggests that it is really to the customer, and not the employer, that workers look for their wages.

While Leidner (1993, 1996) argued that allegiances in the 'service triangle' were constantly shifting, in the case of the restaurant server paid the tipped wage, these relationships take on a very particular formation. This is not a matter of misapprehension on the part of restaurant workers, but the direct result of the codification of a tipped wage. The effect of the court's ruling in *Jacksonville Terminal,* that the tip was a form of legal wage, is to turn the customer, as the provider of this wage, into a secondary employer. As such, a tipped wage redefines, and doubles, the typical employer-employee relationship, as Josephson (1956, p. 89) wrote of mid-century workers wearied of serving 'two bosses'.

On a slow day at Tastee Co., I asked Dori, a server, who she worried about more while she was working: the customers or the managers? 'Oh, the customers', she replied. 'I'm not worried about the managers. They don't do anything. They don't care'. Servers relied on customers for the bulk of their earnings and perceived other workers either as helpmates or impediments to their work, and these two facts combined to contribute to the relative invisibility of management in the labour process and on the dining room floor. Given the choice between those 'two bosses', many servers professed a distinct preference for keeping their interactions limited to the customers, whenever possible. When I asked him about his own interactions with management at work, Jack replied, 'The manager? The less work they have to do, the better. They're happy with you'. Managerial involvement was 'the game changer', he told me, and likely to spark 'a disciplinary action of some sort'. This accords with a finding common in labour process theory: work can be organized in such a way as to obscure the very relations of production by which it is governed (Burawoy, 1979). In the restaurant, where tips are calculated as a percentage of the bill, worker and managerial objectives largely align, and so the 'game' of tip earning comprises the near-entirety of work for many servers. Accordingly, the labour process appears to unfold between the worker and the customer, and management's authority on the floor primarily reemerges in times of strife or, especially, as Sallaz (2002) observes, in the rare occasions when a worker's tip-seeking conflicts with managerial aims.

In this way, beyond simply providing them a subsidy, a tipped wage provides additional services to employers. While real employers retreat behind the screen of the customer-as-employer, workers willingly self-exploit. This vanishing act is reminiscent of an effect Marx describes among workers paid a piece rate, determined not by hours worked but work completed. 'Since the quality and intensity of the work are here controlled by the very form of the wage', he writes, 'superintendence of labour becomes to a great extent superfluous' (Marx, 1867/1990, p. 695). Specifically, tips ensure that workers will generally perform the work that management requires, skilled service customization. As with the piece wage, tipped wages synchronize this managerial aim and workers' own monetary objectives, and so 'it is naturally in the personal interest of the worker that he should strain his labour-power as intensely as possible' (Marx, 1867/1990). Joseph, a Tastee Co. host with little patience for the servers, summarized it thusly: 'If the company was paying you, I highly doubt some of these servers would kiss their tables' asses like they do now. Some servers just do any bitty thing'. He put on a mocking, falsetto voice and continued:

> 'Oh, no, I know my table so well. They don't want green onions in the chicken. Oh, no, don't do that!' The managers probably look at that table fifty-six as dollar signs. And you better take care of that dollar sign, because if the dollar sign doesn't leave with the money we want it to leave, then – well, there's not much they can do, but they're just going to be a little upset. But if they're like, 'Oh my god, your server was wonderful. We're definitely coming back', and they see those dollar signs coming back in ....

As Joseph highlights, were it not for the fact that servers rely on customers directly for such a disproportionate amount of their wages, they would be unlikely to exert nearly as much of this customized service labour. The tipped wage structure itself accomplishes managerial aims more economically than could a traditional wage and direct managerial oversight. Tip earning, as Sallaz (2002, p. 421) observed among casino blackjack dealers, 'spontaneously generates service provision', and so the customer-as-employer is a time- and money-saving boon to restaurant management. In what follows, we will see that for workers, this two-employer situation means something else entirely.

Antisocial Animals: Tips and Cooperative Labour

One significant effect of this two-employer problem, wherein the customer emerges as a secondary employer – informal, yet the server's primary preoccupation – is that tipped workers appear to be engaged in separate and distinct labour processes on the dining room floor. This effect is evident both between tipped workers and between the tipped and non-tipped workers of the front and back of house. Studies of tipped restaurant work have found that tip earning can fuel competition between workers and accentuate extant divisions and hierarchies in the workplace (Gatta, 2009b; Wilson, 2019). In the provision of customized service, tipped service and non-tipped kitchen workers are often at cross purposes, as their modes of income and the requirements of their jobs may suggest opposite courses of action.

Unlike the kitchen staff, tipped restaurant servers, when engrossed in the individuated service interaction, appear to be working for different employers. A server quoted in Brewster and Wills (2013, pp. 200–201) puts it most succinctly:

> This isn't [the restaurant's] table; this is your table. … The way you should look at it, whenever you're serving, is you're renting out, kind of like you're renting out a little section in the mall to have your business. You got your little business stand up there, and that's the way you should look at it and sell yourself. That's basically the way I look at it. *I'm not working for [the restaurant] I'm working for myself.* [emphasis added]

Such entrepreneurialism is a commonly described feature of tipped service work (see, e.g., Paules, 1991; Sallaz, 2009) but is particularly notable here for a couple of reasons. First, this worker articulates the perception that, when engaged in tip earning, they are not, in fact, working for their primary employers. Second, the worker also sums up the non-cooperative, or antisocial, quality of this work. If workers see themselves as 'renting out' tables and 'working for [themselves]', relations-in-production take on an a particularly antisocial form.

Brewster and Wills (2013) understand this feature as a positive avenue for workers' empowerment in the workplace, and it may well be experienced as such. Some Tastee Co. servers enjoyed the apparent autonomy that customer-facing tipped work provides, and in the two-employer context favoured the customer over management, when the two were at odds. They might re-seat customers asking for a coveted booth or a window view to the mall, upsetting the table rotation and its veneer of fairness.[10] They were quick to 'comp' (provide free of charge) and replace items when faced with a frequent customer complaint, hairs in the food, thus infuriating the kitchen staff, who (wearing caps and hairnets) insisted the offending hairs came from the customers themselves.

The fact remains that workers, regardless of how they see themselves on the floor or from where their money comes, *are* employed by the restaurant, and management always retains the ability to fire a worker or to censure them through unfavourable scheduling or section assignments. Tastee Co. workers were always reminded of this last threat by the malign presence of the so-called cursed table near the kitchen, at which customers refused to sit. When, at the beginning of a shift, server Jane saw that she had been assigned this table, she shook her head and said to me in dismay, 'Oh man, I'm in the time out section'. The cursed table was but one reminder that servers' autonomy remains incomplete and that the entrepreneurial server may in fact 'misrecognize … their own agency' (Sallaz, 2009, p. 61).

These qualities recall again the conditions of piece-wage work, to which interactive service work more generally has been compared (see Sherman, 2007), and where 'the wider scope that piece wages give to individuality tends to develop both that individuality, and with it the worker's sense of liberty, his independence and self-control, and also the competition of workers with each other' (Marx, 1867/1990, p. 697). The wage form itself structures relations-in-production, spurring competitiveness between workers who might otherwise experience their work as cooperative. But where the resemblance stops is that in piece-wage work, workers still labour for, and are paid by, the same capitalist employer. They are 'brought together ... employed simultaneously by the same capital, the same capitalist', and 'their labour-powers are bought simultaneously by him' (Marx, 1867/1990, p. 447). In the case of tipped work, workers appear to receive the tipped portion of their wage from separate employers. Because earning this second, and usually larger, portion of the wage requires servers' unfettered access to the customer, servers might see other workers as competition for tables – or jobs – within the workplace.

This was certainly the case at Tastee Co. Servers' anxiety over access to tables typically manifested in their hawkish monitoring of the host stand, and perpetual squabbles with hosts over fairness and adherence to the 'rotation', the order by which tables were allocated. Kyle, a server at a popular downtown restaurant, generally attested to the cordiality of his relationships with coworkers, but admitted, 'If someone gets hired, I do start thinking about my shifts being taken'. At the more extreme end of the spectrum was Jack's workplace, a restaurant notorious among other servers I interviewed for its intense and high stakes dining room. 'I like to spread the wealth, whereas some people like to hoard the wealth', he said.

> To work with strong personalities, you have to be a strong personality, I feel. Because if you're a weak personality you will get taken advantage of, one hundred percent, and you will make $100 to $200 less than that person. So you have to stand on your toes and make sure the people around you understand that you can't just come up and steal a table.

I asked Jack how he projected that to other people, and he laughed. 'Uh, how I project that is, "Stop stealing my tables'. In the restaurant where Jack worked, servers were engaged in constant territorial skirmishes, attempting to eke out additional tips by encroaching on tables and poaching customers. Of course, servers can only maximize their earnings by these means at the expense of their coworkers, and so Jack cultivated an aggressive, imposing posture on the floor to discourage those sorts of advances. At Tastee Co., the functioning of the table rotation system and clear delineation of sections meant that there were rarely direct confrontations between severs over customers or tables. More often, servers would blame the hosts, who mediated between them and who they perceived to be in control of the allocation of customers and tables. When a server named Jeff believed that he had been skipped twice in the table rotation, he harangued my coworker at the host stand, reducing her to tears, insisting that he had earned only half of what the other servers had made that night in tips and that she was to blame.

Conflict also frequently emerges over the distribution of tips themselves, as it is common for non-pooled restaurants to require that servers allocate a portion of their tips to the support staff – usually bussers, runners, and hosts – who are not directly tipped but facilitate service in the front of house. Tastee Co. workers on both sides of the tip out described these kinds of eruptions to me. Server

Kim refused to tip out a busser who she felt had left her in the lurch during an especially busy shift. Afterwards, she faced an oblique censure, akin to being shunned, from our general manager. Joseph, my fellow host at the stand, harboured years-long grudges against the servers he felt had stiffed him when he worked as a runner. In a sense, the tip out functioned as tip work in miniature, making the server the employer of support workers' services. Unlike in the wage relation between servers and customers, however, management still retained some authority over these transactions, and so might step in to curtail any perceived tyranny on the part of servers, as Dale did in the interaction between the server and busser noted above.

Server Alex described her thinking around the tip out, of which she was not especially proud: 'I haven't counted it, but maybe I have $25 in cash, and it's the end of the night, and I'm tired and I don't care, and the host – maybe they didn't help'. This kind of hyper-individualism around the tip also seemed to explain the negative attitudes servers I interviewed expressed about the prospect of tip pooling. Vanessa said of a tip pool, 'The kitchen would get it, the dishwashers would get it, and honestly, I don't think that's fair'. The tip, she said, was 'my money' given by customers who 'just want to see me'. When I asked Kyle if he would want to work in a pooled house, he made a face. 'I don't like that. I'm selling my personality'.

In this context, it is perhaps not surprising that workers' resistance is often highly individualized and directed towards customers or fellow workers. Workers might demonstrate that resistance by refusing to engage emotionally with customers (Erickson, 2004b; Gatta, 2002) or by attempting to influence the rotation system or speed through customers (Paules, 1991). Such resistance does not pose any challenge to capital but may impinge on other workers, especially when workers refuse a task that ultimately falls to a coworker or circumvent the rotation and 'steal' a table. At times, servers might signal refusal by forgoing the tip altogether (Gatta, 2009a), but I would argue that this mode of resistance is also bounded. Restaurant servers, for whom tip earning constitutes the near-entirety of work, cannot make a habit of forgoing their earnings, or refusing to do the job for which they have been hired, and likely reserve these extreme approaches for the worst and most abusive customers. Crucially, tip earning is not only divisive in creating hyper-competitive relations-in-production on the floor. It also performs a further degree of mystification, wherein the subjective experience of the sale of workers' labour-power does not appear to reveal the shared objective sale of their labour-power to a single employer.

One caveat, however, to the heightened divisions of the tipped labour process comes with the pooled house, where tips are shared according to various schemes, either by all servers, all workers in the front-of-house, or throughout the restaurant. My data do not provide sufficient evidence to discuss the pooled context at length; as I noted above, Tastee Co. was a non-pooled house, and while several the workers I interviewed had experience with tip pools, only one was at that time employed in a pooled house. That said, the reports of even these few workers support observations of other studies of tip pooling (see Mulinari, 2019; Sallaz, 2002), that in the pooled house workers may experience more cooperation and solidarity, and such systems may contribute to diminishing, or even eliminating, the two-employer problem. Alex, whose former employer had utilized a tip pool that included the back-of-house workers, said,

> The kitchen was more willing to work with us when we had difficult tables that wanted annoying things. They were less likely to blame us, or be tense, or make it hard on us, because they understood that if they did this annoying thing that the table wanted, they were probably going to get some return on it as well, not just me. Why go out of their way and ruin their flow, and they're not going to see any difference for that?

Compared to her current, non-pooled employer, there was 'a lot more cohesiveness, and the feeling of folks and the way they related in the workplace was great'. Gia, who worked in a restaurant that utilized a tip pool, made frequent reference to the 'team' environment, where her coworkers were generally willing to lend a hand and assist one another in running food out to the floor or handling customer requests. That said, tip pools might pose their own challenges, and Alex described the light-hearted, but nonetheless real, mutual pressure to perform: 'People will be puttin' on their push-up bras like, 'It's for the tip pool'.

Of the workers I spoke to during this ethnography and in interviews, only Alex had any first-hand experience of collective organizing with her coworkers. In her previous, pooled, workplace, workers had banded together and conducted a button-wearing campaign to demand the censure of a manager who had harassed a worker in the kitchen with a racial slur. As a result of the campaign, the restaurant's general manager grudgingly agreed to hold a meeting with the workers, ultimately demoting the offending manager. While these accounts offer just a glimpse into the pooled house, it seems that this would be a fruitful avenue for future study of the tipped labour process.

The Unregulated, Informal Employer

While pooling arrangements may provide workers some buffer from the vicissitudes of tipped work, the worker earning tips directly and individually may be more likely to be subject to uneven, and even exploitative, treatment in the workplace. A worker's legal employer is (or, at least, should be) subject to regulation regarding their treatment of employees, but the same is not true of the customer. As such, and in the interest of tip earning, workers may be subjected to and even feel compelled to tolerate treatment from customers that they would not from their employer of record. Studies of restaurant work suggest this is the case, finding disproportionate rates of workplace sexual harassment reported by tipped restaurant servers (Restaurant Opportunities Center (ROC) United, 2012, 2020). In the 2019 survey of New York State tipped workers, 47 per cent of workers reported that they or a coworker had experienced sexual harassment in the workplace, and 52 per cent said that they or a coworker had experienced verbal abuse. Studies on tipping practices (see Lynn, 2006; Lynn et al., 2008) also demonstrate that customers often discriminate when they tip, and on average leave higher tips for white servers than they do for black servers.

Many of my Tastee Co. coworkers had witnessed or experienced discrimination, racial or otherwise, from customers, and it was commonplace enough that workers were generally unphased by it. When I asked Vanessa about unequal treatment from customers on the floor, she shrugged and responded, 'Yeah, I've had tables turn me down. I'm like, "Hi, my name is Vanessa". And they're like, "We'd like to speak to your manager". They don't even say my name, but they want a male server'. Reflecting on her own workplace, server Alex said that one of her male coworkers, whom she described as 'outwardly queer' and 'fairly effeminate', consistently earned less in tips than did the rest of the servers, something Alex attributed to prejudice on the part of diners. In her own customer interactions, Alex frequently experienced 'subtle', but nevertheless disconcerting, attention, including 'unwelcome looks of appraisal'. I asked her how she handled these situations, and she told me,

> I make a decision about the kind of friendly I'm going to be. It's like a huge, crazy algorithm. ... It's like, am I going to be curt and short? Am I going to make eye contact, and smile, and be like, you're nice, I'm nice ...

She paused and sighed, and I began to ask her if this 'algorithm' of decision making was simply about getting through the night without altercation, or if it meant walking a fine line to maximize her tips. She cut me off, saying bluntly:

> Yeah, frankly. Because you don't want to. In any interaction, even if you're not a server, in the world, when you feel intimidated by a guy like that, or uncomfortable, you're always doing math about, what can I do to not provoke this person, but avoid feeling uncomfortable? It's intensified when there's money involved because *you don't just need them to not harass you. You need them to give you money*.

Alex's description encapsulates the conundrum workers face due to this informal wage relation. In every customer interaction, they must weigh the cost of accepting mistreatment against the cost of refusing to do so. Workers are responsible not only for the management of their own emotions but are also burdened with the onus of managing the behaviour of their customers, including potential harassers. Up to a point, abuse and harassment may be tolerated precisely because refusal comes with the threat of the lost tip. Workers are for the most part left to make these impossible decisions entirely on their own. From the employers' perspective, the tip 'spontaneously generates customized service provision' (Sallaz, 2002, p. 421), but Alex's account demonstrates that only from the *outside* does this customization, and the allocation of workers' efforts, appear spontaneous. What goes unseen is the labour workers perform calibrating each one of these service interactions, tailoring their own behaviour, attempting to smooth ruffled feathers and deflect inappropriate behaviour, and weighing risk against possible reward.

However, accurate is a worker's 'huge, crazy, algorithm' telling them how much and what type of service labour to extend to customers, workers ultimately must perform this labour on faith. Only when the check has been paid do they know how well, and if, they have been remunerated. This is typical of capitalist employment, wherein 'the worker advances the use-value of his labour-power to the capitalist', letting 'the buyer consume it before he receives payment of the price' (Marx, 1867/1990, p. 278). What is different about this 'credit' (Marx, 1867/1990) to the customer, rather than capitalist, is the absence of any contract between worker and customer fixing the tipped portion of the wage at a historically and morally determined rate (Marx, 1867/1990). Workers may employ any number of strategies to influence the amount of the tip, including small actions or subtle cues to the customer (Lynn, 2006; Lynn et al., 2008; Lynn & McCall, 2009), but ultimately there remains an element of divination as servers seek to read the tea leaves in the faces, dress, and behaviour of their customers. Kyle admitted that he expected white, middle-class customers to tip the best and most regularly, and Gia had low expectations of non-American customers or those who were dining in the company of their children.

Tipped workers do seem to have fairly firm ideas of what constitutes an acceptable tipping percentage: when asked, most workers were appalled by anything short of 18 per cent of the check, considering 20 per cent the baseline of decency. While servers may conceive of the tip as a fee for service (Mulinari, 2019), and there exists a broad cultural consensus around tipping percentages, customers are in no way obligated (saving an automatic gratuity charge)[11] to acknowledge it. Nothing prevents the customer from leaving without tipping, even if a server has exerted an enormous amount of service labour. Not surprisingly, servers that I worked with and interviewed frequently told me that restaurant industry workers themselves were the best and most consistent tippers. Complaining one night about a table that had 'stiffed' her, Lauren, a longtime Tastee Co. server, said wistfully, 'Give me a table of industry people, industry people flush with tips'.

As with the piece wage, tips do 'not alter the general relation between capital and wage-labour' (Marx, 1867/1990, p. 697). The core relationship of surplus value extraction remains intact underneath all the apparent particulars of the restaurant labour process, and though tips are both unpredictable and apparently attached to a specific exertion of service labour. However, the unique relationship between customer and server in the context of tipped work sets the restaurant industry apart. For piece-wage workers, the rate attached to a piece was both fixed in advance and a constant source of struggle with their employers (Marx, 1867/1990), as wages are a general ground for economic and political struggle between workers and capital (Mann, 2007).

While food service workers can and do struggle with their employers and, in legislative fights, over the amount of the employer-provided tipped wage, there is no comparable terrain of struggle between workers and customers over the amount of the tip. To put it another way, workers are engaged in a double sale, and double advancing, of the use-value of their labour-power. To their employers, they advance its use-value at a fixed rate that both parties (and state and federal governments) agree is substantially below its exchange value. Then, workers attempt the resale of their labour-power by again advancing its use-value, this time to customers with no guarantee of payment. Moreover, the exchange value of this second iteration of labour-power remains unclear. While there exists a loose social consensus around tip percentages, and workers ('industry people', as server Lauren put it) have clear notions of what constitutes an acceptable tip, these norms may or may not be recognized. Further, the customer might not even be aware they are making a purchase.

All workers can really do is attempt to demonstrate the value of their service labour to the customer through its skilled provision. As a result, many servers place a great deal of importance on the *skill* of service. 'I pride myself on being very personable and giving good service', said Gia, who worked at an upscale restaurant catering to Syracuse's wealthy suburbanites. 'It's something I prioritize'. Kim, a recent hire at Tastee Co., reflected on the high tips that she earned at a previous restaurant job, saying, 'I was recognized for my hard work. … I just have a lot of pride in that'. But workers also frequently acknowledge the fundamental insecurity of seeking the bulk of their incomes from customers who can choose not to pay or who – due to bad weather or some misalignment of the stars – may fail to materialize altogether. Vanessa shrugged, and of this uncertainty told me, 'It's just the name of the game'. Alex, too, said,

> I compare it to a game, like gambling, but not like slots. Like blackjack or something. You can learn to read. It's chance, and you're not going to win every time, but you can be better or worse at it.

They felt they had some control, but it was only ever partial.

Sam, who worked a tipped counter service job, had a somewhat less equivocal take on this extension of credit to the customer and the way it placed workers in the position of perpetual supplicants.

> Everyone's like, 'Oh, you don't like tips? Then I guess you're not a good worker, because you're not getting the tips you want'. And it's not the fact of that. It's the fact that you're relying on other people, outside your employer, for a substantial amount of your living. That's grotesque in a way … asking people to be like, Oh, you have to perform for this stranger, and make sure it's optimal, so that they may or may not give you money.

Sam was clear on the solution to this issue, as well as the crux of the problem. Employers should have to pay more – at least the regular minimum wage, he told me. The 'grotesque' element of tipped service work that Sam describes reflects the real precariousness of tipped service work, where customers 'may or may not give you money'. It is a condition made only more glaring by the COVID-19 crisis, which escalated rapidly in the weeks after I left the field. Most of my former coworkers were by that point out of work and the pandemic continued to make the work of 'good service' largely impossible. It was, after all, difficult to read or communicate emotions behind the masks.

When I asked Sam why he thought restaurant employers did not pay the full minimum wage, he said simply, 'It's just capitalism', an observation that hints at two broader points about this two-employer problem. First, though these wage and workplace dynamics may be so pervasive as to seem an inevitability, they are historically contingent. The profit motive is an ever-present feature of capitalist economies in general, but tipped wages are not. It is primarily in the US, where for workers like Sam an extreme form of free market capitalism is entirely normalized, that this entrepreneurial system persists. That said, while the informality of tip earning may be experienced by workers as intimately tied to their identities or outward presentations, ultimately it is a structural feature of the tipped labour process. It is precisely *because* this tipped labour process is so individualizing that workers generally face each new iteration of the service encounter, where they 'perform for [a] stranger', alone.

CONCLUSION

While tipped restaurant work has long attracted sociological study, in these pages, I have attempted to provide a missing piece of the tipped wage puzzle and to cast tipped restaurant workers in a light in which they are not often considered: as a collective workforce 'brought together ... by the same capital' (Marx, 1867/1990, p. 447). It is precisely this view of tipped work, and the challenges posed to workers collectively, that the two-employer problem lays bare. As I have argued, in the two-employer problem, workers appear to be engaged in separate labour processes, whether they see themselves as employed by the customer or as canny entrepreneurs making sales at a 'rented' table. Tips are an uncertain source of income at best, disbursed by customers who are most likely unaware that the gratuity they provide is a worker's legal (and often primary) wage. Finally, the presence of the secondary employer ultimately obscures workers' objective relationship to their employers, as well as the fact that they share this objective relationship with their coworkers on and off the floor.

Unions recognized the insidious strategic problems lurking within tipped work over a century ago. It was readily apparent that the endeavour of tip earning put workers in direct competition for customers and prompted workers to willingly self-exploit by opting to work longer hours (U.S. Bureau of Labor Statistics, 1919). As a result, and as I found in the Tastee Co. dining room, the constraints of tip-earning function to further mystify the social nature of capitalist work, from which class solidarity develops. Tips also set a ceiling on unions' attempts to win higher wages for workers. A wage from an employer was something that unions could fight to increase, a site of political struggle, 'a functional means through which capital and workers assert, contest, and address workers' interests' (Mann, 2007, p. 150). The value of the tip might be historically and morally determined (Marx, 1867/1990) in the sense that there exists a broad cultural consensus around appropriate percentages. But, any customer may choose to ignore that consensus, and there exists no contract, framework, or other means through which it can be enforced. That is to say, there is no real terrain of struggle between workers and customers, as there is between workers and capital, through which this pseudo-wage can be antagonistically determined (Marx, 1932), forcing workers to 'depend on the generosity of the patron, an uncertain factor at best' (U.S. Bureau of Labor Statistics, 1927).

It is also worth noting that these conditions do not arise endogenously but are actively cultivated by employers and by the food service industry writ large. Service industry employers fought for, and to maintain, this wage system, one that reduces their expenditure on labour to an almost unprecedented low. The National Restaurant Association has been particularly aggressive in defending and suppressing the value of this wage, and, in 1996, successfully lobbied for its decoupling from the regular minimum wage and freezing at $2.13 per hour. The 'other NRA' has also continued to fight any increases to the wage through front groups like the misleadingly named Restaurant Workers of America and astroturfed 'Save Our Tips' campaign (Fang & Jilani, 2018; Thielman, 2018).

Nor does some inherent quality of restaurant work mandate such arrangements, as workers and diners in many other nations can attest. In the US, restaurant workers' wages have stagnated over the last two decades, and food service workers are some of the lowest paid in the country (Jayaraman, 2013; U.S. Bureau of Labor

Statistics, 2020b). In cities and states with separate tipped wages, tipped workers are almost twice as likely to live in poverty as non-tipped workers (Allegretto & Cooper, 2014). As for the organizations representing those workers, today, there is little union presence among tipped workers: only 1.4 per cent of workers in the broad food services and drinking sector, within which most tipped workers are employed, are union members (U.S. Bureau of Labor Statistics, 2020a). As unionized workers predicted a century ago, tip earning, beyond creating unstable work conditions and subsidizing employers, may have contributed to this state of affairs.

These figures, and the dispiriting history of the US tipped wage system, are no less significant today. While tipped work is a longstanding feature of the US restaurant industry, it is spreading to new occupations, as is use of the tipped subminimum wage category (Restaurant Opportunities Center (ROC) United, 2019). As tipped work expands in, for example, the unstable realm of the so-called gig economy, workers' dependence on the good graces of customers is compounded by the facts that they work not only for tips but also for ratings, and that companies eschew an employer status altogether. In these spheres, this story of the customer-as-employer and its effects on the labour process may presage things to come. If the use of tipped wages becomes more widespread and entrenched in these growing industries, it will be incumbent upon researchers to figure out how it is that such workers' undue reliance on customers for their wages shapes the labour process and influences how and whether workers organize (for two recent studies that do examine the role of the customer in the 'gig' labour process, see Belanche, Casaló, Flavián, & Pérez-Rueda, 2021 and Healy, Pekarek, & Vromen, 2020).

To return to the conundrum that began this study and the contentious hearing at which the two workers quoted at the top of this article spoke, I would argue that the concept of the two-employer problem aids in the analysis of contemporary debates over the tipped wage and the very real, impassioned split amongst tipped workers on the issue of their wages. The diner worker quoted above had tears in their eyes as they spoke. The bartender who followed, also quoted, had to pause their speech so that the jeering crowd could be chastised into silence. As Jack, one of the servers I interviewed for this study, put it, 'Change is bad for a lot of people. They don't like it. And that's what it would be for me, is change'. All told, a tipped wage may work to the advantage of some workers and the disadvantage of others and likely increases inequality across the workforce (Haley-Lock & Ewert, 2011). But therein lies the rub: the tipped wage divides workers – certainly across the industry, and even within one workplace. The effects of this wage on the tipped labour process suggest that the continued existence of a two-tier wage system forms an obstacle to the realization of workers' long-term abilities to present the organized front required to shape the terms of their own work.

NOTES

1. Full transcripts from the New York State Department of Labor Syracuse hearing on the subminimum wage are available at https://www.labor.ny.gov/workerprotection/laborstandards/subminimumwage/transcript-syracuse.pdf, while video of the hearing is available at https://www.youtube.com/watch?v=AFgCbuLHZf4. Hearings were conducted throughout the state in the summer of 2018.

2. As a Pullman Company manager put it when questioned about the company's hiring practices during the 1915 Commission on Industrial Relations: 'the Southern negro is more pleasing to the traveling public. He is more adapted to wait on people and serve with a smile' (Scott, 1916, p. 107). At work in the sleeper cars, porters were called 'George' or 'Georgie' after the company's founder George Mortimer Pullman, and were expected to fade unobtrusively into the background (Bates, 2001; 'Pullman Porters', 1928).

3. In a letter to the manager of the Hotel Stowell in Los Angeles, AFL president Samuel Gompers wrote that he opted to tip at hotels while traveling but continued: 'yet I have maintained the principle of tipping to be unwise and that it tends to lessen the self-respect of a man who accepts a tip' (Scott, 1916, p. 146).

4. In 1960, several service industry unions – the Hotel and Restaurant Employees International Union; the Barbers, Hairdressers and Cosmetologists International Union; the National Maritime Union; and the Seafarers International Union – formed a coalition to lobby congress to address the issue of workers' earned tips in the calculation of Social Security benefits (Segrave, 1998). Four years later, a contingent of unionized restaurant workers planned a trip to the capital to argue the case before the Social Security Administration (Arlen, 1964).

5. At the time, employers could only apply this credit toward the wages of workers who earned at least $20 a month in tips. That threshold is now $30, and in addition workers must spend at least 80 percent of their time on the clock engaged in tip-earning activities (Weissner, 2021).

6. The surveys, asking workers about their wages and working conditions, were provided by ROC United, and extended the organization's reach into the upstate New York region.

7. At Tastee Co., this capital intensity was evident in certain surveillance technology, an algorithmic table management system and online scheduling platform, and in a tendency toward pre-made and standardized ingredients and menu items.

8. At the time of this study, the state food service tipped wage was $7.50 per hour, while the regular state minimum wage for New York State (excluding three regions with higher wages, New York City, Long Island, and Westchester County) was $11.10 (Offenhartz, 2018).

9. To protect participants' confidentiality, all names have been changed.

10. In these cases, workers' particular wage structures inclined them toward distinct responses. The servers, who relied for their wages primarily on tips from customers, were wont to placate customers whenever they could, within the bounds of reason. Hosts, who did not receive tips and were subject to greater scrutiny from managers, were far more likely to refuse customer requests to move or be seated at specific tables. Managers instructed hosts explicitly on this point: we were to politely decline requests for booths, saying that they were 'all reserved'. Often, we followed this direction even when the restaurant was nearly empty, and from the customers were met with blank and baffled stares.

11. It is not atypical for US restaurants to apply such automatic gratuity charges, that is, obligatory tips, to the bills of large parties – generally of six to eight or more persons. In these cases, a percentage of the bill (likely 18% or 20%) will automatically be tacked on and will form the server's tip, though diners may choose to supplement that amount. When restaurants opt to use these automatic gratuities, which provide workers some buffer in particularly high-stakes service interactions, it will generally be stated on the menu.

REFERENCES

Alexander, M. (2021). Tipping is a legacy of slavery. *The New York Times*, February 5. https://www.nytimes.com/2021/02/05/opinion/minimum-wage-racism.html

Allegretto, S. (2018). *Should New York State eliminate its subminimum wage?* Berkeley, CA: Center on Wage and Employment Dynamics and Institute for Research on Labor and Employment, University of California.

Allegretto, S., & Cooper, D. (2014). *Twenty-three years and still waiting for change: Why it's time to give tipped workers the regular minimum wage*. Washington, DC: Economic Policy Institute.

Allegretto, S., & Filion, K. (2011). Waiting for change: The $2.13 federal subminimum wage. Briefing Paper #297. Economic Policy Institute and Center for Wage and Employment Dynamics. Retrieved from http://www.epi.org/publications/waiting_for_change_the_213_federal_subminimum_wage

Arlen, M. J. (1964). Tips on tipping and tippees. *The New York Times* (p. 20), May 31.

Azar, O. (2003). The implications of tipping for economics and management. *International Journal of Social Economics*, *30*(10), 1084–1094. https://doi.org/10.1108/03068290310492878

Barber, W. J., II. (2019). The racist history of tipping. *Politico*, July 17. Retrieved from https://www.politico.com/magazine/story/2019/07/17/william-barber-tipping-racist-past-227361/

Bates, B. (2001). *Pullman porters and the rise of protest politics in Black America, 1925–1945*. Chapel Hill, NC: The University of North Carolina Press.

Belanche, D., Casaló, L., Flavián, C., & Pérez-Rueda, A. (2021). The role of customers in the gig economy: How perceptions of working conditions and service quality influence the use and recommendation of food delivery services. *Service Business*, *14*, 45–75.

Brewster, Z., & Wills, J. (2013). The institution of tipping as a source of employee agency: The case of restaurant servers. *Sociological Focus*, *46*(3), 193–210.

Burawoy, M. (1979). *Manufacturing consent: Changes in the labor process under monopoly capitalism*. Chicago, IL: University of Chicago Press.

Burawoy, M. (1998). The extended case method. *Sociological Theory*, *16*(1), 4–33.

Conlin, M., Lynn, M., & O'Donoghue, T. (2003). The norm of restaurant tipping. *Journal of Economic Behavior & Organization*, *52*, 297–321.

Ehrenreich, B. (2001). *Nickel and dimed: On (not) getting by in America*. New York, NY: Henry Holt and Company.

Erickson, K. (2004a). To invest or detach? Coping strategies and workplace culture in service work. *Symbolic Interaction*, *27*(4), 549–572.

Erickson, K. (2004b). Performing service in American restaurants. *Space & Culture*, *7*, 76–89.

Erickson, K. (2009). *The hungry cowboy: Service and community in a neighborhood restaurant*. Jackson, MS: University of Mississippi Press.

Fang, L., & Jilani, Z. (2018). Save our tips, the campaign against D.C.'s minimum wage hike, is run by a Trump consultant. *The Intercept*, June 11. Retrieved from https://theintercept.com/2018/06/11/save-our-tips-initiative-77-dc-minimum-wage-tipped-employees/

Gatta, M. (2002). *Juggling food and feelings: Emotional balance in the workplace*. Lanham, MD: Lexington Books.

Gatta, M. (2009a). Restaurant servers, tipping, and resistance. *Qualitative Research in Accounting and Management*, *6*(1/2), 80–82.

Gatta, M. (2009b). Balancing trays and smiles: What restaurant servers teach us about hard work in the service economy. In S. Bolton & M. Houlihan (Eds.), *Work matters: Critical reflections on contemporary work* (pp. 114–128). New York, NY: Palgrave Macmillan.

Haley-Lock, A., & Ewert, S. (2011). Waiting for the minimum: US state wage laws, firm strategy and chain restaurant job quality. *Journal of Industrial Relations*, *53*(1), 31–48.

Healy, J., Pekarek, A., & Vromen, A. (2020). Sceptics or supporters? Consumers' views of work in the gig economy. *New Technology, Work and Employment*, *35*(1), 1–19.

Jayaraman, S. (2013). *Behind the kitchen door*. Ithaca, NY: ILR Press.

Josephson, M. (1956). *Union house, union bar: The history of the Hotel and Restaurant Employees and Bartenders International Union, AFL-CIO*. New York, NY: Random House.

Koerner, C. (2018). These tipping activists deny being funded by the restaurant lobby. *Buzzfeed News*, June 27. Retrieved from https://www.buzzfeednews.com/article/claudiakoerner/rwa-restaurant-workers-america-grassroots-astroturf-berman

Leidner, R. (1993). *Fast food, fast talk: Service work and the routinization of everyday life*. Berkeley, CA: University of California Press.

Leidner, R. (1996). Rethinking questions of control: Lessons from McDonald's. In C. L. MacDonald & C. Sirianni (Eds.), *Working in the service society* (pp. 29–49). Philadelphia, PA: Temple University Press.

Luker, K. (2008). *Salsa dancing into the social sciences: Research in an age of info-glut*. Cambridge: Harvard University Press.

Lynn, M. (2006). Race differences in restaurant tipping. *Journal of Foodservice Business Research*, *8*, 99–113.

Lynn, M., & McCall, M. (2009). Techniques for increasing servers' tips: How generalizable are they? *Cornell Hospital Quarterly*, *50*(2), 198–208.

Lynn, M., Sturman, M., Ganley, C., Adams, E., Douglas, M., & McNeal, J. (2008). Consumer racial discrimination in tipping: A replication and extension. *Journal of Applied Social Psychology*, *39*(4), 1045–1060.

Mann, G. (2007). *Our daily bread: Wages, workers, & the political economy of the American West*. Chapel Hill, NC: The University of North Carolina Press.

Marx, K. (1867/1990). *Capital volume 1*. (Trans. D. Fernbach). London: Penguin Books in Association with New Left Review Books.

Marx, K. (1932). *Economic and philosophical manuscripts of 1844*. (Trans. M. Milligan). Moscow: Progress Publishers.

Meyer, B. (2017). Mrs. Orville isn't trying to steal tips: An FLSA story. *The University of Chicago Law Review*, *84*(4), 1971–2016.

Mulinari, P. (2019). Weapons of the poor: Tipping and resistance in precarious rimes. *Economic and Industrial Democracy*, *40*(2), 434–451.

Needleman, R. L. (1937). Tipping as a factor in wages. *Monthly Labor Review*, *45*(6), 1303–1322.

The New York Times. (1928). Pullman porters' fight on tipping. *The New York Times* (p. 8), July 23.

Offenhartz, J. (2018). NYC's full $15 minimum wage kicks in on New Year's Eve. *Gothamist*, December 27. Retrieved from https://gothamist.com/news/nycs-full-15-minimum-wage-kicks-in-on-new-years-eve

Ogbonna, E., & Harris, L. (2002). Institutionalization of tipping as a source of managerial control. *British Journal of Industrial Relations*, *40*(4), 725–752.

Paules, G. F. (1991). *Dishing it out: Power and resistance among waitresses in a New Jersey restaurant*. Philadelphia, PA: Temple University Press.

Restaurant Opportunities Center (ROC) United. (2012). Tipped over the edge: Gender inequality in the restaurant industry. Retrieved from https://rocunited.org/publications/tipped-over-the-edge-gender-inequity-in-the-restaurant-industry/

Restaurant Opportunities Center (ROC) United. (2013). Realizing the dream: How the minimum wage impacts racial equality in the restaurant industry and in America. Retrieved from https://chapters.rocunited.org/wp-content/uploads/2014/02/report_realizing-the-dream.pdf

Restaurant Opportunities Center (ROC) United. (2019). The gig is up: The new gig economy and the threat of subminimum wages. Retrieved from https://rocunited.org/wp-content/uploads/sites/7/2020/02/TheGigIsUp

Restaurant Opportunities Center (ROC) United. (2020). Take us off the menu: The impact of sexual harassment in the restaurant industry. Retrieved from https://rocunited.org/wp-content/uploads/sites/7/2020/02/TakeUsOffTheMenuReport.pdf

Ross, J., & Welsh, J. (2021). Understanding the 'tipped minimum wage': Critical directions for US policy research. *Social Policy & Society*, *20*(2), 192–210. .

Sachs, C., Allen, P., Terman, A. R., Hayden, J., & Hatcher, C. (2014). Front and back of the house: Socio-spatial inequalities in food work. *Agriculture & Human Values*, *31*, 3–17.

Sallaz, J. (2002). The house rules: Autonomy and interests among service workers in the contemporary casino industry. *Work and Occupations*, *29*(4), 394–427.

Sallaz, J. (2009). *The labor of luck: Casino capitalism in the United States and South Africa*. Berkeley, CA: University of California Press.

Santino, J. (1989). *Miles of smiles, years of struggle: Stories of Black Pullman porters*. Chicago, IL: University of Illinois Press.

Scott, W. R. (1916). *The itching palm: A study of the tipping habit in America*. Philadelphia, PA: The Penn Publishing Company.

Segrave, K. (1998). *Tipping: An American social history of gratuities*. Jefferson, NC: McFarland & Company.

Sherman, R. (2007). *Class acts: Service and inequality in luxury hotels*. Berkeley, CA: University of California Press.

Specker, S. (2016). Hun, I want *you* for dessert: Why eliminating the sub-minimum wage for restaurant servers will empower women. *University of Pennsylvania Journal of Law and Social Change*, *19*(4), 335–350.

Thielman, S. (2018). One conservative group's successful infiltration of the media. *Columbia Journalism Review*, June 21. Retrieved from https://www.cjr.org/analysis/77-referendum-astroturf-tipping.php

U.S. Bureau of Labor Statistics. (1919). Wages and hours of labor. *Monthly Labor Review*, *9*(3), 176–247.

U.S. Bureau of Labor Statistics. (1927). Opposition of organized labor to the tipping system. *Monthly Labor Review*, *25*(4), 1–4.

U.S. Bureau of Labor Statistics. (2020a). Industries at a glance: Food services and drinking places. Retrieved from https://www.bls.gov/iag/tgs/iag722.htm

U.S. Bureau of Labor Statistics. (2020b). Occupational employment statistics: May 2019 national occupational employment and wage estimates United States. Retrieved from https://www.bls.gov/oes/current/oes_nat.htm#00-0000

U.S. Department of Labor, Wage and Hour Division. (2019). Low wage, high violation industries. Retrieved from https://www.dol.gov/agencies/whd/data/charts/low-wage-high-violation-industries

Weissner, D. (2021). Labor Dept. revives '80/20 rule' for paying tipped workers. *Reuters*, October 28. Retrieved from https://www.reuters.com/legal/transactional/labor-dept-revives-8020-rule-paying-tipped-workers-2021-10-28/

Williams v. *Jacksonville Terminal Co.* (1942). 315 U.S. 386.

Williams, C., & Connell, C. (2010). "Looking good and sounding right": Aesthetic labor and social inequality in the retail industry. *Work and Occupations*, *37*(3), 349–377.

Wilson, E. R. (2018). Bridging the service divide: Dual labor niches and embedded opportunities in restaurant work. *RSF: The Russell Sage Foundation Journal of the Social Sciences*, *4*(1), 115–127.

Wilson, E. R. (2019). Tip work: Examining the relational dynamics of Tipping beyond the service counter. *Symbolic Interaction 42*, 669–690.

CHAPTER 3

'IT'S SIMPLE, IF YOU STAND STILL YOU DO NOT GET PAID': PIECE WAGE GAMES AS INDIRECT MODALITY OF CONTROL IN THE PLATFORM-MEDIATED FOOD DELIVERY SECTOR

Floris de Krijger

Hasselt University, Hasselt, Belgium

ABSTRACT

A growing body of research finds that gig economy platforms use gamification to enhance managerial control. Focusing on technologically mediated forms of gamification, this literature reveals how platforms mobilize gig workers' work effort by making the labour process resemble a game. This chapter contends that this tech-centric scholarship fails to fully capture the historical continuities between contemporary and much older occurrences of game-playing at work. Informed by interviews and participatory observations at two food delivery platforms in Amsterdam, I document how these platforms' piece wage system gives rise to a workplace dynamic in which severely underpaid delivery couriers continuously employ game strategies to maximize their gig income. Reminiscent of observations from the early shop floor ethnographies of the manufacturing industry, I show that the game of gig income maximization operates as an indirect modality of control by (re)aligning the interests of

Ethnographies of Work
Research in the Sociology of Work, Volume 35, 35–72

Published under exclusive licence by Emerald Publishing Limited
ISSN: 0277-2833/doi:10.1108/S0277-283320230000035003

couriers with the interests of capital and by individualizing and depoliticizing couriers' overall low wage level. I argue that the new, algorithmic technologies expand and intensify the much older forms of gamified control by infusing the organizational activities of shift and task allocation with the logic of the piece wage game and by increasing the possibilities for interaction, direct feedback and immersion. My study contributes to the literature on gamification in the gig economy by interweaving it with the classic observations derived from the manufacturing industry and by developing a conceptualization of gamification in which both capital and labour exercise agency.

Keywords: Gig economy; gamification; work games; piece wage; control; food delivery

INTRODUCTION

It's a Thursday in Amsterdam and I am about to deliver my last meal of the evening for Diner Direct. I feel exhausted yet satisfied, as I have met my personal income target (€35) and ended up in an area of town very close to my own house. Right after I swipe 'arrived' on my app and ring my clients' doorbell, my phone rings. 'Beep, beep', a new delivery request. '€4.30 + 0.50 tip'. Although my current order is not yet completed, Diner Direct[1] has already sent me a new one – an algorithmic technique called 'forward dispatch' which platforms have copied from videogames and streaming services (Scheiber, 2017). In the split second before my client opens the door I swipe 'accept', only to regret this right after. Although the new restaurant is close, my new client lives all the way across town, not only making this last order highly unprofitable in terms of effort-to-wage ratio but also leaving me on the road for much longer than I had initially planned. Feeling somewhat defeated and irritated, I promise myself that, next time, I will just stick to my original game plan and not allow Diner Direct to override my personal boundaries.

In the burgeoning literature on platform-mediated gig work, managerial practices like these are known as *gamification*: the repurposing of 'game design elements' to 'non-game contexts' such as gig work (Deterding et al. 2011, p. 10; Van Doorn & Chen, 2021, p. 1347). Gig economy platforms adopt gamification widely, using game design elements ranging from point scoring (Morschheuser et al., 2017), user-generated ratings (Chan, 2019), and employee rankings (Van Doorn & Chen, 2021), to time pressure (Chen & Sun, 2020), challenges and quests (Mason, 2018), and personalized psychological nudges that rearrange workers' decision-making context (Scheiber, 2017). Employers make use of gamification to enhance the level of work engagement and motivation among their workforce. By invoking gamified emotional states like joy, pride and 'flow' in workers, gamification has the ability to positively change how workers perceive their job (Morschheuser et al., 2017; Warmelink et al., 2020). This managerial technique is particularly suitable for the gig economy, it is often stated, as it indirectly stimulates gig workers' motivation for their often repetitive and low-paid work tasks, while simultaneously respecting their on-the-job autonomy – a job characteristic implied in their legal status as 'independent contractors' (Behl et al., 2021, p. 17, 2022, p. 1385; Morschheuser et al., 2017, p. 35; see also Warmelink et al., 2020).

Challenging this positive interpretation, critical scholarship does not conceive of gamification as a playful method to enhance work motivation but as a manipulative tool to strengthen managerial control: the platform's ability to 'obtain desired work behaviour from [gig] workers' (Edwards, 1979, p. 17; Gandini, 2019; Krzywdzinski & Gerber, 2021). This literature shows that platforms use gamification to subtly steer gig workers to work longer, harder, and in a desirable way by taking advantage of their cognitive biases (Scheiber, 2017), prompting their self-discipline (Chan, 2019) and fashioning addictive work environments (Mason, 2018; Vasudevan & Chan, 2022). As platforms' efforts to establish managerial control emanate from their material positioning as 'owners and managers of capital' (Chai & Scully, 2019, p. 946), critics hold that gamification is yet another 'weapon in capital's arsenal to control labour' in the gig economy (Lazzolino & Varesio, 2023, p. 877; also see Woodcock & Johnson, 2018).

Although critical scholarship has developed convincing critiques of gamification's instrumental and manipulative nature, it suffers from two related problems. First, it tends to emphasize the technological 'novelty' of platforms' gamification strategies by focusing on algorithmically enabled game design elements (e.g. user-generated ratings, personalized nudges and quests) and their entanglement in the more comprehensive system of algorithmic control (Kellogg et al., 2020; Rosenblat & Stark, 2016; Vasudevan & Chan, 2022). As a consequence, this literature fails to fully grasp the possible continuities between new and pre-algorithmic forms of gamification known to emerge from piece wages – that is, a type of wage hardly new under capitalism and used by almost all gig economy platforms (Alkhatib et al., 2017; Dublin, 1991; Marx, 1867/2013). Secondly, assuming that the platform initiates, designs, and implements gamification, much of the literature positions gig workers as passive targets of such techniques (Chan, 2019; Morschheuser et al., 2017; Scheiber, 2017; Van Doorn & Chen, 2021) and overlooks whether their game strategies also reduce, complicate, or even actively challenge managerial control (see e.g. Lupton, 1963; Roy, 1952a, 1952b).

To address these two problems, this article draws on 'piece wage games' theories developed in shop floor ethnographies of the manufacturing industry from the 1950s (Dalton, 1948; Lupton, 1963; Roy, 1952a, 1952b, 1953) and 1970s (Burawoy, 1979, 1985). This early scholarship evidences that piece wage games are a much older phenomenon than the gig economy. Piece wage games tend to occur if workers are paid per produced 'piece' and experience enough on-the-job autonomy to develop game strategies that potentially increase their income. These kinds of work games are imbued with antagonism, this literature demonstrates, as they offer opportunities for managerial control as well as for workers' resistance. Depending on the conditions under which they emerge, piece wage games produce different kinds of behaviour in workers, ranging from enhanced work effort and consensual work engagement (Burawoy, 1979, 1985; Dalton, 1948) to intentional slowdowns and collective forms of resistance (Baldamus, 1961; Brown, 1973; Lupton, 1963; Roy, 1952a, 1952b).

Building on these insights, this chapter studies the (in)ability of piece wage games to operate as an indirect modality of control in the platform-mediated food delivery sector of Amsterdam, The Netherlands. To do this, I conducted participatory observations and interviews while working as a delivery courier at two food delivery platforms: Speedily and Diner Direct. Echoing the managerial practices inside manufacturing plants, food delivery platforms are known to rely on gamified forms of control and to pay their delivery couriers by the piece – that is, each delivered meal (Van Doorn & Chen, 2021; Veen et al., 2020). Because of these overlapping conditions, it is possible to study how gamified control changed over time and to analyze in what way new algorithmic technologies accounted for the observed alterations (*cf.* Alkhatib et al., 2017).

This chapter offers two key contributions to the (critical) literature on gamification in the gig economy. First, it complicates the existing understanding of the relationship between gamification and new technologies by showing that algorithmic systems do not establish an entirely new type of gamified control. Instead, this chapter argues that algorithms expand and intensify the much older forms of gamified control associated with piece wage remuneration. Secondly, this chapter demonstrates the agency couriers exercise within the observed piece wage game and connects this behaviour to their role and material interests as workers who aim to sell their labour power for the highest possible wage. More specifically, it contributes to the emerging literature on gig workers' resistance against gamified control by theorizing why individual and concurrent forms of agency were observed in the streets of Amsterdam but collective ones did not materialize.

This chapter is divided into five sections. I start by explaining why gamification provides a solution to the specific managerial challenges food delivery platforms face and continue by elaborating on the two earlier introduced shortcomings of the extant literature. I proceed by introducing the insights from the early shop floor ethnographies of the manufacturing industry. This scholarship offers useful conceptual terminology for capturing the antagonistic nature of piece wage games and provides comparative historical evidence that can be used to evaluate how such work games have changed. After briefly reporting on the employed methodology, I present my findings by documenting how the game of *gig income maximization* exercises indirect control during the different phases of the food delivery process and by comparing in what ways this algorithmically mediated piece wage game differs from the ones observed in the manufacturing industry. The chapter concludes by discussing how my findings contribute to the (critical) literature on gamification and the ethnographic literature on piece wage games and piece wage bargaining.

FOOD DELIVERY PLATFORMS, GAMIFICATION, AND CONTROL

Food delivery platforms are for-profit companies that facilitate and direct interactions between delivery couriers, consumers, and restaurants through their digital platform infrastructure. In Heeks' (2017) typology, these platforms are part of the 'physical gig economy', as the service they offer is 'tangible and delivered to a client in a physical location' (p. 4). By categorizing couriers as 'independent contractors' instead of 'employees', food delivery platforms organize the classic capital-labour relationship outside of formal employment (Gandini, 2019; Joyce, 2020) and avoid some of the costs associated with couriers' social reproduction – that is, pensions, social security, holiday pay, etc. (Zanoni, 2019; Federatie Nederlandse Vakbeweging (FNV), 2019, 2020). In relation to managerial control, however, this employment construction poses problems. The status of 'independent contractor' is legally demarcated and presupposes that workers are granted a degree of on-the-job autonomy (Healy et al., 2017; Shapiro, 2018; Stefano, 2015). As part of this legal classification, managerial control needs to be established without the use of direct force – a requirement food delivery platforms do not always meet and for which many face legal charges in court (Defossez, 2022; Stefano, 2015).[2] Gamification contributes to solving this problem, as the repertoire of nudges, ratings, rankings, and quests does not force but indirectly 'seduces' gig workers to perform desired conduct (Chapman et al., 2021; Scheiber, 2017) and neatly fits gig platforms' ideological narrative of offering workers independence and entrepreneurial freedom (Fleming, 2017; Lazzolino & Varesio, 2023; Manriquez, 2019).

Critical scholarship on platforms' gamification strategies is expanding and tends to revolve around game affordances that are directly enabled by new algorithmic technologies, such as algorithmic rewarding (Rosenblat & Stark, 2016), personalized nudges (Scheiber, 2017), and user-generated ratings (Chan, 2019). At first sight, this is understandable, given the vital role algorithms, and the digital work environment more generally, play in controlling gig workers (Kellogg et al., 2020; Rosenblat & Stark, 2016). By now, it is well known that platforms collect and 'datafy' work-related information (Srnicek, 2016; Van Doorn & Chen, 2021) to design algorithmic choice architectures that subtly steer gig workers' behaviour in the preferred direction (Aneesh, 2009; Kellogg et al., 2020). While platforms use algorithms to present gig workers with a set of preselected choices, monitor workers' performance and reward or penalize their conduct in real time (Kellogg et al., 2020; Newlands, 2021), they employ game design elements, vernacular, and aesthetics to make it appear *as if* this system of restricted choices represents a 'fun' and 'challenging' game (Vasudevan & Chan, 2022). Concomitantly, researchers analogize gig work with an actual *video* game and interpret behavioural patterns such as addiction and zoning out as digital 'player modes' (Manriquez, 2019; Mason, 2018; Scheiber, 2017; Vasudevan & Chan, pp. 866, 875).

Although gamification is certainly embedded in the more expansive system of algorithmic control (Kellogg et al., 2020; Vasudevan & Chan, 2022), there is also a risk in (tacitly) positioning new technologies as *the* decisive ingredient for explaining 'gamified patterns of worker engagement' (Rosenblat & Stark, 2016, p. 3759; Scheiber, 2017). From ethnographic accounts of the manufacturing industry, we know that game-playing at work is a much older phenomenon which the introduction of piece wage remuneration can bring about by itself (Burawoy, 1979, 1985; Dalton, 1948; Lupton, 1963; Roy, 1952a, 1952b, 1953). The literature's fixation on new technologies and its tendency to associate gamification with 'techno-normative' control makes it difficult to fully grasp the potential continuities between the current and pre-algorithmic forms of gamification (Gandini, 2019, p. 1049).

This concern is particularly pressing since piece wages are the dominant mode of remuneration in the gig economy but have thus far received little attention in discussions on managerial control (Joyce, 2020; Joyce & Stuart, 2021). Scholarship that does focus on the gamified piece wage usually conceptualizes this type of remuneration as a (psychological) incentive (see e.g. Morschheuser et al, 2017; Rosenblat & Stark, 2016) rather than an unequal economic exchange between capital and labour (Marx, 1867/2013). As a form of exchange, piece wages exercise material control by tying 'workers to a condition of [economic] dependency upon capital' and by creating a direct connection between produced output and individual wage level (Joyce, 2020, p. 547; Marx, 1867/2013). Therefore, the first goal of this study is to develop an account of gamification in which piece wages take centre stage, and new algorithmic technologies offer opportunities to expand or refine older forms of gamified control. By treating material control exercised by the piece wage as analytically distinct from technological control exercised by algorithms, it responds to recent calls to pay closer attention to the independent role piece wages play in regulating labour in the gig economy (Joyce, 2020; Joyce & Stuart, 2021).

A second problem of gamification scholarship is that it fails to fully capture and theorize the agency gig workers exercise when exposed to gamification. Much literature, for instance, exposes the highly manipulative nature of gamified control by showing that platforms leverage workers' behavioural data to identify and exploit workers' cognitive biases (Mason, 2018; Scheiber, 2017; Van Doorn & Chen, 2021) and purposefully create addictive, game-like, work environments that 'seduce' workers to keep on 'playing' (Chapman et al., 2021, p. 2; Mason, 2018; Scheiber, 2017; Vasudevan & Chan, 2022). Critical scholars hold that playful work behaviour does not necessarily benefit gig workers themselves, as it indirectly prompts their self-discipline (Chan, 2019) and makes their work more intensive and demanding (Gandini, 2019). Chan (2019) and Manriquez (2019), for instance, show how user-generated ratings induce Uber and Lyft drivers to play 'rating games' for five-star ratings by offering passengers free candy or chewing gum, and by tirelessly adjusting their conduct to be talkative, quiet or serious, depending on the type of person entering their car.

Ethnographic research offers detailed accounts of the psychological hardship gamification inflicts on the individual gig worker. Gig workers often feel frustrated, stressed, or even powerless in their confrontation with the highly sophisticated and opaque systems of gamified control (Chan, 2019; Krzywdzinski & Gerber, 202; Rosenblat & Stark, 2016; Van Doorn & Chen, 2021). Moreover, such research finds that gig workers cross personal boundaries once they begin to fixate on completing quests (Mason, 2018) or feel pressured to maintain a high personal rating (Raval & Dourish, 2016). As a consequence, some gig workers work longer hours than they initially plan or expose themselves to higher degrees of risks than they actually want to (Mason, 2018; Raval & Dourish, 2016; Scheiber, 2017; Vasudevan & Chan, 2022).

In sum, extant gamification scholarship reveals accurately how gamification controls, manipulates, and frustrates gig workers but is less explicitly focused on how gig workers resist gamification. As a consequence, gig workers are too often robbed of their agency and (unwittingly) imagined as 'subjectless subject[s]' who adopt game strategies that automatically work in the platforms' favour (Briziarelli, 2018; Burawoy, 1979, p. 77). This tendency is most dominant in the mainstream literature, as this scholarship tests when gamification mobilizes positive emotions and work behaviours but leaves gig workers' potential resistance against such measures outside its analytical purview (Behl et al., 2022; Morschheuser et al., 2017). The second goal of this chapter is, therefore, to better understand how and why gig workers exercise agency when exposed to gamified control. By classifying and explaining the specific forms such agency takes, this study contributes to emergent gamification literature on gig workers' 'oppositional play' (Lazzolino & Varesio, 2023; Vasudevan & Chan, 2022, p. 874) and broader discussions on resistance in the gig economy (Lei, 2021; Tassinari & Maccarrone, 2017; Walker et al., 2021). To deliver on these two analytical ambitions, this study interweaves the contemporary insights from the (critical) gamification literature with the much older (ethnographic) observations on piece wages and piece wage games in the manufacturing industry.

GAMIFICATION IN THE GIG ECONOMY AS CONTEMPORARY 'PIECE WAGE GAME'

As piece wages are often implicated in platforms' gamification strategy, it is necessary to introduce this type of remuneration and explain how it exercises indirect (material) control. In a piece wage system, a worker's wage is proportional to the exact amount of produced output. In its simplest form, 'output' is measured in produced 'units', for which the worker receives a fixed price irrespective of work duration (Lazear, 1986; Schloss, 1892). At the turn of the nineteenth century, the introduction of scientific management refined this simple version by not just assuming workers' productivity but actively evaluating and stimulating it via other performance-related wage incentives. In this so-called 'differential rate' piece wage system (p.100), prices fluctuate per hour or shift, depending on the worker's ability to produce against a predefined productivity level (Edwards, 1979).

A defining characteristic of piece wages is that they reduce the necessity for direct managerial control (Baldamus, 1961; Joyce, 2020; Marx, 1867/2013; Stanford, 2017). Marx (1867/2013) explains that since piece wages establish a direct connection between work effort and wage level, workers have a direct interest in maximizing individual production output. Consequently, piece wages not only stimulate workers to 'strain (...) labour power as intensely as possible' (p. 388) and 'lengthen the working-day' (p. 388) but also create the impression that workers enjoy a high level of autonomy in their work. By increasing competition between workers and incentivising them to outperform past productivity standards, piece wages exert downward pressure on wage levels. After all, if the more skilled workers increase their piece wage by enhancing their work speed, the capitalist can set this new productivity level as the norm, adjust piece prices downwards and lower the average worker's wage. Marx (1867/2013) famously concludes that the piece wage represents the type of remuneration 'most in harmony with the capitalist mode of production', as it can maximize work effort, decrease solidarity, and lower wage levels, all under the pretext of expanded 'freedom' (pp. 388–389).

By studying the work culture piece wages gave rise to, the early shop floor ethnographers revitalized critical scholarship on this form of remuneration (Burawoy, 1979; Dalton, 1948; Lupton, 1963; Roy, 1952a, 1952b, 1953). Observing the labour process from close by, these field researchers discovered that machine operators were not just working for a piece wage, they were also playing a game – a piece wage game. Piece wage games revolved around the goal of 'making out': hitting a time-based production target connected to specific work tasks (Burawoy, 1979; Lupton, 1963; Roy, 1952a, 1952b, 1953). Depending on the piece wage system, pieces produced after this point translated into a wage bonus or nominal wage increase. However, making out was not easy, as it required technical, physical, and social skills, as well as some luck.

In line with contemporary gamification theory, it was the fixation on achieving a concrete goal in combination with uncertainty about success that made engaging in a piece wage game so stimulating (Roy, 1953, p. 511) and seductive (Burawoy, 1985, p. 38). More specifically, game-playing produced four mutually reinforcing rewards: physical, psychological, social, and economic (Burawoy, 1979; Lupton, 1963; Roy, 1953). Roy (1953), for instance, described how the game helped machine operators cope with the physically demanding and psychologically draining nature of manufacturing work by reducing fatigue and infusing the highly repetitive labour process with a sense of uncertainty. Burawoy (1979) and Lupton (1963), in turn, observed that skilled game players reaped social rewards from their status, as the social hierarchy on the factory floor was largely determined by the hierarchy of the piece wage game. Consistent game success also offered economic benefits, as the increased output levels translated into higher wage levels (Dalton, 1948) or better promotion opportunities (Burawoy, 1979).

Unsurprisingly, piece wage games also benefitted capital, as they could align the interests of workers with the interests of management. Similar to observations from the gig economy (Lehdonvirta, 2018; Mason, 2018; Vasudevan & Chan, 2022), the piece wage game improved machine operators' focus and physical stamina (Roy, 1953) and incentivised them to work more intensively and consistently throughout the day (Baldamus, 1961; Dalton, 1948; also see Ranganathan & Benson, 2020). Moreover, they incentivised workers to acquire productivity-enhancing skills as quickly as possible and micro-managed workers' behaviour behind their machines (Burawoy, 1979). In contrast to the despotic (Burawoy, 1985) or simple form of control (Edwards, 1979), piece wage games operated as an indirect modality of control exactly because workers were granted some 'responsible autonomy' (Friedman, 2000, p. 67).

Unlike most contemporary gamification theorists, however, the early shop floor ethnographers were well aware that not all game strategies worked in management's favour. In fact, a key theoretical insight was that the observed interest alignment was always provisional, as game strategies arose from machine operators' own (semi)spontaneous 'initiatives' and fell, to some extent, outside the purview of management (Burawoy, 1979, p. 86; Lupton, 1963; Roy, 1952a, 1952b). Roy (1952b), for instance, found that machine operators would slow down their work pace if they considered the hourly production targets too challenging or the piece price too low. He also observed how experienced workers preferred to hit their base wage targets as quickly as possible, to drastically reduce work effort in the hours after (Roy, 1953, p. 512). Turning in much more production than required was strongly condemned on many shop floors, as this would give management ammunition to 'tighten' the so-called 'gravy jobs' – that is, jobs for which the effort-to-wage ratio was perceived as relatively beneficial to workers (Lupton, 1963; Roy, 1952a, 1952b, 1953; *cf.* Dalton, 1948).

Baldamus (1961) interprets the strategic withholding of work effort through the notion of 'wage-effort bargaining': negotiations about the level of effort expected in return for a wage. In these negotiations, which reflect the fundamental conflict of interest between capital and labour (Thompson, 1990), exerting the least effort for the highest possible wage was the central goal of machine operators. If the relative wage increase was not considered worth the additional effort, playing a piece wage game could also mean slowing down one's work pace (Lupton, 1963; Roy, 1952a).

If piece wage games began to run against management's interests, management usually attempted to adjust the effort-to-wage ratio underlying specific piecework jobs. Concretely, this entailed asking the time study men (Roy, 1952a) and, later, the industrial engineer (Burawoy, 1979) to retime jobs with 'loose' targets in such a way that the perceived disparity between the relatively 'high' piece price and the relatively 'low' work effort was corrected in management's favour (Baldamus, 1961; Burawoy, 1979; Roy, 1952a). Although more direct control instruments such as threats of dismissal (Lupton, 1963) or increased surveillance (Roy, 1952a, 1953) were observed as well (*cf.* Sallaz, 2002), adjusting the piece price was a much more common and effective way management dealt with the problem of workers' output restriction. It should be no surprise that these price adjustments were highly contentious and often actively challenged on the shop floor (Baldamus, 1961; Brown, 1973).

Burawoy (1979) added, last of all, that piece wage games were not only able to align and, subsequently, realign the interests of labour with the interests of capital but also establish control in a much more pervasive, and long-term manner. As almost all interactions on Burawoy's shop floor were infused with the logic of the piece wage game, machine operators expressed work-related grievances within the game's individualistic frame and mostly in the direction of auxiliary workers that damaged their personal success – for example, slow truck drivers who interrupted machine operators' production speed. By redefining the very terms in which workers voiced work-related frustrations and redirecting old hierarchical conflicts between workers and management in a horizontal direction, the game held down class antagonisms. Burawoy (1979) concluded that if piece wage games were to become an end in themselves, they might depoliticize, reroute and reconfigure workplace conflicts in such a way that underlying capitalist social relations are obfuscated and long-term control is guaranteed.

To capture how class antagonisms and associated material interests regulate game-playing in the platform-mediated food delivery sector, this chapter theorizes gamified work behaviour through the notion of the 'piece wage game' and its associated terminology – piece prices, game rewards, wage-effort bargains, and interest (re)alignment. As algorithms have the ability to make existing regimes of managerial control more comprehensive, instantaneous, interactive, and opaque (Kellogg et al., 2020), I evaluate how this contemporary piece wage game compares to the one observed in the manufacturing industry and analyze if algorithmic technologies accounted for observed changes. My two research questions are therefore: (1) how are piece wage games played in the platform-mediated food delivery sector; and (2) in what ways do algorithmic technologies (re)configure their ability to exercise indirect control and bring forth gig workers' resistance?

RESEARCH SETTING, DATA COLLECTION, AND ANALYSIS

Cases: Diner Direct and Speedily

This chapter is based on field research at the food delivery platforms Speedily and Diner Direct in Amsterdam, the Netherlands. Speedily and Diner Direct both arrived in The Netherlands in the second half of the 2010s. In Amsterdam, these platforms operate in a highly competitive market next to market leader Food4Life, specialized food delivery companies (e.g. focused on organic food), and restaurants that organize food delivery in-house (Wijngaarde, 2017). Although Diner Direct paid its couriers by the piece from the start, Speedily changed to this system right before the commencement of my fieldwork. Both platforms use a 'differential rate' piece wage system, indicating that delivery couriers are paid per delivered meal and rewarded extra for high performance. Piece prices consist of two components: a regular price hovering between €4.50 and €8.00 depending on the delivery distance and a variable bonus depending on work performance. In line with the principles of game design, couriers' earnings are tracked in real time and displayed on the home pages of couriers' work applications. Performance-related bonuses are phrased in game-like language and take the form of a fixed wage guarantee, fixed or contingent wage bonus per delivered meal, a progressive wage bonus per x numbers of delivered meals or a fixed recruitment bonus. In contrast to the manufacturing industry, performance-related bonuses are not connected to the produced output per hour but to all sorts of other indicators – that is, availability, work location, reliability, and service quality (for an overview, see Table 3.1).[3] Moreover, there is no predefined wage ceiling, nor a standard wage guarantee, indicating that couriers' wage levels vary much more than those of machine operators. Average wage levels are extremely low and do not include holiday pay, days off or pension contributions. In 2019, net wages were estimated between €5.80 and €7.90 per hour by the biggest Dutch labour union. These estimates fall far below the sectoral minimum of €13.99 (FNV, 2019, p. 2).[4]

At its core, food delivery work consists of an endless reiteration of one deskilled process: picking up meals at a restaurant, transporting them to customers and

Table 3.1. Food Delivery Piece Wage System.

	Speedily	Diner Direct
	Regular Piece Price	
	Fluctuating piece prices per delivered meal depending on delivery distance (± €4.5–8)	Fluctuating piece prices per delivered meal depending on delivery distance (± €4.6–8)
	Variable Wage Bonus	
Location wage bonus	Progressive bonus for delivering an x number of meals within two weeks' time in understaffed areas of Amsterdam	Piece price multiplier bonus per delivered meal in understaffed areas of Amsterdam
Availability wage bonus	Fixed bonus per completed delivery in times of high demand (rainy days, new years', etc.)	Fixed bonus per completed delivery in times of high demand (rainy days, new years', etc.) Guaranteed base wage in times of high demand (dinner time, weekends)
Reliability wage bonus	Fixed bonus after delivering the first 25 number of meals	Progressive bonus for delivering an x number of meals during a single shift
Service wage bonus	Contingent bonus per delivered meal (tips from customers)	Contingent bonus per delivered meal (tips from customers)
Recruitment wage bonus	Fixed bonus for recruiting a new courier	Fixed bonus for recruiting a new courier

waiting for the next order to start over again. Diner Direct and Speedily use algorithms to allocate gigs to couriers and instruct them where to go (addresses), what to pick up (order numbers), and how to get there (fastest routes) via a smartphone app. Work standardization is, however, not the only logic at play. Delivery couriers are left alone in much of their work-related decision making. Delivery couriers can self-schedule work shifts (Speedily) or even work anytime a day (Diner Direct), complete deliveries anywhere in the city, reject incoming orders, cancel assigned orders, leave their shift prematurely, respond to a myriad of different incentives, and choose their own means of transportation. In other words, this labour process provides ample opportunity for game-playing around piece wages. To study how this workplace dynamic plays out in practice, I jumped on a bike myself and joined delivery couriers in their game of gig maximization.

Data Collection

Empirical data was gathered through participatory observations and interviews. In the period between August 2018 and March 2019, I spent 92.5 hours on demand, delivering 191 meals in all corners of Amsterdam. In order to build a comprehensive view of this work, I alternated full-time workweeks with part-time ones, tried out morning, afternoon, and evening shifts and read all internal newsletters meticulously.

Taking notes was easy, as couriers continuously used their smartphones while waiting for their meals to be prepared. Although I tried to rewrite my smartphone jottings into more formal field notes immediately after my shifts, the physical nature of my work rendered this challenging. Fieldnotes were written in the first person and included accounts of my emotional responses to gamification, which I used as 'analytic leads' in my analysis (Emerson et al., 2001, p. 361). As a white male master's student with a (lower) middle-class background, I did not stick out in the mass of couriers, who seemed to consider me normal. In fact, my delivery work did not only have an academic purpose but also a personal one, as it partly covered my personal living expenses at the time. Consequently, I found myself almost as invested in the game of gig maximization as any other part-time courier. I explicitly mention part-time courier here, to signal that it is unlikely that my participatory observations fully grasped what it must feel like – both emotionally and physically – to be wholly financially dependent on gamified algorithmic rewarding. This methodological reservation is especially warranted since research indicates that gig workers' employment history and economic dependency on platform work affect how they experience gamification and their working conditions (Krzywdzinski & Gerber, 2021; Manriquez, 2019).

After a couple of weeks of delivery work, I noticed that it was difficult to learn about couriers' personal work experiences through 'casual conversations' alone (Silverman & Patterson, 2015, p. 51). Not only did I spend most of my hours by myself, cycling from restaurant to customer; the platform structure also made it difficult to build up a 'special bond of trust' with fellow couriers (Schwandt, 2007, p. 149). Running into the same person was extremely rare and conversations tended to be cut off abruptly since they were typically held in restaurants while waiting for a meal to be prepared. To acquire a more in-depth understanding of couriers' work experiences, I recruited delivery couriers (n =19) for more formal, off-site, interviews using various recruitment channels (i.e. online forums, personal contacts, my fieldwork and snowball sampling). Although raw data on the socio-demographic composition of the Dutch food delivery workforce does not exist, in light of several other data sources my interview sample seemed particularly skewed in terms of educational background (89% attained higher education) and 'race' (89% was white).[5] It proved particularly challenging to find full-time couriers from racialized minority groups to participate in my study – a significant part of the local courier community. Although I attempted to include their voices by approaching this group more proactively on the streets, I still remain cautious about extrapolating my findings to this group.

My interviews lasted around 30–40 minutes, were conducted in English or Dutch and were processed anonymously. The interviews consisted of three parts. To give couriers the opportunity to introduce topics of their own choosing, I started with a set of open questions about their motivation to apply for the job and about their general work experiences. In the second part, I attempted to confirm whether or not my personal work experiences were similar to those of other couriers, exploring topics like strategies and routines, work conflicts, interactions with colleagues, and the platforms. In the final part of the interview, I asked couriers to self-identify their age, gender, 'race', and educational background. To increase reliability, all interviews were recorded and transcribed verbatim in their original language.

On the moral continuum from fully covert to completely overt ethnographic research (Bulmer, 1982), I place my study somewhere in the middle. Self-evidently,

I was open about my status as a researcher during the interviews and gathered informed consent from all my respondents. However, I usually kept my status as a researcher hidden from the platforms, my customers, and the majority of my co-workers during my participatory observations. Although I am aware of the ethical dilemmas related to covert observations (Homan, 1980), I opted for this semi-covert approach for several interrelated reasons. First, because I interacted with dozens of restaurants, customers, couriers, and other city dwellers on a daily basis, informing everyone about my research intentions would have been practically impossible. Moreover, since my encounters with fellow couriers were extremely transient and often did not take more than a couple of seconds I was not betraying any long-built-up trust. In fact, couriers often seemed to gain personal satisfaction from the brief moments they talked to me while waiting for their orders, as it allowed them to release some work-related frustrations. The names of customers, restaurants, delivery couriers, and the platforms were not documented or anonymized in the final text of this chapter. Embracing a more situated approach to research ethics (Perez, 2019), I usually announced my academic intentions rather quickly if I spent somewhat more time talking to a courier and planned to invite them for an interview. Diner Direct and Speedily were, however, never formally informed about my study. I consider this less of an ethical concern because in the platforms' own view, I operated as an 'independent' contractor instead of 'their' employee. Furthermore, this semi-covert approach allowed me to actually experience the precarious conditions under which delivery couriers have to work – information that can hopefully contribute to progressive change (Roulet et al., 2017).

Data Analysis

Applying an abductive approach to theory development, I analyzed my data by creating an 'iterative dialogue' between extant understandings of gamified control and my own empirical observations in Amsterdam (Timmermans & Tavory's, 2012, p. 180). Drawing on the Abductive Coding Manual by Vila-Henninger and colleagues (in press), I started this progress by turning to the existing (critical) gamification literature to compile a list of game design elements that platforms are known to repurpose (e.g. point scoring, ranking, rating, nudges, etc.) and a set of codes for the different ways gig workers have responded to them (see e.g. Chan, 2019; Morschheuser et al., 2017; Scheiber, 2017; Van Doorn & Chen, 2021). These codes were divided into emotional (e.g. flow, joy, powerlessness, addiction, etc.) and behavioural responses (e.g. maximizing work effort, lengthening the work days, etc.). This codebook was used to document all the game design elements that Speedily and Diner Direct use and to code what kind of responses to gamification were present in my data. While exploring the coded data, I noticed that much of the strategic, game-like behaviour I observed in the streets of Amsterdam was not captured via this deductive strategy. Not only did it fail to grasp the game strategies that couriers develop out of their own initiative (Burawoy, 1979), but it also largely missed the tactics that did not necessarily work in the platforms' favour (Roy, 1952b). Moreover, my observations seemed to overlap much more with how piece wage games were described in the manufacturing industry than with the literature on algorithmically enabled gamification in the gig economy. As abductive analysis rests on the 'cultivation of anomalous and surprising empirical findings' (Timmermans & Tavory, 2012, p. 169), I recoded my data to better grasp the overlap between older and newer forms of game-playing at work. Echoing the approach of the early shop floor ethnographers, I started by reconstructing how the labour process was perceived from the perspective of delivery couriers and coded all the game strategies they employed (23 in total). To improve validity, I triangulated my data by crosschecking if similar game strategies were mentioned or described in both data sources – that is, fieldnotes and interviews. In turn, I evaluated if the effect of couriers' game strategies aligned with the interests of Diner Direct and Speedily and documented how both platforms responded if they did not. The last step of the analysis was to bring the (critical) gamification literature on the gig economy in direct conversation with the much older studies on the manufacturing industry. Concretely, this entailed mapping the historical differences between the two sectors and evaluating if new algorithmic technologies transformed older game-playing dynamics and associated forms of control (see Table 3.4).

PLAYING FOR A PIECE WAGE, DELIVERING TO CAPITAL

The labour process in the platform-mediated food delivery sector presents itself as one endless piece wage game revolving around the maximization of gig income, and the minimization of work effort. Although not all delivery couriers are equally invested in this game, the large majority of the couriers I met employ at least some game strategies. To maximize their earnings, couriers strategize about when and where to deliver meals, which orders to accept or reject, and how to navigate the busy streets of Amsterdam. In doing so, they aim to increase the average number of deliveries per hour, select gigs with a generous effort-to-wage ratio, and reduce the time spent waiting on demand.

Akin to the manufacturing industry, the piece wage game operates as an indirect modality of control by successfully aligning the interests of couriers with the interests of the platforms (Burawoy, 1979). In establishing a direct connection between individual work effort and wage level, the game incentivises couriers to strain their labour power as intensely as possible and to deliver meals in those areas of town (the centre and *de Pijp*) and at those moments a day (lunch and dinner) in which customer demand, and thereby gig earnings, is the highest. In line with Roy's (1952a, 1952b) and Lupton's (1963) observations, however, the game of gig income maximization *also* gives rise to control problems of its own, as regular piece prices do not incentivise enough couriers to complete deliveries in the less profitable areas of town (e.g. the outskirts) or during times of high demand (e.g. dinner time). To ensure a readily available labour pool seven days a week in all corners of the city, Diner Direct and Speedily do not issue direct work instructions but simply adjust the effort-to-wage ratio connected to certain delivery gigs – a managerial practice also observed in the manufacturing industry.

Next to historical continuity, however, I also observed historical change. New algorithmic technologies heavily influence in what way the piece wage game is played and how its rules are policed, continuously attuned, and rewritten by the platforms. Algorithmic systems not only expand the *reach* of gamified control by producing derivate games around the shift and task allocation, they also increase its *intensity* by expanding the possibilities for interactive decision making, instantaneous feedback, and immersive game experiences. Moreover, algorithms reduce the extent to which physical managers have to interfere in the piece wage game directly, further reinforcing the depoliticized and individualistic mentality that piece wages sometimes incite in workers (Burawoy, 1979; Marx, 1867/2013). My findings are organized around the different courier-platform interests configurations I observed – alignment, misalignment, realignment – and loosely follow the different phases of the food delivery process.

THE COURIER-PLATFORM INTEREST ALIGNMENT

Phase 1. Preparing for a Shift – 'You Should Get an Electric Bike'

Couriers' vehicle choice is the first, very important, strategic decision in the game of gig maximization. The kind of vehicle couriers rides drastically influences the number of deliveries they can complete per hour. Although driving a car is not prohibited, most couriers deliver their meals on a regular push bike, an electric bike or a scooter. On an electric bike, delivering up to four meals per hour was considered relatively 'easy'. However, reaching such output levels on a regular bike proved to be 'very difficult'. Not only does delivering on an electric bike drastically increase couriers' cycling speed, but also lengthens their physical stamina. I delivered my meals on a regular bike, as I considered purchasing or renting an electronic one not worth the hassle and too expensive. At the beginning of a shift, my cycling speed would always start being relatively high, only to deteriorate quickly after my first few deliveries. In the final hours of my shift, I would always cycle at a snail's pace and immediately lie down on my sofa upon my return home.

As most work-related processes acquire meaning through the interpretative frame of the piece wage game (Burawoy, 1979), couriers talk about their vehicles as representing a long-term investment that 'pays itself back' over time. For instance, Jakub, a full-time courier who dropped out of college, told me of his plans to purchase an electric bicycle worth '3,000 euros' to improve his 'delivery rate' (Interview 18-03-2019). Echoing this sentiment, Jack, a migrant from Ghana who combined his work as a courier with cleaning kitchens, considered leasing one a good option but still doubted whether it would be worth the 'extra seven euros a day' (Fieldnote 26-08-2018). Generally speaking, couriers' choice of vehicle is determined by the number of hours spent on the road: full-time couriers ride scooters or electronic bikes, and part-timers mostly stick to regular push-bikes.

Next to the choice of vehicle, delivery couriers also strategize with their work shifts. This game decision has the most significant impact on couriers' hourly pay rates. As already indicated, while Diner Direct couriers can 'go online' at

Table 3.2. Completed Orders Per Hour.

Time a Day	Number of Completed Orders
11:30–12:30	2.75
12:30–13:30	0.25
13:30–14:30	1
14:30–15:30	0
15:30–16:30	1
16:30–17:30	0
17:30–18:30	2
18.30–19.30	4

any time, couriers working for Speedily have to reserve one-hour work shifts through the app – a decentralized shift scheduling system enabled by their digital and algorithmically-mediated platform infrastructure. In their attempt to limit the time waiting for orders, many couriers mould their working hours around the daily demand fluctuations. 'It never really made sense to work in the morning, you just receive way less order requests, it's just way more quiet', Thijs, for instance, explained (Interview 01-04-2019). In the 'dead' hours before and after lunch, I found myself spending extensive amounts of time on demand waiting for incoming orders. Consider, for example, the following overview of my eight-hour shift in March (see Table 3.2).

This work day, I delivered around three to four meals per hour during 'peak hours' and only one or even less in all the hours in between. Although this shift should be considered an extreme case – I waited 108 minutes for one of the orders – it remains illustrative of the significant impact daily demand fluctuations have on couriers' game success. Another way that couriers reduce waiting time is by considering local weather conditions. Jason, for instance, once advised me: 'you should start riding during rainy days. It makes it way easier to make good money!' (Fieldnote 28-03-2019). He was right; after a few drops of rain, the number of available orders always increased drastically, incentivising couriers to quickly hit the wet bike lanes of Amsterdam.

Reminiscent of the observations from the manufacturing industry, in this first phase of the labour process, the piece wage game incentivises couriers to show strategic, game-like behaviour that serve the interests of the platforms and, by extension, capital: investing in speed-increasing vehicles and primarily working during times of high demand. Because couriers materially rely on their piece wage and have a desire to maximize it, Diner Direct and Speedily do not have to force every couriers to adjust their work schedule to the whims of the internal food delivery market but they can, instead, largely rely on the indirect control exercised by the piece wage game. I use the term *largely* on purpose here, since the less profitable work shifts become more difficult to fill as a consequence of couriers' strategic self-scheduling, impelling the platforms to also continuously expand their pool of labour to make sure such shifts do not remain vacant.

In contrast to earlier observations inside factory plants, however, the piece wage game played by delivery couriers has a much wider reach. As demonstrated, this game does not only incentivise couriers to maximize work effort in their primary task of delivering food but also deeply structures their decision making in the organizational process of shift allocation – something over which machine operators had much less control. By directly connecting supply and demand to one another, the digital and algorithmically mediated platform infrastructure made this expansion of gamified control possible.

Phase 2. Selecting an Order

Once assigned an order by the algorithm, couriers have a couple of seconds to press 'accept' or 'reject' in the app – a decision that has the feel of an actual video game. In this second phase, platforms exercise algorithmic control by limiting the amount of information couriers receive about the pending gig at hand (see e.g. Rosenblat & Stark, 2016; Veen et al., 2020). Couriers are informed about the piece price and the name and location of the restaurant, yet do not know how far the customer is removed from the restaurant or if the next gig in line would make a 'better deal'.[6] Nevertheless, couriers still select orders strategically by only accepting gigs in which they consider the effort-to-wage ratio favourable. This algorithmic choice infrastructure infuses yet another organizational process – that is, task allocation – with the logic of a piece wage game. The following three selection criteria are used most often.

Criterion 1. Location of the Restaurant and Consumer – 'Avoid the Financial District'.
First of all, most couriers reject gigs that take them to the outskirts of town. As the likelihood of receiving an order depends on the couriers' location vis-à-vis a restaurant, ending up on the outskirts drastically increases their chance of waiting. 'I know some parts of the city you just do not want to go', George explained, 'you have to cycle there and then cycle all the way back to the centre to get another order' (Interview 18-03-2019). The neighbourhoods which couriers generally avoid are Amsterdam East (not enough restaurants), Amsterdam North (too far from the centre), and the financial district (office buildings are difficult to find and enter). After a few days of work, I already found myself employing this popular game strategy. Like almost all the other couriers I met, I always tried to navigate back to the neighbourhood of *De Pijp*, given its high number and density of restaurants. In fact, of all the 191 meals I delivered, 35% came from restaurants located in this neighbourhood (see Fig. 3.1).

Criterion 2. Average Waiting Time of the Restaurant – 'Stay Away From China Express'.
Secondly, many couriers avoid restaurants notorious for lengthy meal preparation times. Upon arrival at a restaurant, couriers usually wait about five minutes for their order to be ready. This number can, however, rise up to 30 minutes or more in unfortunate circumstances. Some couriers reject incoming orders from slow restaurants to decrease the risk of 'losing money' while waiting. Harry, for instance, told to me that everyone 'hates' the restaurant China Express as they are 'serial offenders of taking a long time' (Interview 15-03-2019). Jack further complained:

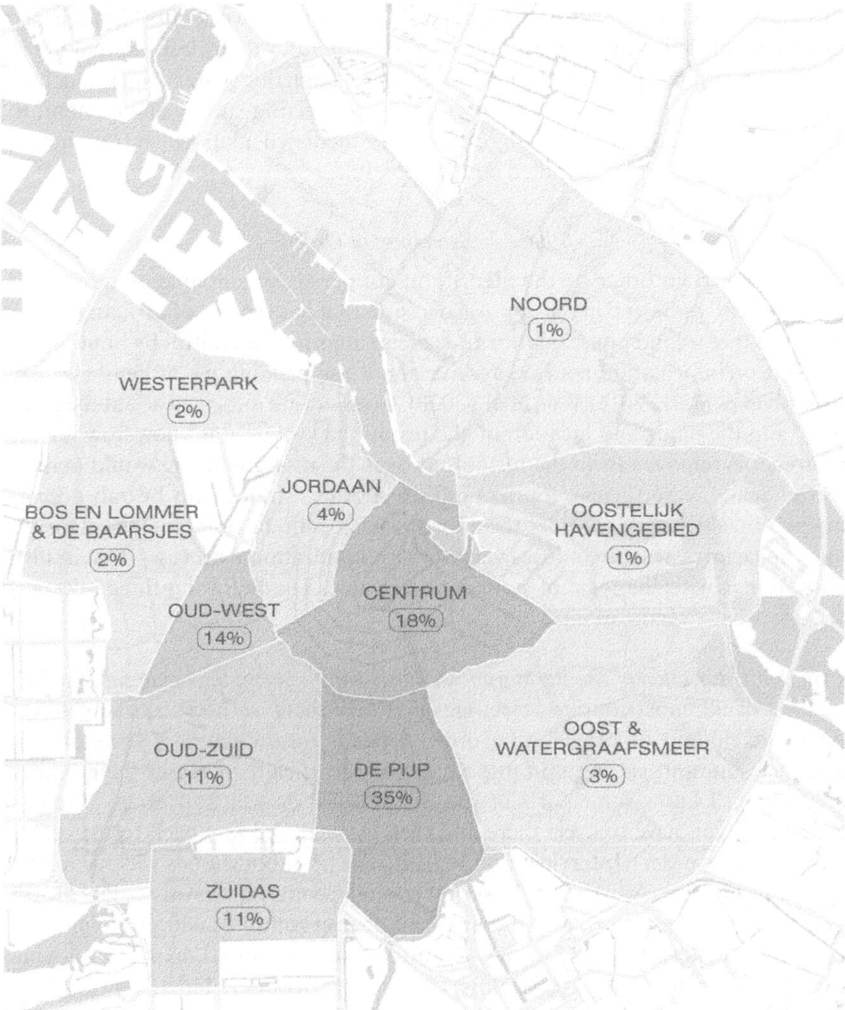

Fig. 3.1. Percentage of Order Pickups Per Neighbourhood ($n = 191$).
Credit line: Original map generated from Google Maps.

'they make you sit around for ages, they are always like "take a seat, have a drink", well that doesn't matter to me, you know!' (Interview 20-03-2019).

Criterion 3. The Piece Price of the Order – 'Take the Shorties'.

Lastly, a small number of couriers take the piece price of incoming orders into account, as they fluctuate depending on delivery distance. As couriers consider the base price relatively high (±€4.30), some of them prefer doing several 'shorties' over only a couple of 'long ones'. Harry, for instance, rejected orders with a piece price over €6: 'it is too far away, and it takes a long time to cycle there' (Interview 15-03-2019). Thijs added that although this strategy increases the chance of encountering slow restaurants, it was worth the risk: 'even if a restaurant takes fifteen minutes to prepare, I am still able to complete three deliveries per hour' (Interview 01-04-2019).

Again, the game dynamics in this second phase confirm what early shop floor ethnographers already noted: piece wage games largely align the interests of capital with the interests of labour. In this phase, the game incentivises couriers to select orders from nearby restaurants and to circle around neighbourhoods where customer demand is highest. As the bulk of all meals are ordered and delivered in such areas, these strategies decrease the transportation time of the majority of the delivery gigs, hence improving the overall quality of the service platforms offer. In later sections, however, I will explain that the strategic selection of gigs also demands additional managerial intervention, as this game tactic produces coordination problems of its own. If all couriers refuse to deliver gigs in the outskirts of town or reject incoming orders from slow restaurants, some meals would, after all, not be delivered.

Algorithmic systems are, at least partly, responsible for making older game dynamics 'new' again. Even if machine operators went at great lengths to secure the 'gravy jobs' by cosying up with the 'scheduling men', in the end it was up to this human actor to decide how the work would be divided (Burawoy, 1979, pp. 51–52). In the gig economy, in contrast, 'gravy jobs' have been replaced by 'gravy gigs' and are no longer allocated by a human being but by a location-sensitive algorithm. Since algorithmic work allocation leaves much more room for individual strategizing, this system imbues yet another organizational process – that is, task allocation – with the logic of the piece wage game. Importantly, it is because of the combination of location-sensitive algorithms and the material control exercised by the piece wage that Diner Direct and Speedily achieve desired conduct from their workforce here. While algorithms make sure that couriers can only see one gig at a time, always from restaurants close to their geographical location, couriers' material dependence on piece wages makes sure that they actually 'listen' to these algorithmic suggestions and (quasi)voluntarily begin to circle around those neighbourhoods in which they are most needed.

Important to note is that the possibilities to strategize about shift and gig selection are unequally distributed between full- and part-time couriers. For the former group, which largely consists of migrant workers, just working the 'peak hours' is not a viable option, as this does not bring in enough money to meet basic survival needs (also see Lazzolino, & Varesio, 2023). To compensate for the lack of orders during the 'dead' hours before and after lunch, many full-time couriers choose to extend their working hours to levels far beyond the full-time workweek. Being less financially dependent on their gig income, part-time couriers – mainly consisting of white students – are better positioned to adjust their personal work schedule to the daily demand fluctuations. By moulding working hours around peak hours, this group minimizes the time waiting on demand and improves their individual bargaining position when selecting gigs. During peak hours, order requests are abundant, which means that part-time couriers can more easily reject

Table 3.3. Game Strategies Full- and Part-time Couriers.

	Game Strategy	Hourly Wage	Monthly Wage
Full-time courier	Lengthening working hours to compensate for unprofitable hours before and after lunch	Relatively low	Relatively high
Part-time courier	Adjusting working hours to daily demand fluctuation	Relatively high	Relatively low

unpopular delivery gigs without having to risk ending up with nothing. From this, it follows that although monthly wage levels of full-time couriers may exceed the one of part-timers, their average hourly wage is significantly lower (see Table 3.3).

Phase 3. Waiting at a Restaurant: 'We Are Very Busy, Consider Cancelling'

After couriers accept an order, they make their way to the restaurant. Upon arrival, couriers first show their order number and then wait for the meal to be prepared. This phase offers limited possibilities for game-playing, as the production speed of restaurants is simply out of couriers' direct control: 'you can try to speak to them [the restaurant] but it won't make much of a difference, you just kind of have to wait', George explained (Interview 18-03-2019). The only avenue for strategizing is to cancel the order if a restaurant is taking a long time – an option enabled by the interactive affordance of the platforms' algorithm (Kellogg et al., 2020). To figure out whether or not this risky strategy is worth pursuing, many couriers ask restaurants to give an estimate of how long the meal preparation is going to take. Mimicking the attitude of the 'rate buster' (Dalton, 1948), only fanatical players regularly cancel orders at this stage of the food delivery cycle. Bram, a part-time courier who utilized almost every opportunity to strategize his work behaviour, for instance, stated:

> If I drove a long time to get there [the restaurant] I tend to wait, as this otherwise would mean I drove all those kilometres for nothing. However, if it [the restaurant] was around the corner and they make me wait fifteen minutes, I tend to go to a new restaurant. In these occasions moving on is just worth doing, as I can make around five euros every quarter-hour. (Interview 14-03-2019)

Phase 4. Biking to the Customer: 'It Is Truly a Race Against the Clock'

In the last phase of the food delivery process, couriers cycle from the restaurant to the customer, usually with hot food in their backpacks. Although the incentive to maximize one's cycling speed permeates the entire labour process, it is most pressing when couriers cycle from a restaurant to a customer. Thijs explained:

> You want to get yourself as fast as possible from the restaurant to the customer. The other way around does not matter that much, as the moment I arrive at a restaurant one minute later there is still a big chance that it [the food] is not ready yet. (Interview 01-04-2019)

Being on the road myself, I repeatedly observed how couriers push themselves physically to maximize their speed and how some of them only use the intermediate moments at restaurants to catch their breath. A few couriers not only increase their cycling speed but literally accelerate *all* of their physical movements:

> It is a sunny afternoon when I make my way to a customer in Amsterdam East. While cycling through the *Piet Heinkade* a fellow courier overtakes me at great speed. Everything about him emanates hurry: he rides a racing bike, wears a colourful cycling outfit and a pair of flashy sunglasses. As we are sent to the same office building, I can see him putting his bike as close to the office entrance as possible and ringing the bell without taking off his backpack. 'BEEEB' the door clicks open. While I take the elevator to the third floor – the location of both our customers – he runs up the staircase, taking three steps at a time. Upon my arrival, he is already agitatedly knocking on the lobby door, as the secretary did not see him immediately. After the door is unlocked, he storms in, drops off his meal and exits the lobby before I had even managed to take off my backpack. (Fieldnote 15-11-2018)

Many couriers reap psychological rewards from this strategy as they described cycling as fast as possible as more 'exciting' or 'fun', and carried the status of adept deliverer with a sense of pride. Most of them, however, rationalized this behaviour by referring to the economic rewards it produces: 'it's simple, if you stand still you do not get paid [...]. Every minute of inactivity just feels like a waste of time. It is truly a race against the clock', Bram explained (Interview 14-03-2019). The fact that the income balance is prominently displayed as a game 'score' in the apps and adjusted in real time only intensifies this gamified work experience (also see Ranganathan & Benson, 2020). While it is most likely that machine operators were tracking their progression towards 'making out' in their heads, delivery couriers are continuously reminded of their real-time progress by the app – a dynamic enabled by the ability of algorithms to provide instantaneous feedback (Kellogg et al., 2020):

> [I]t feels like a game sometimes, when you are like cycling to all these different places across the city [...] and you see your balance going up, and up, and up, it is kind of strange, much more than with other jobs. You wouldn't be in a bar and be like: 'bam, I am on thirty euros already', you be like: 'I'm working for 5 hours'. (Interview 18-03-2019)

Unsurprisingly, couriers often express feeling 'rushed' and admit that they occasionally take more risks in traffic than they would like to. For instance, Sophie specified:

> You are on a mission, you know. A mission of delivering this package in which it can be difficult to hold yourself in check. While cycling, I sometimes think, I am doing this work exactly because I am healthy and I have well-functioning legs, if I would risk all that [by getting into an accident] I also wouldn't be able to continue doing this work. (Interview 14-03-2019)

My observations corroborate Sophie's concerns, as I frequently witnessed couriers cutting off other road users, taking shortcuts, ignoring traffic rules or even smashing into fellow cyclists. For some couriers, an 'aggressive' cycling style even functions as a conscious game tactic. Jakub, for instance, proudly stated that he often skipped red lights in order to maximize his delivery speed: 'I am going recklessly, but I am good, you know, I can really predict things', referring to the movements of his fellow road users (Interview 18-03-2019). Similarly, Gabriel admitted that his fast cycling style was, at least partly, the reason why he hit a fellow cyclist:

> It's like you are doing your job, you have an order, so you are biking fast, you are in your world and if somebody doesn't have light on you don't see them, especially because you are going fast. (Interview 18-03-2019)

Although not all couriers engage in this kind of high-risk behaviour, these accounts demonstrate the piece wage game's ability to produce gamified feelings of 'rush' which diminishes couriers' awareness of their own driving style and their fellow road users. Even if Diner Direct and Speedily do not directly instruct couriers to engage in these cruel forms of self-discipline, they do benefit from them as they reduce the average delivery times: a key variable over which food delivery platforms compete.

In this last two phases of the labour process, historical continuity is, again, incisive. In line with the observations conducted in manufacturing plants, couriers reap economic, psychological, and, to a lesser extent, social rewards from their participation in the piece wage game. The game increases couriers' wage levels and produces positive, game-like mental states that render the repetitive and deskilled food delivery labour process somewhat more bearable (Roy, 1953). As is well documented in the contemporary gamification literature, this psychological effect also has a much darker side: couriers have a hard time holding on to a safe driving style and expose themselves to high degrees of physical risk (also see Chen & Sun, 2020; Mason, 2018; Vasudevan & Chan, 2022). Algorithmic systems only refine and strengthen the infatuating nature of the piece wage game. By adding the number of decision moments, tracking couriers' income progression in real time and displaying individual game 'scores' in the app, new technologies make couriers' piece wage game more interactive, instantaneous, and immersive than the one played by machine operators. Next to *expanding* gamified logics to the organizational activities of shift and task allocation, algorithmic systems also *strengthen* and *intensify* the indirect control exercised by piece wage games.

THE COURIER-PLATFORM INTEREST MISALIGNMENT

As evidenced, the game of gig income maximization largely aligns the interests of delivery couriers with the interests of the platforms. In attempts to raise their piece wage, couriers (semi)voluntarily decide to invest in vehicles, work during times of high demand, repeatedly return to densely populated neighbourhoods and accelerate their delivery speed – behaviour from which the platforms, and by extension capital, also benefit. Akin to observations in the manufacturing industry, however, not all couriers' game strategies work in the interest of the platforms, especially not if they are employed by large groups of workers at the same time. I interpret these forms of 'counter gamification' (Woodcock & Johnson, 2018, p. 549) as acts of agency, as they stem from couriers' class-informed desire to establish a more favourable effort-to-wage ratio, usually run against the interests of capital and demand additional managerial intervention from the platforms.

The first way couriers exercise agency and resist gamified control is by consciously breaking the platforms' wage bonus rules. The fact that all the wage bonuses are allotted through an algorithm rather than a physical manager creates ample opportunities for 'cheating'. To receive Diner Direct's guaranteed 'peak hour' base wage Bram, for instance, explained that he would first secure this bonus by delivering the indicated amount of meals during a 'peak hour' time slot (usually between 6.00 and 7.00 p.m. or 7.00 and 8.00 p.m.) and, subsequently, switch to Speedily's app: 'I would just not check the box "delivered" so I would not receive any new order requests [from Diner Direct]' (Interview 14-03-2019). Similarly, Sem recounted how he was able to collect this same guaranteed wage bonus without doing any work at all. His 'cheating' strategy entailed cycling to the outskirts of town, ordering a meal from the only restaurant close by, counting on his proximity to this remote restaurant to be allocated to the gig, picking up the meal himself and eating it afterwards (Interview 27-03-2019). Sem and Bram, however, also added that it did not take long before their 'cheating' strategies were flagged by the algorithm and quickly made impossible by a change of bonus rules. These observations highlight that delivery couriers act as active agents who identify and exploit the regulatory loopholes of algorithmic rewarding in pursuit of their material interests. These findings, however, also demonstrate that platforms' algorithms heavily police such individual forms of resistance and severely narrow the space individual couriers have to break the rules of the piece wage game.

The second way couriers exercise agency is by concurrently employing game strategies that have a wage-increasing effect for the individual courier but result in coverage problems for Diner Direct and Speedily. As yet indicated, since large groups of delivery couriers avoid the morning shifts, refuse to bike to the outskirts of the city, and reject orders from slow restaurants, platforms have to take additional measures to make sure all gigs are delivered within a reasonable amount of time. Although these synchronized game strategies arise in a largely uncoordinated fashion, they do demonstrate that the game of gig income maximization does not automatically work in the platforms' favour. Moreover, these tactics help some couriers to shake off the feeling of being a passive target of top-down gamified control. Maria, for instance, disclosed that she initially felt 'very manipulated' by the platforms' gamification strategy and even compared herself to Super Maria 'jumping for coins'. However, once she began to take advantage of gamified rewarding by selecting gigs more strategically and avoiding the unprofitable neighbourhoods, these negative feelings subsided (Interview 29-03-2019).

This is not to say that coordination does not occur at all. As couriers play the piece wage game more *with* than *against* each other, tactical knowledge about wage-increasing game strategies is shared within the workforce. For instance, couriers often update each other in real time about which restaurants to avoid or which neighbourhoods to cycle towards for an uninterrupted delivery 'flow'. Secretive information about 'cheating' strategies is not passed on so overtly and is mostly circulated within smaller groups of befriended couriers. By sharing game tactics, couriers essentially teach each other how to obtain delivery gigs with greater effort-to-wage ratios and, thus, retain a larger share of the economic value they produce. Tellingly, couriers interpret one another as colleagues rather than competitors. In doing so, they defy the part of platforms' ideological interpellation that constructs them as competing entrepreneurial subjects (also see Fleming, 2017; Lazzolino & Varesio, 2023; Manriquez, 2019).

Although these two modalities of agency should not be ignored or treated as insignificant, they do not fundamentally challenge the reality of poverty wages or question the highly exploitative class relations the piece wage game presupposes.

For instance, avoiding the outskirts of town does not function as a bargaining strategy that couriers collectively leverage to demand higher wages but rather as a concurrently occurring individual game tactic that unintentionally produces coverage problems for the platforms (*cf.* Briziarelli, 2018). Individual delivery couriers may, thus, break the piece wage game's rules or concurrently develop wage-increasing game strategies; these practices are still far removed from the combative and collective piece wage bargaining tactics machine operators contrived in the darker corners of the shop floor (Brown, 1973; Lupton, 1963). The absence of a physical workplace and the algorithmic allocation of work tasks does, of course, make organizing collective actions in pursuit of higher wages much more difficult – especially in comparison with the closed workspaces of industrial capitalism. Although there are many examples in which gig workers do engage in such collective forms of wage bargaining and manage to push back against the individualistic and depoliticized work attitudes that piece wages under certain circumstances engender, these findings show that algorithmic management functions as a structural hindrance to such forms of collective resistance (see also Wood et al., 2019).

THE COURIER-PLATFORM INTEREST REALIGNMENT

To resolve the interest misalignment caused by couriers' individual and concurrent game strategies, Diner Direct and Speedily do not intervene in the game directly but primarily turn to the controlling capacity of the piece wage itself. To improve the appeal of delivering meals in Amsterdam North, Speedily, for instance, offers couriers a *location bonus* after completing 10 (€15), 25 (€25), 50 (€50), or 125 (€60) deliveries in this understaffed area of town. Similarly, Diner Direct, grants couriers an *availability bonus* to those couriers who are available during dinner time (base wage of ±€11) or contingent peaks in customer demand (e.g. rainy days). By slightly improving the effort-to-wage ratio of unpopular delivery gigs, Diner Direct and Speedily make sure that enough couriers consider it *in their own interest* to bike to the outskirts of town or be available for gigs during lousy weather. In other words, these piece price adjustments realign couriers' interests to those of the platforms and contribute to a situation where there is always a sufficient amount of available couriers throughout the day and in all parts of town.

Although new technologies, indeed, enable platforms to establish this complex system of gamified algorithmic rewarding, adjusting piece prices and performance bonuses in response to workers' game strategies has a much longer lineage. In the manufacturing industry, the repricing of piecework jobs was also continuous and often initiated if management found out that groups of machine operators withheld work effort for tactical reasons. For instance, Roy (1952a, pp. 238–240) observed how the time study man patrolled his shop floor, stopwatch in hand, to identify jobs where the piece price was considered too generous or where machine operators were suspected of restricting output levels. Establishing and recalibrating a piece price was a highly contentious process in which both parties mobilized their bargaining power, and labour did not shy away from calling a strike if consensus could not be reached (Baldamus, 1961; Brown, 1973). In the platform-mediated food delivery sector, however, algorithmic systems depoliticize the repricing process, subdue its contentious nature, and ensure that the game also contributes to establishing more long-term control.

First, algorithmic systems *depersonalize* the process of piece price setting and adjustment by making it appear *as if* a physical manager is no longer involved in this process. Algorithms calculate the piece price per delivered meal on the basis of the delivery distance and by evaluating if the delivery satisfies wage bonus criteria. Although Diner Direct and Speedily are, of course, in charge of the actual price setting and make sure that piece prices vary within a competitive price range, for delivery couriers, the human involvement in this process is completely removed from view. Unsurprisingly, most delivery couriers take piece prices and their adjustments for granted and do not understand them as something over which they can actively bargain or play 'resistance games' (Brown, 1973; Sallaz, 2015, p. 6). In this sense, algorithmic repricing further intensifies the process of depersonalization long underway, as this activity was initially carried out by the physically present time study men, later by a more distant industrial engineer and today by the completely invisible software programmer (Roy, 1952a, pp. 238–240; Burawoy, 1979, pp. 167–170).

Secondly, algorithmic systems *obfuscate* the repricing process by making it difficult for couriers to assess whether changes in the piece wage rules are in their material interests. In the course of my fieldwork Speedily, for instance, changed from a flat piece price of €5.00 per delivered meal to a distance-based piece price hovering between €4.50 and €8.00. This policy change improved the effort-to-wage ratio of delivery trips to the outskirts of town – the areas many couriers were hitherto avoiding. Under the new system, a more complex algorithm calculated a unique piece price for every delivery gig based on the exact distance between the restaurant and the customer. Jakub was very content about the change, as the combination of his good physical shape and the professional racing bike made him well-equipped for the long-distance – and now higher-paying – delivery gigs. Those couriers preferring the 'shorties', on the other hand, were less happy, as the new ruling could imply a lower hourly income. The standard response was, however, compliant confusion: the new algorithmic, piece-by-piece price calculation made it tremendously difficult to compare the old and newer price systems, which depoliticized the issue from the start.

Thirdly, algorithmic systems make it difficult for individual couriers to influence the practice of piece price setting and adjustment by completely *automating* this process. In the manufacturing industry, in contrast, the piece price of a piece-work job was determined manually and usually based on direct observations of the productivity of the 'average' worker. This practice left much room for individual manipulation, as the observed worker could make it appear *as if* a job was more arduous than it in reality was (Brown, 1973, pp. 69–72; Roy, 1952a, pp. 241–254). Instead of drawing on performance data of the average courier, food delivery platforms use real-time data on the behaviour of all couriers (e.g. location, availability, vehicle choice) in combination with several additional sources of information (e.g. delivery distance, customer demand, etc.) to determine the standard and contingent piece price. This diminishes the space for resistance, as this means that couriers cannot exercise agency in the price setting process by, for instance, making a delivery trip appear longer than it was and can only occasionally exploit the loopholes in the complex system of algorithmic rewarding – behaviour these same algorithms attempt to identify and heavily police.

GAMIFYING WAGE LEVELS, DEPOLITICIZING UNDERPAYMENT

Despite couriers' ardent efforts to maximize their gig income, many couriers assured me that the overall wage levels remain low and have only deteriorated over the years. Especially, senior couriers revelled in memories of the 'good old days' when food delivery platforms still had enough venture capital at their disposal to offer couriers generous wage bonuses (Van Doorn & Chen, 2021). Similar to piece price adjustments, structural underpay has historically functioned as a catalyst for collective wage bargaining and associated forms of mobilizations (e.g. strikes) that challenged any kind of managerial control (Baldamus, 1961). In my field site, however, there was no sign of this: couriers usually took their low and unstable wage levels for granted and preferred to quit prematurely than to actively fight for change. George, for instance, explained that he stopped working for Speedily after his income dropped below an acceptable level: 'it kinda [sic] kept getting worse and worse after they changed to distance fees, your fee per order would get less and less, so I was just like, this is not worth it anymore' (Interview 18-03-2019). I argue that the depoliticized mentality the piece wage game produces and algorithms further reinforce can explain, at least partly, why individual and concurrent expressions of resistance against gamification were present in the streets of Amsterdam but collective resistance against the accompanying structural underpay did not materialize.

Firstly, the piece wage game narrows the terms in which classic wage-effort bargains take shape. From my interviews, I learned that most couriers rarely reach out to their platform employers and if they do mostly discuss small technical issues related to single gigs. Instead of challenging the deteriorating wage bonus levels or the structural underpay, couriers mostly file complaints when they were held up in the game of income maximization for reasons outside their own control. Couriers tend to reach out to the platforms when they are sent to the wrong address, encounter exceptionally uncooperative restaurants, or do not receive their wage bonus. Delivery couriers thereby present grievances about wage-related issues as individual game players and in relation to single gigs and do not fundamentally question the low average wage itself. The fact that platforms are hard to reach directly, and often reply to couriers' messages with algorithmically generated responses (especially Diner Direct), reinforces this depoliticized mentality about wages.

Secondly, the piece wage game creates the impression that individual skills and strategy significantly impact individual wage levels. Since the platforms' interactive algorithms bombard couriers with a continuous flow of 'choices' and 'opportunities', some couriers develop the belief that they exercise more control over their income level than is actually the case. In this sense, it is revealing that the less 'successful' couriers often relate their low income to personal shortcomings instead of the platforms' exploitative wage policy. For instance, Chen, a Chinese-Canadian courier who had recently moved to The Netherlands and who had a hard time finding a 'real' job, explained that her work as a delivery courier provided her with just enough money to 'survive'. Paradoxically, however, she also indicated that she had 'nothing to complain about'. Her low income was, after all, the consequence of her bad physical shape and unwillingness to work in bad weather: 'if you are really athletic and you do not care about the weather, you can earn a very good living of it. But for me, I barely do any sports and get this cold head when it's windy' (Interview 14-03-2019). The fact that couriers draw on past work experiences in their decision making and bear the financial costs of a failed strategy instantaneously makes it even more difficult to not blame oneself if things do not go as planned:

> It's a Friday afternoon when my phone starts ringing. "Beeb, Beeb". It is an incoming order request from China Express. I hesitate whether to accept it, as this restaurant is notorious for its long waiting times. Since I am already waiting 20 minutes on demand without receiving any gigs I decide to accept it anyways. Upon arrival, it is quiet inside. Would this mean that my meal is going to be ready quickly? I show my order number and start to wait outside. 10 minutes pass. I decide to go inside to ask if it is almost done. Another 10 minutes pass. I am getting frustrated, why did I accept this order when I knew this restaurant always keeps couriers waiting for ages? After another 5 minutes, the meal is finally ready. I continue my journey being frustrated about my stupid decision. (Fieldnote 15-03-2019)

The flip side of the individualizing effect of piece wages is that some of the more 'successful' gameplayers feel no need to resist policy changes that effectively lower the wage level of the average courier – something Marx (1867/2013, p. 388) already warned about long ago. Their exceptional skills and physical stamina enables them to earn a decent wage regardless of minor rule adjustments, so this group reasons. Gabriel, for instance, acknowledged that Speedily's decision to let go of the flat fee of €5 per delivery was probably 'quite unfair for the people that work full-time', at the same time he did not 'really mind' himself, as he still knew how to select the profitable orders, avoid the slow restaurants and navigate to those areas in town with a high density of restaurants (Interview 18-03-2019).

Thirdly, the nature of the piece wage game makes couriers deflect frustrations about low wage levels in the horizontal direction of colleagues, consumers, or restaurants, especially since no physical manager is present on the work floor to take the blame. A first source of wage-related frustration was the ever-expanding pool of labour. In the course of my fieldwork, I noticed how the increasing popularity of food delivery work had a very direct impact on my income. Where it used to be relatively easy to secure a significant amount of work shifts with Speedily, once the number of couriers started to increase this became almost impossible. At the end of my fieldwork, the work schedule would always be fully booked the second after its release, leaving me, and many other couriers, without any shift and, thus, no gig income for the week.

Slow restaurants function as the most direct source of frustration for couriers. Mimicking the role of the uncooperative 'truck drivers' of the manufacturing industry (Burawoy, 1979), restaurants are an unavoidable hurdle in the delivery process but do not have a direct stake in couriers' delivery speed. Especially when restaurants provide couriers with no or wrong information about how long the preparation of a meal is going to take, conflict tends to occur. For instance, Thijs explained: 'If they would just tell me straight up it is going to take fifteen minutes, I can just decide to reject the order [...] the moment they keep stringing me along, I can do nothing at all!' (Interview 01-04-2019). Similarly, Oliver recounted that a pizzeria chef once called him a 'fucking asshole' for not treating their pizza with great care: 'I was just like, you lied to me at the beginning [about the preparation time] you have to treat us with respect. He costs me five euro you know' (Interview 11-03-2019). In sum, in the food delivery sector, the gamification of the wage levels and the depoliticization of structural underpay operate as two sides of the same coin. By enabling the platform to completely withdraw from the contested terrain of the work floor, algorithmic systems merely reinforce the individualistic attitudes piece wages are able to produce (Burawoy, 1979; Marx, 1867/2013, pp. 388–389). In combination, these dynamics reduce the possibilities for collective resistance against structural underpay to erupt from the point of production and strengthen Diner Direct's and Speedily's long-term control over the labour process (Table 3.4).

Table 3.4. Piece Wage Games in the Platform-mediated Food Delivery Sector: Historical Continuity and Change.

	Short-term Control		Long-term Control	
Interest (mis) alignment between delivery couriers and platform	Aligned interests	Unaligned interests	Realigned interests	
Historical continuity	The piece wage (game) produces self-discipline among couriers by establishing a direct connection between work effort and individual wage level	The piece wage game produces game strategies among couriers which run against the platform's interests and demand intervention	Platforms re-align the interests of couriers to the interests of the platforms by adjusting the effort-to-wage ratio of certain piecework jobs (i.e. delivery gigs)	The piece wage (game) exert a downward pressure on wages and depoliticise structural underpay
Historical change	Algorithmic technologies expand gamified control by gamifying shift and task allocation and intensify gamified control by making piece wage games more interactive, immersive, and instantaneous	Algorithmic technologies expand the possibilities for individual and concurrent strategizing but limit the possibility for collective and coordinated strategizing	Algorithms technologies depersonalize, obfuscate and automatize the otherwise contentious process of determining and recalibrating piece prices	Algorithms intensify the process of depoliticization by increasing the physical gap between wage-earning couriers and price-setting platforms

CONCLUSION AND DISCUSSION

This study begins to unpack how piece wage games are played and operate as an indirect modality of control in the platform-mediated food delivery sector. Instead of assuming that gamification in the gig economy is inherently tied to platforms' algorithmically enabled managerial techniques, I tracked the historical continuities and transformation between present and much older – pre-algorithmic – forms of gamified control. To do this, I compared how piece wage games indirectly controlled the conduct of machine operators working in the manufacturing industry with the way they do in the platform-mediated food delivery sector. More specifically, this study evaluated how new algorithmic technologies affected the observed piece wage game's ability to align delivery couriers' interests with those of the platforms in the different phases of the food delivery process. My findings contribute to the (critical) literature on gamification in the gig economy and the ethnographic literature on piece wage games and bargaining in the following ways.

First of all, this study challenges the ways in which the contemporary literature on gamification theorizes the relationship between technology, gamification, and control. In this scholarship, new digital technologies are often treated as the 'crucial technical enabler' for the rise of gamification in the workplace (Deterding, 2019, p. 131). Technologies have made it, after all, much easier to track and quantify workers' work performance and translate this information into personal game rankings and scores (also see Nacke & Deterding, 2017; Ranganathan & Benson, 2020; Warmelink et al., 2020). Correspondingly, the literature on the platform-mediated gig economy has paid much attention to algorithmically enabled game design elements (i.e. personalized nudges, user-generated ratings, etc.) and showed how platforms' repurposing of such elements produce gamified attitudes and behaviours in gig workers from which platforms themselves primarily benefit (Chan, 2019; Mason, 2018; Rosenblat & Stark, 2016; Scheiber, 2017; Vasudevan & Chan, 2022).

My study complicates this narrative by treating the omnipresence of piece wage remuneration as the second *crucial enabler* of the rise in gamified control in the gig economy. More specifically, my study shows that there is a remarkable continuity between the way piece wage games exercised control over labour in the pre-algorithmic manufacturing industry and the way they do in the platform-mediated food delivery sector. Akin to ethnographic research on this latter sector (Burawoy, 1979), I observed how the game of gig income maximization yokes the interests of delivery couriers to the interests of the platforms and thus capital (*cf.* Manriquez, 2019). By materially incentivising couriers to deliver faster, longer and in densely populated neighbourhoods, this game produces economic (i.e. increasing piece wage income) and some psychological (i.e. feelings of joy, flow, etc.) rewards for the individual delivery couriers, while simultaneously lowering the platforms' average delivery times – a key variable over which food delivery platforms compete.

Furthermore, my findings corroborate classic observations about the conditional nature of such interest alignment, as some of the game strategies couriers employ also run against the interests of the platforms (Roy, 1952a, 1952b) and prompt them to re-establish control by changing bonus rules or adjusting piece prices (Baldamus, 1961; Brown, 1973). Taken together, the results of this study support the growing body of scholarship which suggests that the emergence of the platform-mediated gig economy does not herald a completely new way of ensuring labour control and surplus value extraction under capitalism (Srnicek, 2016), but instead signifies the continuation of preceding ones (Alkhatib et al., 2017; Finkin, 2016; Joyce, 2020; Moore & Joyce, 2019; Quinlan, 2012; Stanford, 2017). My study expands this literature by more explicitly pointing at the historical continuity between the present and earlier forms of gamified control.

This is not to say that new technologies do not play a role in establishing gamified control at all. On the contrary, my study demonstrates that algorithmic technologies refine, strengthen, and expand earlier forms of gamified control in multiple ways (*cf.* Cameron, 2022). By treating the material control exercised by piece wage (games) as analytically distinct from the control exercised by algorithms, I was able to systematically evaluate how algorithmic systems make the classic form of gamified control 'new' again and avoid the common pitfall of uncritically tracing game-playing to the introduction of new technologies.

More concretely, the findings of this study show that algorithmic systems *refine* and *strengthen* gamified control by making the piece wage game couriers play more interactive, instantaneous and immersive than the one played by machine operators. Once a machine operator realized that hitting the production target was no longer feasible, and the stimulating uncertainty about potential game success vanished, the game of 'making out' was over. For delivery couriers, in contrast, the game is seldom 'over', as their game success is dependent on an array of interactive algorithmically regulated decisions (e.g. selecting an order or shift, cancelling an order, playing for a bonus, etc.) that (re)inject a sense of uncertainty in all phases of the delivery process. Algorithms make it, moreover, possible to track and digitally display couriers' game success in a real-time 'score', magnifying gamified patterns of behaviour even more.

Furthermore, my study reveals that algorithmic systems *expand* gamified control by enabling the logic of a piece wage game to spill over to shift and task allocation – organizational processes that remained largely outside the scope of the piece wage games of the manufacturing industry. While delivery couriers experience a relatively high degree of freedom when it comes to selecting work shifts and delivery gigs, the game of gig income maximization incentivises them to exercise this freedom in such a way that platforms also largely benefit – that is, working in times of high demand and in areas with a high number of restaurants. New location-sensitive algorithmic technologies are, again, vital for ensuring that these decentralized shift and task allocation systems continue to work in the platforms' favour.

An additional benefit of understanding algorithmic control as analytically distinct from the material control exercised by the piece wage, is that this approach demonstrated that the former is often only 'effective' when combined with the latter – a finding downplayed, if not ignored altogether, in the literature on algorithmic control (Kellogg et al., 2020; Rosenblat & Stark, 2016). Although Diner Direct's and Speedily's algorithms subtly steer couriers' behaviour in the preferred direction by assigning them one gig at a time and only from restaurants close by, my study shows that it is still because of couriers' material reliance on a piece wage, and their class-informed desire to maximize it, that they 'listen' to these algorithmic suggestions and collectively position themselves in those neighbourhoods in which they are most needed. Similarly, couriers do not only respond to algorithmically allocated wage bonuses because these opaque incentive schemes make the psychological experience of work more game-like, exciting and 'fun' (Kellogg et al., 2020, p. 382) but also because some piece wage bonuses rather clearly improve the effort-to-wage ratio of unpopular delivery gigs. Future research should continue to explore how the interplay between algorithmic systems and piece wages creates unique configurations of control in other platform-based gig economy sectors.

These findings speak to the recent critique of Joyce (2020, p. 542) and Moore and Joyce (2020, p. 932) on the 'resurgence of technological determinism' in the literature on the platform-mediated gig economy. More specifically, they argue that gig economy scholarship has a tendency to attribute almost all platforms' controlling capacity to opaque algorithms or some other 'technological trickery' (Joyce, 2020, p. 547). Such reasoning creates the impression that the power asymmetry between platforms and gig workers is reducible to unequal access to new technologies instead of their respective material positions as capital and labour, and disregards that some of platforms' power-infused decision making – for example, related to piece wages prices – actually occurs in plain sight (Joyce, 2020; Moore & Joyce, 2020). Although my empirical study largely confirms the empirical relevance of this critique and seconds the importance of 're-centring capital in the analysis of platform work' (Joyce, 2020, p. 546; also see Chai & Scully 2019), it also challenges the simple dichotomy these critics create between technical control of algorithms and the material control of the piece wage. My findings indicate, after all, that algorithmic control is often dependent on material control to produce desired conduct in gig workers.

This chapter updates the classic ethnographic literature on piece wage bargaining by revealing that algorithmic systems can depoliticize the potentially explosive processes of piece price setting and adjustment. In many classic accounts, the workplace culture of piece wage factories is characterized as a dog-eat-dog world in which the struggle between capital and labour is continuous and manifests in everyday interactions (Roy, 1952a). Piece workers are known to exercise pressure towards looser productivity targets and higher piece prices by manipulating the rate-setting process, increasing absenteeism, restricting output, working to rule, or calling strikes (Alkhatib et al., 2017; Baldamus, 1961; Brown, 1973; Lupton, 1963; Roy, 1952a, 1952b). In the platform-mediated food delivery sector of Amsterdam, in contrast, piece prices are not actively bargained over and are perceived as an unquestionable given. This is particularly surprising, as Diner Direct and Speedily are continuously altering their bonus rules, overall bonus levels have been deteriorating for a while and couriers are officially operating as 'independent contractors' – a legal status which, at least in theory, presupposes price bargaining (also see Van Doorn & Chen, 2021). Instead of relating this low degree of piecework bargaining to the level of class consciousness of the workforce, the size of the reserve army of labour, or the involvement of unions (Baldamus, 1961; Brown, 1973; Burawoy, 1979), this study points at the importance of new technologies. Although Diner Direct and Speedily are, of course, in charge of determining the final piece price, my study shows that algorithms depoliticize this otherwise contentious process. Algorithms depersonalize and automate the process of piece price setting and adjustment and obfuscate if new piece wage rules are negatively impacting workers' material interests.

Lastly, this chapter contributes to the emerging literature on gig workers' resistance against gamified control by documenting how delivery couriers push back against this managerial technique and by developing a theoretical explanation for the specific forms such resistance takes. Challenging the idea that gamification is either imposed by management (Scheiber, 2017; Van Doorn & Chen, 2021) or emerges from the bottom-up (Cameron, 2022), this study shows that gamification is best understood as an interactive process imbued with antagonisms. Although Diner Direct and Speedily may have designed the food delivery labour process with a (video)game in mind (see e.g. Mason, 2018; Scheiber, 2017), my findings demonstrate that delivery couriers also take initiative and develop game strategies that serve their own instead of the platforms' interests. Acting upon their class-informed desire to maximize wages and minimize work effort, couriers exercise individual forms of agency by identifying and exploiting the regulatory gaps in the platforms' algorithmic rewarding system and concurrent forms of agency by collectively avoiding the morning shifts, refusing to cycle to the outskirts of the city, and rejecting orders from slow restaurants. By interpreting these expressions of resistance as reflecting the process of 'wage-effort bargaining' (Baldamus, 1961) and, thus, stemming from the fundamental conflict of interest between capital and labour (Thompson, 1990), this study not only identifies and describes these forms of resistance but also explains them (*cf.* Veen et al., 2020).

Diner Direct and Speedily, in turn, respond to such acts of 'counter-gamification' (Woodcock & Johnson, 2018, p. 549) by policing piece wage rules, changing bonus schemes in response to 'cheating' strategies and slightly adjusting the effort-to-wage ratio of unpopular delivery gigs – all with the help of algorithms. Because these interventions are highly effective in curbing individual forms of resistance, this finding highlights the limited opportunities solitary couriers have to 'game' algorithmic systems and to successfully mobilize their individual bargaining power to acquire more favourable effort-to-wage distributions in their jobs.

In contrast to the Italian (Tassinari & Maccarrone, 2017) and Chinese (Lei, 2021) food delivery sectors, collective expressions of resistance against gamified control were not observed in the course of my fieldwork. Scholars who have studied other cases where collective forms of resistance did not occur usually point to the way platforms organize the labour process. Collective resistance might be difficult to realize, they argue, because the gig workforce is spatially dispersed, controlled through impersonal algorithms, and often largely consists of financially vulnerable and migrant workers with limited resources to participate in overt resistance (Anwar & Graham, 2020; Lazzolino & Varesio, 2023; Stanford, 2017; Veen et al., 2020; Walker et al., 2021; Wood et al., 2019; *cf.* Lei, 2021). My ethnographic field research, however, enabled me to focus not only on how platform work is organized and structured but also on how it is practised and experienced. Focusing on the potentially explosive issue of structural underpay, my observations reveal that the game of income maximization contributes to a depoliticized workplace culture in which wage-related grievances about low pay are individualized and redirected away from the platforms. Confirming previous research on piece wages games (Burawoy, 1979; Marx, 1867/2013; Ranganathan, & Benson, 2020), the game of gig income maximization interpellates couriers as skilful go-getters who grab small opportunities for some extra income but who leave the capitalist logics responsible for establishing the high rates of exploitation largely unchallenged. This depoliticized work culture can, at least partly, explain why individual and concurrent forms of resistance against gamification were observed in Amsterdam but collective mobilizations against the accompanying structural underpay did not materialize.

These findings, however, beg the question: why did collective forms of struggles against structural underpay emerge in many parts of the gig economy but not in Amsterdam? (see e.g. Lei, 2021; Tassinari & Maccarrone, 2017). One possible explanation for this could be that the Dutch consensus-oriented approach to industrial relations, and the associated culture of conflict avoidance, offers a poor foundation for such forms of resistance to arise from the point of production in this sector (see e.g. Becker, 2001). Due to this ideological climate, piece wage games may have been particularly powerful in producing a depoliticized work culture around piece wages. The city of Amsterdam provides, moreover, nearly perfect material conditions for work practices of solitary strategizing to gain traction: Amsterdam is home to a relatively large pool of delivery couriers and dozens of restaurants, has flat and well-maintained bike lanes, hosts several electric bike rentals, and offers couriers the option to work for multiple food delivery platforms at the same time (*cf.* Tassinari & Maccarrone, 2017, p. 354). Under such material conditions, individual forms of resistance can easily emerge but collective ones may materialize less quickly. A last reason less directly connected to gamification relates to the legal battles the biggest labour union and one individual gig worker were fighting on behalf of all Dutch couriers in the course of my fieldwork. Although their cases revolved around couriers' legal (mis)categorization instead of their structural underpayment, these long and eventually successful legal actions may have moved activist attention away from the last-mentioned matter. Comparative ethnographic research is, however, necessary to ascertain if gamified work cultures differ from city to city and to establish if these differences can explain why collective forms of resistance (do not) emerge. All of this implies that if we want to develop powerful critiques of the way platform capitalism (re)produces class and intersectional inequalities, we need to keep in mind that gamified piece wage systems can produce depoliticized class subjectivities and acquire a better understanding of the conditions under which such subject positions can be undermined, subverted, or wholly rejected.

NOTES

1. All the names of delivery couriers, restaurants and food delivery platforms have been replaced by pseudonyms in the empirical sections of this chapter.

2. In The Netherlands, for instance, the food delivery platform Deliveroo faced several lawsuits for mis-categorizing their delivery couriers as 'independent contractors'.

The central accusation in the biggest case (*Deliveroo* v. *FNV*) was that delivery couriers do not experience the kind of on-the-job autonomy associated with the status of 'independent contractor' (especially in relation to shift allocation, the allocation and selection of gigs, piece price determination). Although Deliveroo expanded couriers' on-the-job autonomy over the years, it has lost most lawsuits thus far. In March 2023, the highest Dutch court (*De Hoge Raad*) resolved the issue once and for all by ruling that Dutch delivery couriers should be treated as employees (*Deliveroo* v. *FNV*, 2021, 2023; Klein, 2023).

3. Food delivery platform's wage bonus rules change regularly. The presented bonus rules of the two platforms were in place during my fieldwork but may have changed by now.

4. FNV's (2019) estimates are based on empirical data collected in the second half of 2018 and thus largely overlap with the period of my fieldwork. To compare the hourly wage levels of freelance delivery couriers with the wage of comparable workers receiving the sectoral minimum, FNV estimated the average amount of meals couriers are able to deliver per hour ($n = 2$) and multiplied this number with the average piece price of each platform. In turn, they added the average wage bonus and deducted estimates of pension and social security premiums, income tax and individual business expenses (e.g. bike maintenance costs). This careful calculation yielded a net hourly wage far below the sectoral minimum. Although FNV's (2020) estimates for the year after were somewhat higher, they still remained below the sectoral minimum.

5. On the basis of survey data, anecdotal evidence and my own observations in the streets of Amsterdam, I conclude that particularly white (89% in my sample) and university-level educated (89% in my sample) couriers were overrepresented in my interview sample. For instance, in surveys from SEO Economic Research the percentages of food delivery couriers that obtained university-level education lie between 40% (2018, $n = 113$) and 50% (2020, $n = 142$) (ter Weel et al., 2018, p. 33, 2020, p. 10). As 'race' and ethnicity are generally not covered in Dutch surveys on delivery work, reliable estimations of the racial composition of the workforce are wholly unavailable. Much anecdotal evidence suggests, however, that (undocumented) migrant workers from racial minority groups make up a large part of all delivery couriers in the Netherlands – an observation corroborated by my own field research and echoed in the international literature on migrant labour in the gig economy (Rengers, & Houtekamer, 2022; Van Doorn et al., in press). The fact that platform workers with a non-Dutch nationality are overrepresented in some surveys further points in this direction (43% of all respondents in the study by Verbiest, et al., 2020).

6. The level of transparency is somewhat higher for Speedily, as this platform also shows couriers the location of the customer.

REFERENCES

Alkhatib, A., Bernstein, M. S., & Levi, M. (2017). Examining crowd work and gig work through the historical lens of piecework. In G. Mark, S. Fussel, C. Lampe, M. C. Schraefel, J.P. Hourcade, C. Appert, & D. Wigdor (Eds.), *Proceedings of the 2017 CHI conference on human factors in computing systems* (pp. 4599–4616). ACM Press. https://doi.org/10.1145/3025453.3025974

Aneesh, A. (2009). Global labor: Algocratic modes of organization. *Sociological Theory*, *27*(4), 347–370. https://doi.org/10.1111/j.1467-9558.2009.01352.x

Anwar, M. A., & Graham, M. (2020). Hidden transcripts of the gig economy: Labour agency and the new art of resistance among African gig workers. *Environment and Planning A: Economy and Space*, *52*(7), 1269–1291. https://doi.org/10.1177/0308518X19894584

Baldamus, W. (1961). *Efficiency and effort: An analysis of industrial administration*. London: Tavistock Publications.

Becker, U. (2001). 'Miracle' by consensus? Consensualism and dominance in Dutch employment development. *Economic and Industrial Democracy*, *22*(4), 453–483. https://doi.org/10.1177/0143831X01224002

Behl, A., Jayawardena, N., Ishizaka, A., Gupta, M., & Shankar, A. (2022). Gamification and gigification: A multidimensional theoretical approach. *Journal of Business Research*, *139*, 1378–1393. https://doi.org/10.1016/j.jbusres.2021.09.023

Behl, A., Sheorey, P. A., Chavan, M., Jain, K., & Jajodia, I. (2021). Empirical investigation of participation on crowdsourcing platforms: A gamified approach. *Journal of Global Information Management, 29*(6), 1–27. https://doi.org/10.4018/JGIM.20211101.oa14

Briziarelli, M. (2018). Spatial politics in the digital realm: The logistics/precarity dialectics and Deliveroo's tertiary space struggles. *Cultural Studies, 33*(5), 823–840. https://doi.org/10.1080/09502386.2018.1519583

Brown, W. (1973). *Piecework bargaining*. London: Heinemann Educational Books.

Bulmer, M. (1982). When is disguise justified? Alternatives to covert participant observation. *Qualitative Sociology, 5*(4), 251–264. https://doi.org/10.1007/BF00986753

Burawoy, M. (1979). *Manufacturing consent – Changes in the labour process under monopoly capitalism*. Chicago, IL: University of Chicago Press.

Burawoy, M. (1985). *The Politics of production: Factory regimes under capitalism and socialism*. London: Verso Books.

Cameron, L. D. (2022). "Making out" while driving: Relational and efficiency games in the gig economy. *Organization Science, 33*(1), 231–252. https://doi.org/10.1287/orsc.2021.1547

Chai, S., & Scully, M. A. (2019). It's about distributing rather than sharing: Using labor process theory to probe the "sharing" economy. *Journal of Business Ethics, 159*, 943–960. https://doi.org/10.1007/s10551-019-04210-y

Chan, N. K. (2019). The rating game: The discipline of Uber's user-generated ratings. *Surveillance & Society, 17*(1–2), 183–190. https://doi.org/10.24908/ss.v17i1/2.12911

Chapman, C., Chua, W. F., & Fiedler, T. (2021). Seduction as control: Gamification at foursquare. *Management Accounting Research, 53*, 1–14 https://doi.org/10.1016/j.mar.2021.100765

Chen, J. Y., & Sun, P. (2020). Temporal arbitrage, fragmented rush, and opportunistic behaviors: The labor politics of time in the platform economy. *New Media & Society, 22*(9), 1561–1579. https://doi.org/10.1177/1461444820913567

Dalton, M. (1948) The industrial 'rate-buster': A characterization. *Applied Anthropology Winter, 7*(1), 5–18. Retrieved from https://www.jstor.org/stable/44135193

Defossez, D. (2022). The employment status of food delivery riders in Europe and the UK: Self-employed or worker? *Maastricht Journal of European and Comparative Law, 29*(1), 25–46. https://doi.org/10.1177/1023263X211051833

Deliveroo v. *FNV*, ECLI:NL:GHAMS:2021:392 (Court of Amsterdam, 2021). Retrieved from https://uitspraken.rechtspraak.nl/#!/details?id=ECLI:NL:GHAMS:2021:392

Deliveroo v. *FNV*, ECLI:NL:HR:2023:443 (Dutch Supreme Court, 2023). Retrieved from https://uitspraken.rechtspraak.nl/#!/details?id=ECLI:NL:HR:2023:443

Deterding, S. (2019). Gamification in management: Between choice architecture and humanistic design. *Journal of Management Inquiry, 28*(2), 131–136. https://doi.org/10.1177/1056492618790912

Deterding, S., Dixon, D., Khaled, R., & Nacke, L. (2011). From game design elements to gamefulness: Defining 'gamification'. In A. Lugmayr, H. Franssila, C. Safran, & I. Hammouda (Eds.), *Proceedings of the 15th International Academic MindTrek conference: Envisioning future media environments* (pp. 9–15). https://doi.org/10.1145/2181037.2181040

Dublin, T. (1991). Rural putting-out work in early nineteenth-century New England: Women and the transition to capitalism in the countryside. *The New England Quarterly, 64*(4), 531–573. Retrieved from https://www.jstor.org/stable/366187

Edwards, R. (1979). *Contested terrain*. London: Basic Books.

Emerson, R. M., Fretz, R. I., & Shaw, L. L. (2001). Participant observation and fieldnotes. In P. Atkinson, A. Coffey, S. Delamont, J. Lofland, & L. Lofland (Eds.), *Handbook of ethnography* (pp. 352–368). Thousand Oaks, CA: Sage.

Finkin, M. (2016). Beclouded work in historical perspective. *Comparative Labor Law & Policy Journal, 37*(3), 1–20. Retrieved from https://ssrn.com/abstract=2712722

Fleming, P. (2017). The human capital hoax: Work, debt and insecurity in the era of uberization. *Organization Studies, 38*(5), 691–709. https://doi.org/10.1177/0170840616686129

FNV. (2019). Riders verdienen beter – De maaltijdbezorgsector in Nederland. Retrieved from https://www.ridersunion.nl/getmedia/6a0b6589-712a-4be8-accf-3e1603655d53/Riders-verdienen-beter-zwartboek.pdf

FNV. (2020). Bezorgd om maaltijdbezorgers – Te laag inkomen, opgejaagd en geen zekerheid. Retrieved from https://www.fnv.nl/getmedia/dfbee842-a80f-4af1-8a16-c00d842ece65/Rapport-Bezorgd-om-maaltijdbezorgers-2-0.pdf

Friedman, A. L. (2000). Microregulation and post-Fordism: Critique and development of regulation theory. *New Political Economy*, *5*(1), 59–76. https://doi.org/10.1080/13563460050001989

Gandini, A. (2019). Labour process theory and the gig economy. *Human Relations*, *72*(6), 1039–1056. https://doi.org/10.1177/001872671879000

Healy, J., Nicholson, D., & Pekarek, A. (2017). Should we take the gig economy seriously? *Labour & Industry: A Journal of the Social and Economic Relations of Work*, *27*(3), 232–248. https://doi.org/10.1080/10301763.2017.1377048

Heeks, R. (2017). Decent work and the digital gig economy: A developing country perspective on employment impacts and standards in online outsourcing, crowdwork, etc. Development Informatics Working Paper Series No. 71. http://dx.doi.org/10.2139/ssrn.3431033

Homan, R. (1980). The ethics of covert methods, *British Journal of Sociology*, *31*(1), 36–59. https://doi.org/10.2307/590062

Joyce, S. (2020). Rediscovering the cash nexus, again: Subsumption and the labour–capital relation in platform work. *Capital & Class*, *44*(4), 541–552. https://doi.org/10.1177/030981682090635

Joyce, S., & Stuart, M. (2021). Digitalised management, control and resistance in platform work: a labour process analysis. In J. Haider & M. Keune (Eds.), *Work and labour relations in global platform capitalism* (pp. 158–184). London: Edward Elgar Publishing Limited. https://doi.org/10.4337/9781802205138.00017

Kellogg, K. C., Valentine, M. A., & Christin, A. (2020). Algorithms at work: The new contested terrain of control. *Academy of Management Annals*, *14*(1), 366–410. https://doi.org/10.5465/annals.2018.0174

Klein, C. (2023). Laatste weekend Deliveroo: Bezorgdienst verloor van Uber, Thuisbezorgd en FNV. *NOS*. Retrieved from https://nos.nl/artikel/2454025-laatste-weekend-deliveroo-bezorgdienst-verloor-van-uber-thuisbezorgd-en-fnv

Krzywdzinski, M., & Gerber, C. (2021). Between automation and gamification: Forms of labour control on crowdwork platforms. *Work in the Global Economy*, *1*(1–2), 161–184. https://doi.org/10.1332/273241721X16295434739161

Lazear, E. P. (1986). Salaries and piece rates. *Journal of Business*, *59*(3), 405–431. http://dx.doi.org/10.1086/296345

Lazzolino, G., & Varesio, A. (2023). Gaming the system: Tactical workarounds and the production of antagonistic subjectivities among migrant platform workers in Italy. *Antipode*, *55*(3), 877–896. https://doi.org/10.1111/anti.12917

Lehdonvirta, V. (2018). Flexibility in the gig economy: Managing time on three online piecework platforms. *New Technology, Work and Employment*, *33*(1), 13–29. https://doi.org/10.1111/ntwe.12102

Lei, Y. W. (2021). Delivering solidarity: Platform architecture and collective contention in China's platform economy. *American Sociological Review*, *86*(2), 279–309. https://doi.org/10.1177/0003122420979980

Lupton, T. (1963). *On the shop floor: Two studies of workshop organization and output*. Oxford: Pergamon Press.

Manriquez, M. (2019). Work-games in the gig-economy: A case study of Uber drivers in the city of monterrey, Mexico. In S. P. Vallas & A. Kovalainen (Eds.), *Work and labor in the digital age* (pp. 165–188). Bingley: Emerald Publishing. https://doi.org/10.1108/S0277-283320190000033010

Marx, K. (2013). *Capital – A critical analysis of capitalist production (Vol. 1 and 2)*. Stansted: Wordsworth Editions Limited. (Original work published in 1867).

Mason, S. (2018). High Score, low pay: Why the gig economy loves gamification. *The Guardian*. Retrieved from https://www.theguardian.com/business/2018/nov/20/high-score-low-pay-gamification-lyft-uber-drivers-ride-hailing-gig-economy

Moore, P. V., & Joyce, S. (2020). Black box or hidden abode? The expansion and exposure of platform work managerialism. *Review of International Political Economy*, *27*(4), 926–948. https://doi.org/10.1080/09692290.2019.1627569

Morschheuser, B., Hamari, J., Koivisto, J., & Maedche, A. (2017). Gamified crowdsourcing: Conceptualization, literature review, and future agenda. *International Journal of Human–Computer Studies*, *106*, 26–43. https://doi.org/10.1016/j.ijhcs.2017.04.005

Nacke, L. E., & Deterding, S. (2017). The maturing of gamification research. *Computers in Human Behavior*, *71*, 450–454. https://doi.org/10.1016/j.chb.2016.11.062

Newlands, G. (2021). Algorithmic surveillance in the gig economy: The organization of work through Lefebvrian conceived space. *Organization Studies*, *42*(5), 719–737. https://doi.org/10.1177/0170840620937900

Perez, T. S. (2019). In support of situated ethics: Ways of building trust with stigmatized 'waste pickers' in Cape Town. *Qualitative Research*, *19*(2), 148–163. https://doi.org/10.1177/1468794117746553

Quinlan, M. (2012). The 'pre-invention' of precarious employment: the changing world of work in Context. *The Economic and Labour Relations Review*, *23*(4), 3–24. https://doi.org/10.1177/103530461202300402

Ranganathan, A., & Benson, A. (2020). A numbers game: Quantification of work, auto-gamification, and worker productivity. *American Sociological Review*, *85*(4), 573–609. https://doi.org/10.1177/00031224209366

Raval, N., & Dourish, P. (2016). Standing out from the crowd: Emotional labor, body labor, and temporal labor in ridesharing. In D. Gergle, M. R. Morris, P. Bjørn, & J. Konstan (Eds.), *Proceedings of the 19th ACM conference on computer-supported cooperative work & social computing* (pp. 97–107). https://doi.org/10.1145/2818048.2820026

Rengers, M., & Houtekamer, C. (2022). Fietskoeriers Uber en Deliveroo werken zonder papieren. *NRC*. Retrieved from https://www.nrc.nl/nieuws/2022/09/15/fietskoeriers-uber-en-deliveroo-werkenzonder-papieren-2-a4142077

Rosenblat, A., & Stark, L. (2016). Algorithmic labour and information asymmetries: A case study of Uber's drivers. *International Journal of Communication*, *10*, 3758–3784. http://dx.doi.org/10.2139/ssrn.2686227

Roulet, T. J., Gill, M. J., Stenger, S., & Gill, D. J. (2017). Reconsidering the value of covert research: The role of ambiguous consent in participant observation. *Organizational Research Methods*, *20*(3), 487–517. https://doi.org/10.1177/1094428117698745

Roy, D. (1952a). *Restriction of output by machine operators in a piecework machine shop: A preliminary analysis*. Unpublished Ph.D. thesis. University of Chicago, Chicago, IL.

Roy, D. (1952b). Quota restriction and goldbricking in a machine shop. *American Journal of Sociology*, *57*(5), 427–442. Retrieved from https://www.jstor.org/stable/2772323

Roy, D. F. (1953). Work satisfaction and social reward in quota achievement: An analysis of piecework incentive. *American Sociological Review*, *18*(5), 507–514. https://doi.org/10.2307/2087434

Sallaz, J. J. (2002). The house rules: Autonomy and interests among service workers in the contemporary casino industry. *Work and Occupations*, *29*(4), 394–427. https://doi.org/10.1177/0730888402029004002

Sallaz, J. J. (2015). Permanent pedagogy: How post-Fordist firms generate effort but not consent. *Work and Occupations*, *42*(1), 3–34. https://doi.org/10.1177/0730888414551207

Scheiber, N. (2017). How Uber uses psychological tricks to push its drivers' buttons. *The New York Times*. Retrieved from https://www.nytimes.com/interactive/2017/04/02/technology/uber-drivers-psychological-tricks.html

Schloss, D. F. (1892). *Methods of industrial renumeration*. London: Williams & Norgate.

Schwandt, T.A. (2007). *The Sage dictionary of qualitative inquiry*. London: Sage Publications.

Shapiro, A. (2018). Between autonomy and control: Strategies of arbitrage in the "on-demand" economy. *New Media & Society*, *20*(8), 2954–2971. https://doi.org/10.1177/1461444817738236

Silverman, M., & Patterson, K.L. (2015). *Qualitative research methods for community development*. London: Routledge.

Srnicek, N. (2016). *Platform capitalism*. London: Polity Press.

Stanford, J. (2017). The resurgence of gig work: Historical and theoretical perspectives. *The Economic and Labour Relations Review*, *28*(3), 382–401. https://doi.org/10.1177/10353046177243

De Stefano, V. (2015). The rise of the just-in-time workforce: On-demand work, crowdwork, and labor protection in the gig economy. *Comparative Labor Law Policy Journal*, *37*(3), 471–504. http://dx.doi.org/10.2139/ssrn.2682602

Tassinari, A., & Maccarrone, V. (2017). The mobilization of gig economy couriers in Italy: Some lessons for the trade union movement. *Transfer*, *23*(3), 353–357. https://doi.org/10.1177/1024258917713846

Ter Weel, B., van Kesteren, J., van der Werf, S. (2020). *Meting kluseconomie.* Seo Economisch Onderzoek. Retrieved from https://www.seo.nl/wp-content/uploads/2020/10/2020-04-Meting-kluseconomie.pdf

Ter Weel, B., van der Werff, S., Bennaars, H., Scholte, R., Fijntje, J., Westerveld, M., & Mertens, T. (2018). *De opkomst en groei van de kluseconomie in Nederland.* Seo Economisch Onderzoek. Retrieved from https://www.seo.nl/wp-content/uploads/2020/04/2018-30_De_opkomst_en_groei_van_de_kluseconomie_in_Nederland.pdf

Thompson, P. (1990). Crawling from the wreckage: The labour process and the politics of production. In D. Knights & H. Willmott (Eds.), *Labour process theory* (pp. 95–124). London: MacMillan.

Timmermans, S., & Tavory, I. (2012). Theory construction in qualitative research: From grounded theory to abductive analysis. *Sociological Theory*, *30*(3), 167–186. https://doi.org/10.1177/0735275112457914

Van Doorn, N., & Chen, J. Y. (2021). Odds stacked against workers: Datafied gamification on Chinese and American food delivery platforms. *Socio-Economic Review*, *19*(4), 1345–1367. https://doi.org/10.1093/ser/mwab028

Van Doorn, N., Ferrari, F., & Graham, M. (in press). Migration and migrant labour in the gig economy: An intervention. *Work, Employment and Society*, 1–13, https://doi.org/10.1177/09500170221096581

Vasudevan, K., & Chan, N. K. (2022). Gamification and work games: Examining consent and resistance among Uber drivers. *New Media & Society*, *24*(4), 866–886. https://doi.org/10.1177/14614448221079028

Veen, A., Barratt, T., & Goods, C. (2020). Platform-capital's 'app-etite' for control: A labour process analysis of food-delivery work in Australia. *Work, Employment and Society*, *34*(3), 388–406. https://doi.org/10.1177/0950017019836911

Verbiest, S. E., van de Ven, H. A., & van den Bergh, R. E. C. (2020). *Platformarbeid in kaart brengen – Een verkennend onderzoek uitgevoerd binnen het Kennisinvesteringsprogramma Future of Work 2019–2020.* TNO. Retrieved from https://wp.monitorarbeid.tno.nl/wp-content/uploads/2020/11/TNO-verkenning-platformarbeid-in-kaart-brengen-.pdf

Vila-Henninger, L., Dupuy, C., Van Ingelgom, V., Caprioli, M., Teuber, F., Pennetreau, D., … Le Gall, C. (in press). Abductive coding: Theory building and qualitative (re) analysis. *Sociological Methods & Research*. https://doi.org/10.1177/00491241211067508

Walker, M., Fleming, P., & Berti, M. (2021). 'You can't pick up a phone and talk to someone': How algorithms function as biopower in the gig economy. *Organization*, *28*(1), 26–43. https://doi.org/10.1177/1350508420978831

Warmelink, H., Koivisto, J., Mayer, I., Vesa, M., & Hamari, J. (2020). Gamification of production and logistics operations: Status quo and future directions. *Journal of Business Research*, *106*, 331–340. https://doi.org/10.1016/j.jbusres.2018.09.011

Wijngaarde, Y. (2017). Food delivery tech: Battle for the European consumer [PowerPoint slides] Dealroom. Retrieved from https://www.slideshare.net/yoramw/food-tech-battle-for-the-european-consumer

Wood, A. J., Graham, M., Lehdonvirta, V., & Hjorth, I. (2019). Good gig, bad gig: Autonomy and algorithmic control in the global gig economy, *Work, Employment and Society*, *33*(1), 56–75. https://doi.org/10.1177/0950017018785616

Woodcock, J., & Johnson, M. R. (2018). Gamification: What it is, and how to fight it. *The Sociological Review*, *66*(3), 542–558. https://doi.org/10.1177/0038026117728620

Zanoni, P. (2019). Labor market inclusion through predatory capitalism? The "sharing economy," diversity, and the crisis of social reproduction in the Belgian coordinated market economy. In S. P. Vallas & A. Kovalainen (Eds.), *Work and labor in the digital age* (pp. 145–164). Bingley: Emerald Publishing. https://doi.org/10.1108/S0277-283320190000033009

CHAPTER 4

WORK AND SUSTAINABILITY AT TWIN OAKS INTENTIONAL COMMUNITY

Monica Bhatia

University of Texas at Austin, Austin, TX, USA

ABSTRACT

A growing body of literature suggests that creating a just sustainable society will require reorganizing economic arrangements and, in particular, rethinking work. Previous studies have recognized alternative organizations, such as cooperatives and intentional communities, as sites for building more democratic, sustainable models of work. This study contributes a description and analysis of work and sustainability at Twin Oaks Intentional Community, an 80-person income- and resource-sharing commune in Louisa, Virginia. Some measures show that Twin Oaks members live more sustainably in terms of energy consumption than the average US resident. In this article, I investigate the relationship between sustainability and work at Twin Oaks. I find that sustainable work is linked to the following key principles: broadening definitions of work, prioritizing community well-being, and democratizing decision making. In doing so, I contribute to previous literature on work, sustainability, and alternative organizations by suggesting that (1) sustainability in intentional communities is deeply intertwined with systems of work; (2) broadening definitions of work to include social reproductive labour contributes to sustainability; and (3) the democratization of work can further goals of sustainability.

Keywords: Intentional communities; sustainability; work; alternative organizations; reproductive labour; environmentalism

Ethnographies of Work
Research in the Sociology of Work, Volume 35, 73–93

ISSN: 0277-2833/doi:10.1108/S0277-283320230000035004

INTRODUCTION

As climate scientists continue to point to the dire impacts of deleterious human activity on the planet, sociologists are increasingly addressing the importance of rethinking work in constructing a sustainable society (Bell et al., 2020; Coulter, 2017; Daggett, 2019; Magdoff & Foster, 2010; Magdoff & Williams, 2017). In her Presidential Address to the American Sociological Association, Christine Williams (2021) described the problems with working for a living, including lack of access to jobs, poor job quality, and inequality in the workplace and advocated for expanding social safety nets. An environmental perspective would add that work, as we know, it is also *not sustainable*. Environmental sociologists have long argued that environmental degradation results from overconsumption, overextraction, and exploitation (Magdoff & Foster, 2010; Magdoff & Williams, 2017; Plumwood, 1997). Our current neoliberal economic systems value infinite growth – a value that is incompatible with the finite nature of Earth's natural resources.

Constructing a sustainable society will require rethinking work, what it is, and who does it (Agyeman et al., 2003). In this study, I consider the relationship between work and sustainability in one intentional community which has created alternative mechanisms and definitions of work. Alternative organizations, such as cooperatives and intentional communities, have been identified as sites for empirical research on building more democratic, sustainable models of work (Battilana et al., 2022; Jarvis, 2019; Kociatkiewicz et al., 2021; Meyers, 2022). In this paper, I investigate the model of work developed at Twin Oaks, an ecological intentional community (EIC) of 85 adult members located on a 100-acre farm in rural Virginia (Bhatia, 2021). The community was founded in 1967. The community's land, building, cars, and businesses are all cooperatively owned and operated. As an income-sharing community, members are expected to freeze their assets and live collectively off shared resources during their time there. The community provides its members with housing, food, and healthcare. The basic values of Twin Oaks are cooperation, egalitarianism, non-violence, and importantly for this study, *sustainability*. According to the Twin Oaks website, 'Twin Oaks incorporates a variety of ecological practices' including sharing houses and cars, working on the land, carpooling, sustainable building, alternative energy, permaculture landscaping, growing organic food, and bulk purchasing (Twin Oaks, n.d.).

By some measures, the community has been successful in achieving its environmental goals. Twin Oaks members consumed about 17% less electricity in 2022, drove about 82% fewer miles in 2021, and used about 76% less natural gas in 2022 as compared to the average US resident in 2020 (Office of Highway Policy Information, 2022; U.S. Energy Information Administration, 2022; 2023).[1,2] Significantly, these figures are inclusive of both Twin Oaks' residential consumption and Twin Oaks' community businesses (except for electricity usage for the tofu business). This is not to mention the reduction in carbon footprint achieved by growing their own organic food, and sharing housing, clothing, appliances, and other resources, for which no specific data on Twin Oaks is available, but which has been shown by other studies to be a significant contributor to sustainability in intentional communities (Jarvis, 2011; Nelson, 2018). In this study,

I consider the mechanisms that make such reductions in carbon footprint at Twin Oaks possible.

Previous studies of intentional communities have primarily focused on resource sharing in creating sustainable living arrangements (Jarvis, 2011; Nelson, 2018; Sargisson & Sargent, 2017). In this study, I expand on this research, by considering alternative work arrangements as a fundamental component of creating more sustainable communities. I ask: What is the relationship between work and sustainability in intentional communities? Specifically, how does Twin Oaks' alternative organization of work address the community's goal of sustainability? Sustainable work is linked to the following key principles: broadening definitions of work, prioritizing community well-being, and democratizing decision making. I argue that Twin Oaks offers lessons for how work, in general, might be reconfigured for a more sustainable society.

This study contributes a description and analysis of one small-scale model for environmentally just and sustainable economic arrangements. In this study, I contribute to previous literature on work, sustainability, and alternative organizations in three ways. First, I argue that sustainability in intentional communities goes beyond previous descriptions of resource sharing and is also deeply intertwined with systems of work. Second, I contribute an empirical description of how broadening definitions of work to include social reproductive labour contributes to sustainability in one ecological intentional community. Third, I consider how the democratization of work in intentional communities can further goals of sustainability.

LITERATURE REVIEW

The definition of 'sustainability' is contested. Traditionally, sustainability is defined as 'the use of environment and resources to meet the needs of the present without compromising the ability of future generations to meet their own needs' (Berkes et al., 2001, p. 3, as cited in Cruz-Torres & McElwee, 2019, p. 134). This means that humans and other species are able to thrive now and in the future, that resources are not depleted, and that the serious negative impacts of human activity such as pollution, global warming, habitat destruction, and extinction will end. From an environmental justice perspective, however, sustainability also means addressing problems of inequality, so that *all people* are able to thrive, rather than just an elite few (Cole & Foster, 2001; Di Chiro, 1996). From this perspective, solving environmental problems must address questions of social and economic inequalities (Agyeman et al., 2003).

Mainstream solutions to the problem of climate change have focused almost entirely on implementing new technologies, such as renewable energy and electric cars (Bell et al., 2020; Coulter, 2017; Günel, 2019; Howe, 2019; Magdoff & Williams, 2017). 'Green jobs' are the proposed new, high-quality jobs that will arise from environmentally sustainable industries, such as those created in the transition from carbon-based production to renewable energy. However, these mainstream solutions do not address social inequities, reduce fossil fuel use, or promote environmental justice (Bauhardt, 2014; Coulter, 2017; Littig, 2019).

A more radical approach to environmental justice is to completely change our economic systems (Bell et al., 2020; Magdoff & Williams, 2017). Current institutions of work are undemocratic and authoritarian, in which employers exercise arbitrary control over people's lives while workers have little to no say, including over the environmental impact of their work (Sobering, 2022). Further, current systems of work are embedded in the dynamics of global capitalism and neoliberalism which increase wealth at the top and withhold access to resources for the majority. Critics of current work institutions advocate for alternative systems of work, including cooperative economics, universal basic income, and increasing social safety nets (Daggett, 2019; Sobering, 2022; Weeks, 2011; Williams, 2021).

Environmental feminists (or ecofeminists) draw attention to the ways in which women's domestic labour and nature are considered externalities under the market economy (Bauhardt, 2014). These scholars argue that the externalization of social reproductive labour is ecologically dangerous because it obscures the embodiment of humanity and the material basis of human existence in nature (Mellor, 2019; Plumwood, 1997). The term 'social reproductive labor' is used to describe the activities and relationships involved in maintaining people's well-being both on a daily and on an intergenerational basis (Glenn, 1992). This includes the work of 'purchasing household goods, preparing and serving food, laundering and repairing clothing, maintaining furnishings and appliances, socializing children, providing care and emotional support for adults, and maintaining kin and community ties' (Glenn, 1992, p. 1). Similarly, ecofeminist scholars have argued for recognizing care as labour (Cudworth, 2022). Ecofeminist scholars have suggested that implementing a universal basic income and a shorter work week, and prioritizing time spent engaging in low-carbon care work and leisure activities such as art, music, and social engagement, could have the dual benefit of lowering emissions and increasing happiness and fulfilment (Bell et al., 2020; Daggett, 2019).

Some ecofeminists advocate sufficiency provisioning, which is imagined as a way of living within ecological means (Mellor, 2019). Under this framework, communities would focus on meeting people's needs by prioritizing social reproductive labour rather than wealth accumulation. When thinking about the future of work, Battistoni (2021) begins with question, 'What kinds of work does the low-carbon good life require?' and imagines creating economic systems that value those kinds of work. From an ecofeminist perspective, the experiences of working-class women could play a crucial role in the transition from exploitative, unsustainable capitalist system to more sustainable alternatives (Giacomini, 2020). Materialist ecofeminists argue that women are uniquely positioned as an economic underclass with the motives and alternative life-giving skills to challenge oppressive systems (Salleh, 2017). Ecofeminist scholars advocate transitioning to a commons-based society in which there is collective control over the means of life (Giacomini, 2020). As Giacomini writes, a 'just transition involves a fundamental shift from all forms of exploitative, capitalist relations to more life-centered social relations' (Giacomini, 2020, p. 195).

There are few opportunities to empirically study what these 'more life-centered social relations' might look like in practice. Prior scholarship identifies cooperatives, intentional communities, and anarchist collectives as sites for empirical studies of democratization and sustainability (Jarvis, 2019; Nelson, 2018; Sargisson & Sargent, 2017). For example, Battilana et al. (2022) suggested that the democratization of work may play a key role in solving social and environmental problems in society and identified cooperatives as a potential site for empirical research on this question. Furthermore, Meyers (2022) considers the possibilities of worker cooperatives in reducing social inequalities. Taking up this call, I investigate the democratization of work at one cooperatively organized ecological intentional community.

An intentional community is a communal living experiment that includes cohousing communities, housing cooperatives, ecovillages, communes, and community farms. Such communities are defined by 'expression of resistance to dominant social norms and expectations of home, work and family life', an ethic of shared care and responsibility, and collectively agreed upon shared visions and values (Jarvis, 2019, p. 435). An *ecological* intentional community (EIC) attempts to develop sustainable alternatives to the dominant society (Bhatia, 2021).

Collective living has been shown to reduce overconsumption and resource use per capita, leading some to consider intentional communities as models for addressing sustainability challenges (Jarvis, 2011; Nelson, 2018). For example, Nelson (2018) notes that because conventional housing models contribute to overconsumption both directly (the material costs of residential construction and servicing residential homes) and indirectly (the resource costs of nuclear families living in larger-than-necessary suburban homes), intentional communities may provide a sustainable alternative. However, these studies do not focus on how the reconfiguring of *work* in intentional communities is related to sustainability. In this study, I take up this question through an empirical analysis of the relationship between work and sustainability at Twin Oaks Intentional Community.

CASE

Twin Oaks Intentional Community is an income-sharing commune on approximately 100 acres of communally owned land in Louisa, Virginia. The community was founded in 1967 by a group of eight people who were inspired by B. F. Skinner's *Walden Two* to form a utopian community founded on the principles of behaviourism (Kinkade, 1973). Today, the primary guiding principle of the community is egalitarianism, which is carried out through a complex system of checks and balances in decision making with the intention of equitably distributing resources amongst all community members (see Fig. 4.1).

As an income-sharing community, Twin Oakers collectively own their community businesses, land, and resources. Most Twin Oakers do not have outside jobs and instead work to sustain the community in exchange for room and board, healthcare, childcare, and a small monthly allowance (about $115 in 2022). While on the farm, Twin Oakers agree not to use their individual assets in order to maintain a sense of egalitarianism and classlessness within the community. Twin Oakers work approximately 42 hours per week in a community labour system, which encompasses the community's community businesses as well as other types

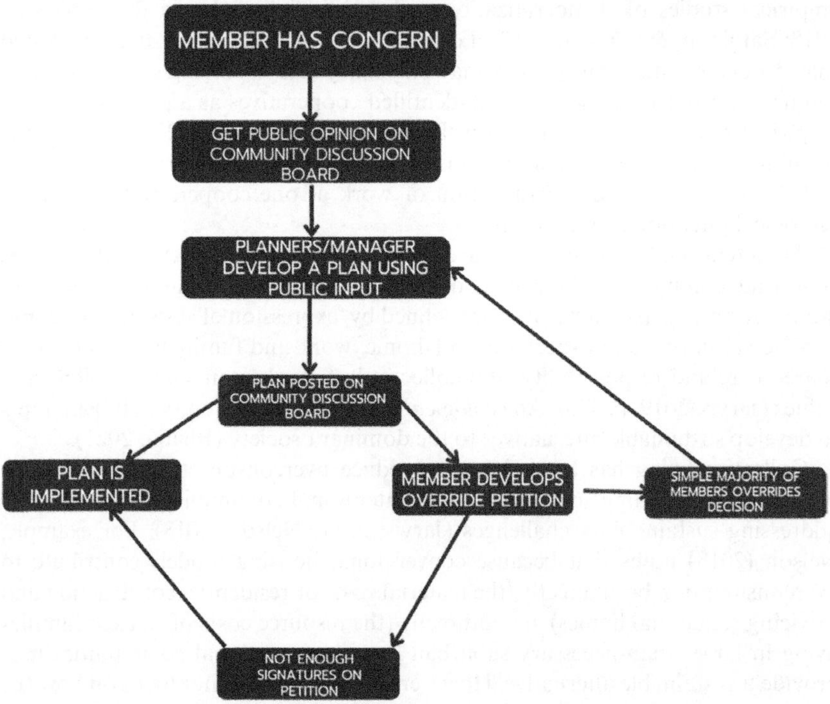

Fig. 4.1. Twin Oaks' Decision-making Process.

of labour that the community designates as work. When a Twin Oaker does work outside the community, the member either gives this money to the community in exchange for labour hours or keeps the money as vacation earnings which can only be spent off the farm.

The initial purchase of the community land was funded by a loan from a community member (Kinkade, 1973). Initially, the group intended to fund the community through farming, but over the years, the community has evolved to include a number of businesses reflecting the interests and skills of the current members. Today, the community's oldest business is its hammock business, which peaked under a contract with Pier 1 in the 1990s, and has since been scaled back. The community puts the majority of its income-producing labour hours into its tofu business. The community's most profitable business is contracted work for a neighbouring commune's organic heirloom seed business.

Twin Oaks is composed of an ever-evolving membership of long-term and short-term members. The last founder who remained in the community, Kat Kinkade, died in 2008 and is buried on the property in the community graveyard. However, there are several members who have been a part of the community for decades, including one who has lived at Twin Oaks for 50 years. At a given time, about 20% of the community has been there a year or less, about 20% of the community has been there for 20 years or more, and most people fall somewhere in between. The community is truly intergenerational with residents spanning from newborn babies to members in their 80s. Every new member undergoes a membership process which includes visiting for three weeks, an intensive interview, a six-month probationary period, and a vote of the current membership.

Each member of the community receives their own room in one of eight community houses. Food is provided in the form of two community meals per day and access to multiple kitchens stocked with pantry staples, homegrown fruits, vegetables, dairy and eggs, and homemade tofu. After the six-month probationary period, members are guaranteed healthcare from the community which is provided through a variety of means. First, members are strongly encouraged to sign up for Medicaid, which almost all members qualify for due to the Twin Oaks' frugal lifestyle and tax status. Second, the health team provides basic first aid and over the counter medicines, and a list of low-cost and free doctors in the area. Third, Twin Oaks is part of a healthcare insurance network called Peach with other income-sharing communities in which the communities all pay into a pool that pays out in the case of large, unexpected healthcare expenses. Lastly, the community will pay out of pocket for any healthcare expenses for its members that cannot be covered through other means.

The community exists in stark contrast with its neighbourhood, being both more white and more politically liberal than its home county of Louisa, Virginia, which voted for Trump in the 2020 presidential election. Twin Oaks is approximately 90% white and 10% members of colour, according to data from tax reports compiled by a member in 2022. In comparison, Louisa County is approximately 78% non-Hispanic white, 15% black, and 7% other races (United States Census Bureau, 2021). Despite the differences between Twin Oaks and the surrounding community, the neighbours generally are friendly with and tolerate the community, which at this point is a longstanding institution in the county. In fact, Twin Oaks now exists in what could be called a 'neighbourhood of communities' in which approximately six intentional communities exist within the area of Louisa County, and share in social events, resources, and labour. These communities all exist in Louisa County with the intention of being near each other in order to share community and resources. Mostly, they are founded by ex-Twin Oakers or through support from Twin Oaks.

METHODOLOGY

This study investigates how Twin Oaks Intentional Community redefines and reorganizes work to promote the goal of environmental sustainability. To understand how work is organized at this community, I visited Twin Oaks once in 2019 and again in 2022. In total, I conducted seven weeks of participant observation and 21 interviews at Twin Oaks. At the time of my first visit, Twin Oaks had a population of approximately 80 members, and when I returned in 2022, the population was down to approximately 65 members. I completed 21 in-depth interviews with 20 individuals (19 interviews with current members, one of whom

Table 4.1. Characteristics of Interview Respondents.

Characteristic	# Respondents
Gender	
Women	10
Men	5
Non-binary	5
Race	
White	16
Multiracial	4
Length of Membership	
1 year or less	6
1–10 years	6
11+ years	7
Age	
21–30	6
31–40	6
41–50	2
51–60	4
61–70	1

I interviewed in 2019 and in 2022, and one interview with a former member). I took care to sample a diversity of community perspectives, including length of membership, gender, age, and race (see Table 4.1).

I participated in the community's visitor program, which is designed to recruit prospective members. During each visit, I lived full-time at Twin Oaks for three weeks: I participated in the labour system, attended decision-making meetings, ate communal meals, and socialized at community gatherings. In 2019, I spent an additional week at the community's annual Queer Gathering at the community's conference site.

As a participant in the Twin Oaks labour system, I was expected to perform 42 hours of labour every week, to record my labour as if I were a member, and to follow community norms and expectations such as not driving my personal vehicle, not spending more than $115/month, and not using my cell phone in public spaces. During my first visit to Twin Oaks, I spent many of my labour hours working in the garden which provides produce for the community, and I also worked in the daycare, tended the chickens, cooked and cleaned, and performed agricultural labour for the community seed business. During my second visit to Twin Oaks, I worked in the three community businesses: tofu, seed packing, and hammocks. I also spent time cooking and cleaning.

I observed community members as they participated in decision making. Every day, I would read the message board in the community dining hall, which is the main forum for community input on group decisions (more on this below). In 2019, I attended a meeting of the planners, which is the body that makes long-term community decisions. In 2022, I attended a meeting of engaged community members who were drafting a proposed overhaul to the labour system. As a member of the community visitor program, I also attended a series of orientations designed to teach prospective members about various community functions, and I was able to audio record and transcribe these orientations.

Field research allowed me to understand how labour discourses and practices are operationalized, translated, and understood from various member perspectives. Additionally, participating in the community's labour system allowed me to experience it for myself. While a longer stay would be necessary to fully grasp the meanings, motives, and backgrounds of the participants, for my purposes – understanding the organization of the labour system and its relationship to environmental sustainability – my time in the field was appropriate.

In addition to participant observation, I also conducted 21 in-depth interviews. I recruited participants for interviews through a variety of methods, including posting publicly on the community notice board in the dining hall, directly approaching community members with whom I formed rapport or whom I was recommended to speak, and participants approached me when they learned of my study through word of mouth or in casual conversations with me.

I have been a member of the intentional communities movement since 2016, a position that assisted me in gaining access to my field site and building rapport with my research participants. I have called three intentional communities my homes, served on the board of two intentional communities, and participated in multiple meetings and conferences of intentional community networks. Through these experiences, I have built a particular vantage point that includes knowledge of the values, goals, and dilemmas frequently a part of community life.

My position as a member of intentional communities and a visitor, and my race, age, and gender, impacted my perspective and access in the field (Reyes, 2018). At Twin Oaks, new members tend to be younger while long-term members are often older although this is not always the case. The newer members, who are often looking to make friends, sat with me at meals and shared their thoughts about community life. I was able to connect with long-term members on the basis of being a member of intentional communities. During my first visit to Twin Oaks, invested community members were eager to give me advice for my growing community back home. By the time I visited in 2022, many of the long-term members remembered me, and I perceived an increased sense of trust. I was also able to build rapport with women and queer members of the community, as is reflected in the demographics of my interview participants, due to our shared identities. In the primarily white context of Twin Oaks, my multiracial identity as a white and Indian person allowed me to connect with other multiracial individuals around shared experiences. On the other hand, I was not able to connect with the two Black members of the community, who were both senior members who seemed reluctant to engage with visitors (different members have differing levels of engagement with visitors). Some members take it upon themselves to socialize with visitors because they see it as important for recruiting new members to the community, while others dislike constantly having new people to host in their home and tend to avoid interacting with visitors at all.

FINDINGS

Work is reorganized at Twin Oaks to promote the community's values of egalitarianism and environmental sustainability. Each community member is expected to work about 40 hours per week (give or take a few hours depending on the season), which they can fulfil in any of Twin Oak's labour areas. Members do not have to do the same jobs every day. Each week, they submit requests to the labour manager, who makes the schedules. Members have the option of having scheduled work or more varied and flexible work schedules as long as they are consistently meeting quota.

The only required labour is one weekly shift in the tofu hut and one shift cleaning the kitchen where lunch and dinner are served every day. There are exemptions and reductions in the labour quota for the elderly and people with disabilities. In community orientations, the labour system is described as having achieved 'equal work for equal pay' because an hour of any kind of work counts equally in the community's labour system, whether it is cleaning toilets, feeding chickens, filing community taxes, cooking dinner, building maintenance, beekeeping, working in the tofu hut or any other income-producing business, or any other kind of approved community work.

Each member's labour balance is tracked weekly and members who work under quota face consequences for being 'in the labor hole'. These consequences accumulate on an escalating scale, starting with a contract to work extra hours to get out of the hole and leading to expulsion if not corrected. Members who work over quota accrue hours that can be used for vacation on or off the farm. Working quota guarantees each member 3.3 weeks of vacation per year.

In this section I will explain three ways that Twin Oaks labour system addresses the community's stated values of sustainability and equality. First, Twin Oaks broadens definitions of work. Second, Twin Oaks' labour system is designed to prioritize community well-being over profit. Third, Twin Oaks' labour system is managed by democratic decision-making processes which incentivize adherence to community values, including sustainability and egalitarianism. Through these alternative definitions, goals, and management of work, Twin Oaks' labour system contributes to the environmental sustainability of the community.

Broadening Definitions of Work

Twin Oaks' labour economy is managed through 'labor areas', each of which has a 'labor budget'. There is a complex budgeting process that determines how labour hours are allocated into each of Twin Oak's 100 different labour areas every year. The budgets are set by the budgeting team every year based on community input. Members determine what counts as labour, how much of each type of labour is creditable each year, and what activities are prioritized. Through this process, members co-create their community definitions of work based on what type of labour they value in order to sustain community well-being.

At Twin Oaks, many forms of social reproductive labour are considered creditable labour under the labour system. This includes cooking, cleaning, elder care, and childcare. While these activities are considered 'domestic' responsibilities in mainstream society, and are traditionally performed by unpaid or underpaid women, they are formally considered work at Twin Oaks. While I was at Twin Oaks, I received labour credit for cleaning the house I was staying in, cooking dinner for the community, washing dishes after dinner, and working in the community's daycare centre.

Furthermore, Twin Oaks' labuor system also considers what I call 'sustaining labor' as work under the labour system. Sustaining labour is the labour of generating and maintaining resources for community self-sufficiency. This includes the work of gardening to produce food, harvesting firewood, maintaining buildings, and composting. These are forms of labour with the goal of sustainably generating resources for community use which also reduce the community's need to generate income in order to purchase commodities through the mainstream capitalist economy.

In general, Twin Oakers speak highly of the 'flexibility' of their labour system. Members can choose how to spend the majority of their labour hours in any given week. In fact, one of the big draws of Twin Oaks for many members is that they were unhappy with their opportunities for employment in mainstream society and found more satisfaction with the Twin Oaks labour system. Maria, a 24-year-old, white, non-binary queer person came to Twin Oaks because they were feeling dissatisfied with life in the mainstream and 'wanted to try something else'. During my time at Twin Oaks, Maria was working as the manager of one of Twin Oaks non-income-producing labour areas, and they expressed appreciation for the many types of work included in Twin Oaks labour system, including social reproductive labour:

> I can take care of children, I can manage the conference site, I can try to install flooring in my new room, I can cook dinner for 100 people. And I can do that, I can work in the factory, and I can do all of that within a week. I can move the milk; I can bake bread. Those are all things that I do every week.

Maria speaks with great joy about the work that they do every week, which includes both income-producing work and social reproductive work. Much of the work that they describe doing would not be credited in mainstream society and would instead most likely constitute a 'second shift' (Hochschild, 1990). However, Twin Oaks' broadened definition of work specifically encompasses domestic responsibilities.

Importantly, Twin Oaks' definition of work includes *care work*. At Twin Oaks, this includes caring for children, elders, and anyone who needs care due to an illness or disability. For example, at the end of my stay in 2022, a member of Twin Oaks was recovering from surgery. She was able to stay in Twin Oak's accessible care building originally built as a hospice care facility which now serves a variety of needs including childbirth, COVID-19 quarantine, and sick care. The recovering member had a care team of 13 community members who received labour credit for tasks like driving her to doctors' appointments, cooking her food, and giving her medications.

One of Twin Oaks' two labour requirements is cleaning labour. A 'K' (kitchen) shift is a weekly labour requirement, which every able member of the community is required to complete. This labour consists of cleaning the community kitchen after a lunch or dinner. As such, cleaning labour is not just *allowed* to be counted as work under Twin Oaks' labour system, but it is *prioritized* on the same level as producing income for the community. Rosa, a multiracial 43-year-old mother of two, told me that she spends two-thirds of her labour hours doing domestic work:

> I also do a lot of domestic work, you know, cleaning. And to me, it's huge that that counts as much as work as anything else. Like, I think that's an important feminist thing.

Whereas in mainstream society, Rosa would not be credited for cleaning her own home, at Twin Oaks, Rosa is able to count this work towards her 42 hour per week labour quota. Rosa mentions that this is a feminist practice because this is the kind of work that feminists have critiqued as being devalued in mainstream society but is being counted equitably at Twin Oaks.

One sustaining labour area where many Twin Oakers find meaning and satisfaction is their work in the community's organic gardens, where members grow a large variety of produce. A couple of members mentioned their work in the garden as being particularly rewarding. For example, Rosa, a multiracial woman in her forties, spends most of her time raising her children and working in the garden. Rosa is drawn to working in the garden because she finds this work to be meaningful.

> Garden is my biggest work area, because a thing that I can do that I feel sure is doing a good thing is helping produce more of our own food. I feel like in the huge scheme of the world, it's small. But yeah, it feels like an important and significant thing. I can do this. Yeah. Be part of us growing our own food.

Paul, a 25-year-old white man who lives at Twin Oaks, specifically mentioned the opportunity to work in the garden when asked about his reasons for joining Twin Oaks:

> I think I was really into growing my own food and so I did some WWOOFing [Worldwide Organization of Organic Farmers] beforehand, but I'm like, you know, it's a really cool community because it's more like a worker-owned sort of thing. You're not just working for somebody else, you potentially have a lot of equity, and a lot of, I guess, power and decision making …. And you're working toward sustainability with the goal of the community, which I really like.

For Paul, the draw of Twin Oaks was not only the opportunity to grow his own food but to do so in a context where he feels ownership and the ability to contribute to decision making. While there are other opportunities to work growing food, such as WWOOFing, which is a work-trade program for organic farming, or working as a wage labourer on a farm, Twin Oaks' cooperative structure is what made the community stand out to Paul.

In general, what counts as work at Twin Oaks is much broader than mainstream society and includes many types of non-incoming producing labour. Broadening the definition of work at Twin Oaks contributes to environmental sustainability by cutting down on the hours spent working for production. Twin Oaks' broadened definition of work prioritizes sustaining the community over capitalist profit. Twin Oakers spend less of their work time on high-emissions, productive labour than they would in mainstream society. Instead, their labour hours are devoted to the low-emissions work of maintaining their daily lives. This labour system is sustainable because Twin Oakers use enough resources and work enough to meet their basic needs, without participating in systems that encourage production for the sake of production and consumption for the sake of consumption.

Prioritizing Community Well-being

Whereas a traditional corporation attempts to maximize profits for shareholders, Twin Oaks' labour system is designed to prioritize community well-being. At Twin Oaks, the goal is to *sustain* the community rather than to profit, consume, or grow. This goal of sustainability and community well-being are laid out in the Twin Oaks Articles of Incorporations, which read:

> The Corporation shall form and become a self-contained intentional community, having a common treasury and *providing for its members and for persons who wish to become members an environment in which they may live in harmony with nature and their fellow humans* [emphasis added], a community designed and maintained according to principles of harmony and love. In furtherance of these purposes the community shall endeavor to: eliminate hierarchical relationships between people; promote the practice of non-violence in personal, interpersonal, and political relationships; respect and preserve the natural environment for the use of all species, now and in the future; eliminate classism, racism, ageism, patriarchy, and other forms of oppression, both within and outside of the community; practice community of property, with all those in the community sharing what they are, have, and can produce with one another.

According to these Articles of Incorporation, the goal of the organization is to meet the needs of the members. Additionally, the Articles specifically emphasize meeting these needs *in an environment in harmony with nature and fellow humans*. This very first statement in the Articles of Incorporation lays out the community's goal to provide for the needs of the members with environmental and social sustainability in mind.

The goals of the community are reflected in the community's tax structure – a rare tax status called 501(d) which is reserved for religious organizations such as monasteries which operate all businesses to the benefit of its members. Under this tax status and the Articles of Incorporation, Twin Oaks commits to holding resources in common for the benefit of the community, with the goal of sustainability in mind.

The Twin Oaks' businesses are an area where community members have to balance their need to bring in some income to maintain their lifestyle with community values and interests. The Twin Oaks tofu business is controversial among members of the community because it is labour intensive, and the business is in debt over machinery upgrades. As one member described to me during an orientation:

> It's a very controversial business right now. Tofu, mostly because of an upgrade that has been in the works for around, I think, 15 years now? We are trying to use this huge machine to automate a lot of the labor of the tofu business because it can be really grueling work. We have unfortunately spent over a million dollars on this thing in those 15 years, and it is still not done. And meanwhile, like, morale about tofu has kind of waned. There was a crew very interested in making and working the tofu business that is not here anymore. They moved away. So there was a proposal from the tofu team to get, like more money, like 100,000 more dollars to put into the upgrade. Above the spending cap that the community had given them before that and someone, I think it was a planner decision to allow this budget increase, and someone tried to override it and get enough signatures so that we wouldn't spend this money. [The override] didn't happen. Didn't get enough numbers. But it was exciting to watch.

The community has invested a very significant amount of money into upgrading the tofu business, which has turned into a much longer and more complicated process than anyone expected. Meanwhile, many members express disinterest or disdain at working in the tofu factory and choose to put their labour hours into other areas. Right now, Twin Oaks makes tofu about two days per week even though the demand for Twin Oaks tofu is significantly greater than current production levels. If Twin Oaks were to make tofu more days per week, the community would be able to generate more profit from the business. If the community were operating as a for-profit corporation, they might even expand their business by building more tofu infrastructure or hiring outside workers to meet the demand for their product. However, Twin Oaks doesn't operate from a profit motive and Twin Oakers would rather spend their time working other labour areas. As long as their businesses generate enough income to provide for the basic necessities that they can't make at home, they don't feel a need to increase production. By shifting the goal from profit to well-being, Twin Oakers have the opportunity to make different decisions about how to spend their time and resources than is the case in a typical corporation.

However, members do not necessarily agree about what is in the best interests of the community. In the case of additional funding for the tofu upgrades, the planners decided that it was in the best interest of the community to approve additional funding for the project. Even in a community where the goal is community well-being and not profit, sometimes the interpretation of what is best for the community means bringing in more income. However, Twin Oakers have still managed to move away from the goal of infinite profit and infinite growth, and instead are having conversations about how much income is necessary to sustain their community.

Democratic Decision Making

Rather than a hierarchical corporate structure, decision-making power is distributed widely among members of the community. All full members have the opportunity to participate in decision making, and all decisions can be challenged by a single member or vetoed by the community-at-large. Planners and managers make decisions about all aspects of life at Twin Oaks, such as what kinds of building materials to use, what kind of food to buy or grow and in what quantities, and how land is managed. These decision makers have the responsibilities of upholding the community's values, which include sustainability, of making decisions for the well-being of the community as a whole, and of considering the input of community members.

Twin Oaks was originally modelled after behavioural psychologist B.F. Skinner's *Walden Two*, which inspired its egalitarian non-hierarchical decision-making structure. Skinner's behaviourist model used positive reinforcement and the restructuring of the social environment to eliminate the violence and chaos of modern life. He imagined a utopia with plenty of leisure time and a non-competitive economy. Although Twin Oaks today has largely abandoned the theory and the ideology of behaviourism, it does retain much of Skinner's structure, including the planner-manager system for decision making.

Twin Oaks is led by three *planner-managers* who serve 18-month staggered terms. Planners decide issues like changes to policy, budgeting of the labour system and community finances, how to handle emergencies and crises, and exceptions to community rules, based on the needs and opinions of the community members. These decision makers also take into consideration the community's official values, one of which is environmental sustainability. Their decisions may be overruled if the community-at-large disagrees with their decisions. Candidates for planner can be vetoed by 20% of the full membership of the community.

At the planners meeting I attended in 2019, all three planners were present, sitting in mismatched chairs in the living room of the Oneida house where I had recently attended a community karaoke night. One topic discussed was the wastewater produced by the tofu factory, the community's main source of income. The planners discussed a community board post about making a pond to store the wastewater. Some members supported this course of action because they believed it to be a low-cost solution to the expensive wastewater problem until a better solution is found. Other members raised concerns about whether there should be an environmental impact study and whether the smell of the pond will be unpleasant. The planners discussed whether there was enough community support to require an environmental impact study and whether they felt that it was in the best interest of the community to spend time and money on an environment impact study. Ultimately, the planners decided that more information and community input were needed and did not come to a decision at that meeting.

When I visited again in 2022, the community had implemented the tofu wastewater pond. I spoke with a long-term member of the community after our visitor group's orientation about the new system. He explained to me that the new system filters the tofu wastewater in the ponds before distributing it to the fields as fertilizer. According to this member, the system is more environmentally friendly than the previous system, which did not filter the wastewater and was therefore creating overly nutrient rich runoff. When I asked about the environmental impact study, he told me that the new system had been approved by the Virginia Environmental Quality Commission.

The case of tofu wastewater demonstrates the kinds of decisions that are made by Twin Oaks' planner-managers – in which they must consider the community's financial well-being and the value of sustainability and come to a decision that reasonably balances these interests based on the input of the community. Meanwhile, the community's veto structure provides a system of accountability in the case that Twin Oaks' members feel that these interests are not being upheld by the planner-managers or area managers.

While the tofu wastewater was considered a long-term investment and ultimately decided by the planners, most day-to-day decisions in the community are made by *area managers* who oversee activities including food processing, accounting, and mental health care. Councils are made up of managers from related areas. An area manager may remain in their position as long as they like or may be asked to step down through a community process if there is discontent with their performance in the position. Once an area manager position opens up, anyone can nominate themselves for the position and the council in that area will decide amongst them using community input. Community input generally takes the form of written communication on the public messaging board in the main dining hall, where members can post opinion papers on any issue of concern. Other members will write their input on the topic before the paper is taken to the area manager or the planner-managers who will then make decisions based on that input. The community does not regularly hold meetings, but they can be called in relation to particular topics when there is enough support. Even then, decisions are never made at meetings. Meetings are discussion forums and then decisions are ultimately made by the area managers or planner-managers.

I spoke with Sam, the area manager of Twin Oaks' dairy program, who makes decisions about animal health, infrastructure, and animal product processing including slaughtering. In this position, Sam makes decisions that impact animal health and welfare. She mentioned that one of her joys about the position is her relative autonomy. She has the power to make day-to-day decisions with the animal's well-being in mind, and as long as she delivers the animal products to the community and no one has a reason to contest her decisions, she can make the decisions that feel right to her. She has used this position to implement new systems which she views as having greatly improved the cows' well-being, including ending cow-calf separation, reducing the size of the herd, and improving the cow's diets. Sam appreciates that Twin Oaks' labour system has allowed her to participate in producing her own food in a way that feels healthier to her. She explained,

> Self-reliance and sustainability is a big factor. It feels healthier to me. I think there's so much existential dread that people have in the world of like, they don't know what the future is going to be. And they also don't know what to do with themselves, or like how to make meaning of their life. And I think, for so long, humans have been making meaning by just learning to survive, or having to survive, and having to be connected to the land to survive. And so that feels like, in some ways, [producing my own food] takes away the sense of like, what do I do? What's my purpose? Because it's like, I know my purpose is just to live and sustain myself and do what I need to do to live and do that with other people.

For Sam, being the area manager of Twin Oaks' dairy program has allowed her to reconnect with the land and participate in sustainable and fulfilling work. The decentralized distribution of decision-making power at Twin Oaks has allowed Sam to manage the dairy program in accordance with her values, which gives her a sense of autonomy and fulfilment that might be hard to find working in a hierarchical environment.

DISCUSSION

Twin Oakers use significantly less electricity, gasoline, and natural gas than the US average while also living below the poverty line. Most Twin Oakers agree that they live a good life – and that their life is better at Twin Oaks than it would be in mainstream society. How are Twin Oakers able to live a good life below the poverty line while drastically reducing their energy consumption compared to the national average? In the following section, I analyze how the three characteristics of Twin Oaks' labour system described above – broadening definitions of work, prioritizing community well-being, and democratizing decision making – contribute to the

Table 4.2. Mainstream Economic Model Versus Twin Oaks Economic Model.

	Definitions of Work	Priorities	Decision Making
Mainstream Economic Model	Income-producing labour	Profit maximization	Authoritarian; hierarchical
Twin Oaks Economic Model	Broadened definitions of work: income-producing labour, resource-generating labour, social reproductive labour	Prioritizing community well-being	Democratized decision making

community's goal of environmental sustainability. In all three of these dimensions, Twin Oaks' provides alternatives to mainstream economic arrangements (see Table 4.2).

A crucial element to environmental sustainability at Twin Oaks is the fact that the community considers social reproductive labour and sustaining labour equally to income-producing work. At Twin Oaks, work of cooking, cleaning, and taking care of children are all credited under the labour system. Additionally, sustaining work that regenerates resources for the community through sustainable practices, such as organic gardening, collecting firewood, and installing solar panels also counts as labour. According to ecofeminist economics scholars, prioritizing this type of work has the double-impact of increasing social equity and lowering carbon emissions.

Twin Oaks' inclusion of social reproductive labour in their definitions of work is particularly important for social equity. The labour of social reproduction has traditionally been an externality in capitalist systems, the burden of which has been placed on unpaid or underpaid women, especially women of colour (Glenn, 1992). By broadening their definition of work to include social reproduction, Twin Oakers have the dual benefit of shifting their labour economy towards low-emissions, low environmental impact work, and also increasing social equity, as those who do this labour, particularly women, are able to have their work valued equitably in the labour system.

Social reproductive labour and sustaining labour is relatively low-emissions work which is necessary for sustaining human life. Therefore, prioritizing this type of work can create green jobs while also meeting real human needs. At Twin Oaks, members of the community spend large portions of their 42-hour work week on domestic responsibilities. This work improves their quality of life without promoting overconsumption and over-extraction.

Twin Oakers have revolutionized what counts as work in their community. To Twin Oakers, producing food to feed themselves, maintaining their homes, raising their children, cooking meals, planning cultural events, and contributing to social activism are all work. Twin Oaks' approach provides an answer to Alyssa Battistoni's (2021) question, 'What kinds of work does the low-carbon good life require?': the labour that goes into maintaining liveable lives.

The practices that Twin Oakers point to as ecologically sustainable – sharing houses and cars, working on the land rather than commuting, carpooling, sustainable building practices, alternative energy, permaculture landscaping, growing organic food, and purchasing in bulk – are all enabled by the labour system. All of these practices are labour creditable to the people who participate in them. Similarly, Twin Oakers are able to claim labour hours for the work that they do building and maintaining their own homes, including installing alternative energy features. Considering this kind of labour as legitimate work under Twin Oaks labour system, even though it does not produce profit for the community, allows the community to consume fewer resources than they would under a mainstream definition of work.

The prioritization of community well-being as a goal of work at Twin Oaks' contributes to community sustainability. By reconsidering the motivations for labour, Twin Oakers are *not* incentivized to increase profit for the few at the expense of the many, including the Earth. Twin Oakers have largely stepped off the treadmill of production because there is no incentive to produce profit in their system (Gould et al., 2008). Instead, Twin Oakers focus their attention on maintaining the needs of everyday life. There are no incentives to increase shareholder value at Twin Oaks, only whether everyone's needs are being met adequately. According to an ecofeminist economics perspective, this is very close to meeting the definition of a sustainable lifestyle, in that people's needs are being met, without the overconsumption, over-extraction and exploitation that comprises the livelihoods of future generations and the planet.

Finally, Twin Oaks' decision-making structures contribute to the community's goal of environmental sustainability in two ways. First, planners and managers make decisions for the well-being of the community with the community's explicitly stated value of sustainability in mind. Second, the democratic, decentralized, and public ownership of decision-making processes encourages accountability for decision makers in upholding this value.

Environmental sustainability is at the forefront of decision-making conversations. Although this does not mean that all community members agree about every issue (e.g. some community members debate whether the tofu industry is ecologically sound), planner-managers are expected to consider environmental sustainability in all decisions. Because environmental sustainability is an explicitly stated value, all decisions are expected to be made with environmental impact in mind.

Furthermore, Twin Oakers express ownership of their community's decision-making processes. This is important, because as Bell and colleagues (2020) note, the implementation of technologies like renewable energy without democratic decision making does not guarantee justice or democracy, or even sustainability. When political decision making is undemocratic, environmental sustainability is likely to take a backseat to profit-making and political manoeuvring, and the benefits and burdens of environmental practices are likely to be distributed inequitably. At Twin Oaks, the area manager and council system decentralize decision making so that many Twin Oakers hold decision-making roles. The community message board system means that everyone has a chance to express their opinion on any topic, and every voice is heard by decision makers. Furthermore, the community's veto system holds decision makers accountable to community input. Therefore, decision making at Twin Oaks is relatively protected from the influence of self-interest, and the community's values, including sustainability, are protected.

CONCLUSION

Between the need to rapidly curb greenhouse gas emissions, growing income inequality, underemployment, and the economic impacts of a global pandemic and rapid technological change, major transformations in our economic system are necessary to maintain the habitability of our planet and create a just society (Fred & Williams, 2017). There is growing support for postwork futures, universal basic income, and the creation of alternatives to reliance on waged work for survival (Daggett, 2019; Weeks, 2011; Williams, 2020). What would it look like to step off the treadmill of industrial production and prioritize meeting real human needs instead? This study of Twin Oaks offers us a glimpse into such a world, and the contradictions and questions inherent in creating an economic system focused on providing 'enough' for the low-carbon good life.

I have argued that Twin Oak demonstrates the role of transforming work in creating sustainable communities. Twin Oakers have broadened their definition of work to include the work of sustainable practices, while discouraging overproduction and overconsumption. In particular, Twin Oakers' broadened definition of work includes social reproductive labour and sustaining labour. Decision makers at Twin Oaks prioritize the community's value of environmental sustainability in accordance with the well-being of the community as a whole. The democratic and decentralized decision-making processes hold decision makers accountable to this community value.

While mainstream solutions to climate change have prioritized technological fixes to environmental problems without considering social and economic arrangements, this study of an intentional community provides an empirical case of how reorganizing work arrangements can contribute to building a just sustainable society. Ecofeminist scholars have long theorized how capitalist systems exploit women and nature, and about alternative economic systems, such as sufficiency provisioning and the prioritization of social reproductive labour (Mellor, 2019; Plumwood, 1997). This study of Twin Oaks demonstrates how broadening definitions of work, prioritizing community well-being, and democratic decision making can play a role in an ecofeminist transition from capitalist economics of exploitation to a just sustainable commons-based society (Giacomini, 2020). Furthermore, this study furthers environmental studies of intentional communities by considering how systems of work contribute to sustainability in intentional communities in addition to previous research which has recognized resource sharing as a primary mechanism through which intentional communities achieve sustainability.

One limitation of this study is that these findings may not be generalizeable outside of the context of Twin Oaks, which is a relatively self-contained and homogenous community. Further research must consider how the lessons of intentional communities are transferable to society in general. Furthermore, future research should compare Twin Oaks' labour system to models in other intentional communities. It is essential to note that Twin Oaks is overwhelmingly composed of white, middle-class members and to consider intentional communities with more diverse demographics, and those which primarily serve people of colour.

While Battistoni asks the question, 'What kind of work does the low-carbon good life require', Twin Oakers have provided one answer for their community and are living with the intended and unintended consequences. While their labour system is not perfect, Twin Oakers can lead us to imagine alternative models for a just sustainable society.

NOTES

1. At the time of this writing, the most recent available annual data from the Federal Highway Administration (FHWA) and U.S. Energy Information Administration (EIA) is for 2020. It is important to note that in 2020 the United States experienced a 13.8% decrease in driving miles compared to 2019, largely attributable to the COVID-19 pandemic.
2. Thank you to Mark and Valerie from Twin Oaks for your assistance in providing the data for these numbers.

REFERENCES

Agyeman, J., Bullard, R. D., & Evans, B. (Eds.). (2003). *Just sustainabilities: Development in an unequal world* (1st ed.). Cambridge, MA: MIT Press.

Battistoni, A. (2021, November 15). Climate futures and the future of work: Rethinking 'green jobs,' revaluing care work. Rapoport Center for Human Rights and Justice.

Battilana, J., Yen, J., Ferreras, I., & Ramarajan, L. (2022). Democratizing work: Redistributing power in organizations for a democratic and sustainable future. *Organization Theory*, *3*(1). doi:10.1177/26317877221084714

Bauhardt, C. (2014). Solutions to the crisis? The green new deal, degrowth, and the solidarity economy: Alternatives to the capitalist growth economy from an ecofeminist economics perspective. *Ecological Economics*, *102*, 60–68. doi:10.1016/j.ecolecon.2014.03.015

Bell, S. E., Daggett, C., & Labuski, C. (2020). Toward feminist energy systems: Why adding women and solar panels is not enough. *Energy Research & Social Science*, *68*, 101557. doi:10.1016/j.erss.2020.101557

Berkes, F., Colding, J., & Folke, C. (Eds.). (2001). *Navigating social-ecological systems: Building resilience for complexity and change* (1st ed.). Cambridge: Cambridge University Press.

Bhatia, M. (2021). Gender and sustainability in ecological intentional communities. *Environmental Sociology*, *8*(2), 199–210. doi:10.1080/23251042.2021.1998297

Cole, L. W., & Foster, S. R. (2001). *From the ground up: Environmental racism and the rise of the environmental justice movement*. New York, NY: New York University Press.

Coulter, K. (2017). Towards humane jobs: Recognizing gendered and multispecies intersections and possibilities. In M. G. Cohen (Ed.), *Climate change and gender in rich countries: Work, public policy and action, Routledge studies in climate, work and society* (pp. 167–182). Abingdon: Routledge.

Cruz-Torres, M. L., & McElwee, P. (2019). Gender, livelihoods, and sustainability: Anthropological research. In S. MacGregor (Ed.), *Routledge handbook of gender and environment* (pp. 133–145). London and New York: Routledge.

Cudworth, E. (2022). Labors of love: Work, labor, and care in dog–human relations. *Gender, Work & Organization*, *29*(3), 830–844. doi:10.1111/gwao.12814

Daggett, C. N. (2019). *The birth of energy: Fossil fuels, thermodynamics, and the politics of work*. Durham, NJ: Duke University Press.

Di Chiro, G. (1996). Nature as community: The convergence of environment and social justice. In W. Cronon (Ed.), *Uncommon ground: Rethinking the human place in nature* (pp. 298–320). New York, NY: Norton.

Giacomini, T. (2020). An ecofeminist perspective on the just transition from capitalism to commons. In B. Tokar & T. Gilbertson (Eds.), *Climate justice and community renewal: Resistance and grassroots solutions* (pp. 194–205). London: Routledge, Taylor & Francis Group.

Glenn, E. N. (1992). From servitude to service work: Historical continuities in the racial division of paid reproductive labor. *Signs: Journal of Women in Culture and Society*, *18*(1), 1–43. doi:10.1086/494777

Gould, K. A., Pellow, D. N., & Schnaiberg, A. (2008). *The treadmill of production: Injustice and unsustainability in the global economy*. Boulder, CO: Paradigm Publishers.

Günel, G. (2019). *Spaceship in the desert: Energy, climate change, and urban design in Abu Dhabi*. Durham, NC: Duke University Press.

Hochschild, A. R., & Machung, A. (1990). *The second shift: Working parents and the revolution at home*. London: Piatkus.

Howe, C. (2019). *Ecologics: Wind and power in the anthropocene*. Durham, NC: Duke University Press.

Jarvis, H. (2011). Saving space, sharing time: Integrated infrastructures of daily life in cohousing. *Environment and Planning A*, *43*, 560–577.

Jarvis, H. (2019). Pragmatic utopias: Intentional gender-democratic and sustainable communities. In S. MacGregor (Ed.), *Routledge handbook of gender and environment* (pp. 433–446). London and New York: Routledge.

Jensen, P. R. (2018). 'People can't believe we exist!': Social sustainability and alternative nonprofit organizing. *Critical Sociology*, *44*(2), 375–388. doi:10.1177/0896920517691106

Kinkade, K. (1973). *A Walden two experiment: The first five years of twin oaks community*. New York, NY: Morrow.

Kociatkiewicz, J., Kostera, M., & Parker, M. (2021). The possibility of disalienated work: Being at home in alternative organizations. *Human Relations*, *74*(7), 933–957. doi:10.1177/0018726720916762

Littig, B. (2019). Good green jobs for whom? A feminist critique of the green economy. In S. MacGregor (Ed.), *Routledge handbook of gender and environment* (pp. 318–330). London and New York: Routledge.

Magdoff, F., & Foster, J. B. (2010). What every environmentalist needs to know about capitalism. *Monthly Review*, *61*(10), 1–30.

Magdoff, F., & Williams, C. (2017). *Creating an ecological society: Toward a revolutionary transformation*. New York, NY: Monthly Review Press.

Mellor, M. (2019). Ecofeminist political economy: A Green and feminist agenda. In S. MacGregor (Ed.), *Routledge handbook of gender and environment* (pp. 86–100). London and New York: Routledge.

Meyers, J. S. M. (2022). *Working democracies: Managing inequality in worker cooperatives*. Ithaca, NY: ILR Press, an imprint of Cornell University Press.

Nelson, A. (2018). *Small is necessary*. London: Pluto Press.

Office of Highway Policy Information. (2022). *Travel monitoring: Traffic trends*. Washington, DC: U.S. Department of Transportation Federal Highway Administration.

Plumwood, V. (1997). *Feminism and the mastery of nature*. London: Routledge.

Reyes, V. (2018). Ethnographic toolkit: Strategic positionality and researchers' visible and invisible tools in field research. *Ethnography*, *21*(2), 1–21.

Salleh, A., Shiva, V., & Clark, J. (2017). *Ecofeminism as politics: Nature, Marx and the post modern* (2nd ed.). London: Zed Books.

Sargisson, L., & Sargent, L. T. (2017). Lived utopianism: Everyday life and intentional communities. *Communal Societies*, *37*(1), 1–23.

Sobering, K. (2022). *The people's hotel: Working for justice in Argentina*. Durham, NC: Duke University Press.

Twin Oaks Intentional Community. (n.d.). *Twin oaks intentional community – More about*. Louisa County, VA: Twin Oaks Community.

United States Census Bureau. (2021). QuickFacts: Louisa County, Virginia. Retrieved from https://www.census.gov/quickfacts/louisacountyvirginia. Accessed on September 27, 2022.

United States Energy Information Administration. (2022). *State Energy Data System (SEDS): 1960–2020 (Complete)*. U.S. Energy Information Administration. Retrieved from https://www.eia.gov/state/seds/seds-data-complete.php

United States Energy Information Administration. (2023). *Natural gas consumption by end use*. U.S. Energy Information Administration. Retrieved from https://www.eia.gov/dnav/ng/ng_cons_sum_dcu_nus_a.htm

Weeks, K. (2011). *The problem with work: Feminism, marxism, antiwork politics, and postwork imaginaries*. Durham, NC: Duke University Press.

Williams, C. L. (2021). Life support: The problems of working for a living. *American Sociological Review*, *86*(2), 191–200. doi:10.1177/0003122421997063

Wright, E. O. (2013). Transforming capitalism through real utopias. *American Sociological Review*, *78*, 1–25.

[illegible]
[illegible] *Rural Sociology* [illegible]
[illegible]

CHAPTER 5

WHO IS A DIGITAL NOMAD? THE EVOLVING IDENTITIES OF THE NEW NOMADIC WORKFORCE

Alma Andino-Frydman

Stanford University, Stanford, CA, USA

ABSTRACT

In this paper, I explore what shapes the identities of digital nomads (DNs), a class of remote workers who travel and work concurrently. Through extensive fieldwork and interviews with 50 digital nomads conducted in seven coworking hostels in Mexico in 2022, I construct a theory of DN identity. I base this upon the frequent transformations they undergo in their Circumstances, which regularly change their worker identity.

DNs relinquish traditional social determinants of identity, such as nationality and religion. They define their personal identities by their passions and interests, which are influenced by the people they meet. DNs exist in inherently transitive social spaces and, without rigid social roles to fulfil, they represent themselves authentically. They form close relationships with other long-term travellers to combat loneliness and homesickness. Digital nomads define their worker identities around their location independence. This study shows that DNs value their nomadic lifestyle above promotions and financial gain. They define themselves by productivity and professionalism to ensure the sustainability of their lifestyle. Furthermore, digital nomad coworking hubs serve focused, individual work, leaving workplace politics and strict 'office image' norms behind. Without fixed social and professional roles to play, digital nomads define themselves personally according to their ever-evolving passions and the

Ethnographies of Work
Research in the Sociology of Work, Volume 35, 95–137

Published under exclusive licence by Emerald Publishing Limited
ISSN: 0277-2833/doi:10.1108/S0277-283320230000035005

sustainability of their nomadic life. Based on these findings, I present a cyclical framework for DN identity evolution which demonstrates how relational, logistical, and socio-personal flux evolves DN's worker identities.

Keywords: Digital nomadism; remote work; value of work; WFH; WFA; digital work; COVID-19; productivity; motivation; tourism; identity; identity evolution; role theory; professional identity; worker identity; relational identity; workplace identity

INTRODUCTION

The COVID-19 pandemic drastically transformed how people work. Before the pandemic, only 5% of American workdays were work from home (WFH); as the pandemic engulfed the world, this number rose to a staggering 50% (Barrero, Bloom, & Davis, 2021). For many, the pandemic forced a natural divergence from the '9 to 5' work structure. The 40-hour work week aimed to remedy the harsh conventions of the Industrial Revolution. Despite being challenged by many labour groups for its effects on worker's well-being, this labour convention has remained the traditional norm for knowledge workers in the United States. Many workers have questioned this structure, but the conversation on work-life balance was reimagined during the COVID-19 pandemic.

Working from home allowed people to work on the schedule that suited them. While workers in many occupations were not afforded the luxury of work from home during the pandemic, many knowledge workers realized they were just as, or even more, productive in this arrangement (Barrero et al., 2021). These employees began to value lifestyle choices more in their quotidian lives. They had more time to dedicate to wellness, friends, family, adventure, hobbies, and personal fulfilment. For many, there was no going back to the office.

A particular group of workers has long capitalized on the newfound freedom of a fixed office. First described by Makimoto and Manners (1997), digital nomads (DNs) are location-independent workers who travel the world while working remotely. The US Chamber of Commerce built upon this definition, stating, 'Digital nomads are remote workers, including self-employed individuals, freelancers, and employees. They may travel domestically or overseas, and the internet keeps them connected to jobs, co-workers, and clients' (Elliot, 2022).

While they vary in age, profession, and duration in travel destinations (Sutherland & Jarrahi, 2017), I define DNs as location-independent workers who rely on information and communication technologies (ICTs) to work remotely while they travel. They make residential decisions based on interests and passions rather than proximity to a fixed workplace. They seek new experiences to enrich themselves personally, culturally, and professionally (Müller, 2016). With no fixed itinerary or plans to return home, DNs are a compelling case study into how people make choices about their lives independently from the demands of a static job.

Digital nomadism has increased dramatically since the pandemic transformed work. 16.9 million Americans describe themselves as DNs, a staggering 131% increase from 2019 to 2022 (MBO Partners, 2022). Countries such as Colombia, Costa Rica, and Portugal are trying to attract nomads; 54 nations now offer 'digital nomad visas' (Valencia, 2023). Nomads with proof of income live tax-free in attractive destinations. News coverage on DNs in Mexico described growing anger among locals and this massive migratory movement (Linthicum, 2022). Although many countries are desperate to attract these workers, academic research on DNs is limited (Muller, 2016; Nash et al., 2020; Reichenberger, 2021; Thompson, 2021). Few investigations have examined the evolution of DN's worker identities. Digital nomads tend to work high-impact knowledge jobs, such as programming and marketing, which have concrete impact on our society. One's moral and social self-image impacts the work produced in these fields (Schauster, Ferrucci, & Tandoc, 2021). Thus, understanding what this class of workers value and how they view themselves will yield novel insights around how this nomadic work structure changes the work they conduct.

The central research question this study investigates is, 'How does the logistical, socio-personal, and relational flux experienced by digital nomads shape their worker identity?' This paper illustrates the regular social, physical, and ideological changes DNs undergo and their impact on their professional self-image. It contributes significantly to the literature by presenting an in-depth case study on their novel work arrangements and priorities. The identity evolution of DNs has not been investigated deeply despite their lifestyle uncertainty being conducive to more frequent identity work (Brown, 2014). While past studies analyzed components of DNs' work styles, careers, and infrastructure demands, this study is the first to detail the cycle of worker identity evolution that arises from the inherent transitions that define their lives. In illustrating how digital nomads' identities change as they travel, we will gain clarity on how their professional, political, and financial choices are impacted as a result. Their identities dictate where they spend their Western income, what jobs they work, and what products and services they demand to sustain this lifestyle.

This paper makes three significant contributions to the academic literature on worker identities and digital nomadism. It establishes (a) how DNs pursue and are defined by a state of professional liminality; (b) the workplace dynamics that characterize DN cowork offices within social role theory; and (c) most importantly, presents a novel model of the cycle by which DNs evolve their identities. Ultimately, this paper concludes that these very cyclical changes define digital nomads.

LITERATURE REVIEW

Understanding the construction of workers' identities is increasingly relevant for management and work studies. Identity theory (IT) states, 'An identity [is] a shared set of meanings that define individuals in particular roles in society' (Stets & Serpe, 2013, p. 31) (i.e. role identities). Identity is defined by belonging to groups (i.e. group identities) and the unique ways in which individuals see themselves (i.e. personal identities) (Burke & Stets, 2009). Identity is an attempt to determine 'who am I?' and 'how should I act?' (Alvesson, Ashcraft, & Thomas, 2008).

Traditionally, identity was considered a stable state (Albert & Whetten, 1985), but more recently, it has been seen as a permuting process (Rodgers & Scott, 2008).

Identity reconstruction occurs as individuals renegotiate their roles within evolving organizations and networks (Beech, 2011). Identity evolution is more frequent and profound in times of uncertainty, chaos, or strain when individuals must reevaluate themselves in new circumstances and among new people (Brown, 2014). This uncertainty defines digital nomads; they regularly change the entire cities they live in. For these reasons, digital nomads regularly experience tension and ambiguity in their residential and professional environments. I aim to explain how this instability, along with the uncertain norms of remote work, defines DN worker identity.

To answer 'How does the logistical, socio-personal, and relational flux experienced by digital nomads shape their worker identity?', several sub-questions surface. I identify such questions from the extensive literature on identity described in the below sections on worker identity, relational identity, and socio-personal identity.

Worker Identity

There has been a significant academic discourse on work identity and how it is developed. In understanding who digital nomads are as workers, I must establish the differences between professional identity and worker identities and what comprises each. In this section, I define professional and workplace norms, determine why these are critical to Americans' self-image, and how WFH affects this. I can then analyze transformations in worker identity and use the lens of liminality – the state of transition from one occupational state to the next – to consider the identities of DNs. Finally, I identify key gaps in the literature to establish the necessity of this research.

Summarizing the extant literature on worker identity is well beyond the scope of this paper, but it is vital to shine a light on concepts relevant to our investigation. Individual worker identity is created from a worker's interpretation of organizational and occupational identity (Walsh & Gordon, 2008). This is distinct from professional identity, which is traditionally defined as 'an individual's self-definition as a member of a profession and is associated with the enactment of a professional role' (Chreim et al., 2007, p. 1515). For those in formal professions, such as accountants, lawyers, or doctors, professional identity is characterized according to one's adherence to the historical norms of said role (Alvesson & Sandberg, 2013), the relationships within a workplace (Abbott, 1988), and the labour markets and institutions of said job. Thornton, Ocasio, and Lounsbury (2013) posit that professional identity is shaped and affirmed by reputations within professional institutions. In essence, professional identity is strictly defined and applicable, within the literature, only to those in formal professions. Here is where this paper deviates; many DNs work non-traditional jobs without formal norms and institutions and are thus not formally defined as 'professionals'. When I discuss how digital nomads define themselves professionally, I am referring to their 'worker identity', rather than their 'professional identity'. The paper highlights how career ambitions, workplace culture, and networking shape one's worker identity. However, for this review, worker identity can encompass four key concepts: professional role expectations, organizational hierarchy, workplace identity, and societal role as a worker.

Beyond the professional norms and historical definers of a worker, organizational hierarchy often defines 'who [workers] are, their logics of action, how they act, their vocabularies of motive, and what language is salient' (p.54). Organizational association is and has always been key to answering the question of 'Who am I?' and 'Whom am I becoming?' (Beijaard, Meijer, & Verloop, 2004; Hatch & Schultz, 2002). Organizational identity is defined as the 'central, distinctive, and enduring' qualities of an organization (Albert & Whetten, 1985, p. 265). As such, an individual's role within this organization yields their own distinct identity (Dutton et al., 1994). The organizational work identities of digital nomads have never been closely investigated. Notably, DNs exist occupationally within remote roles, either at a company or working with clients directly. Most literature on professional identity focuses on its development within organizations, but digital nomads often work outside of organizations and formal professions. Many DNs work as freelancers and entrepreneurs within digital industries that lack rigid professional norms (LSE, 2017). As such, professional identity, as traditionally defined, does not apply to them. Thus, it is relevant to understand how hierarchy affects worker identity construction when workers work physically apart from their intra-company coworkers or clients.

Another key element of a worker's identity is workplace identity, or 'the sense of individual identity that an employee derives from being part of a particular workplace' (Agostino, 2004). Workplace behaviour norms, interpersonal workplace dynamics, and logistical demands of a particular workplace shape workplace identity. In 'Workplace Identities', garbage collectors describe structuring their entire lives (e.g. mortgages, daily schedules, families) around this identity (Agostino, 2004). One's workplace identity can be shaped around the quality of relationships with superiors and colleagues (Sias, 2005). The space, time constraints, and relationships within a workplace significantly determine one's worker identity (Mikkola et al., 2020). DNs, however, lack a fixed physical workplace. Coworking spaces – shared work offices dedicated to remote workers – have emerged as valuable infrastructure to keep DNs accountable, find stable internet, and rigidly separate their social and professional lives (Chevtaeva, 2021). Nomads change cowork spaces regularly and, thus, change their workplace and all the norms and dynamics accompanying it. As this study aims to grasp how logistical flux changes DN's worker identities, it is relevant to understand how regularly changing physical workplaces impact DN's worker identity.

Finally, worker identity is shaped by the societal expectations of the role work plays in one's life. In the United States, complete integration of work objectives and personal fulfilment was encouraged by employers, as described in 'The Time

Bind'. As a result, the lines blurred, forcing people to spend more 'face time' in the office or risk falling behind their peers. Hochschild delineates how work transitioned to fulfil personal and social needs.

> Employees were permitted – nay encouraged – to socialize through self-managed teams at the office and the factory and, thus, were offered an attractive means to fulfill social, esteem, and even self-actualization needs on the job – all functions that used to be met by family, friends, and community. (Hochschild, 2018, p. 359)

While people are encouraged to spend more time in their workplace, they are unhappy at work (Biskup et al., 2019). In the United States, people will spend one-third of their lives at work (Vaughn, 2018), meaning most of their social interactions, spatial engagement, and identity formation revolve around work. On top of this, long working hours affirm worker identities (Lewis, 2003), so the lines between work and personal validation are further erased. People do not necessarily choose for work to become their whole identity, but rather esteem and recognition are only allowed to come from work (Kofodimos, 1993) and the value added from their role. This notion is reinforced by Vallas and Cummins who noted how 'employees feel compelled to remake themselves in ways that willingly embrace the demands of the marketplace' and change their identities to accommodate such expectations (2015, p. 297).

The role of work in society has seen the most dramatic shift resulting from pandemic-induced forced remote work. Even before the pandemic, workers valued a flexible remote work arrangement highly; in a 2017 study, call-centre workers were willing to accept 8% lower wages for a remote work option (Mas & Pallais, 2017). The pandemic caused remote work to skyrocket from 5% in 2018 to 60% in May 2020 (Barrero et al., 2021). WFH allows workers the time and flexibility for healthier eating, more physical exercise, and better sleep quality while minimizing wasted commuting hours by 1.3 billion hours per month (Barrero et al., 2021). Remote work allowed American workers to reevaluate the role of work in their lives and the importance of professionalism to their identity. Thus, it is important to investigate how DN's worker identity changes when the role of work in their lives changes.

Worker identity is constructed from the knowledge, skills, societal implications, hierarchical positions, ambitions, social dynamics, and norms accompanying a role or career trajectory (Barbour & Lammers, 2015). Thus, in analyzing how DNs transform their identities, I pay close attention to 'shifts and transformations to personal and professional knowledge, skills, and dispositions' (Trede, Macklin, & Bridges, 2011, p. 365). This evolution may result simply from necessity. Sennett argues that the modern worker must constantly transform and augment themselves to secure jobs because precarious labour conditions require a constant permutation skillset (Sennett, 2006). Reed and Thomas argue that liminality creates a distinct worker identity (2019).

> Liminality thus refers to a temporary phase, with the liminal person being caught 'betwixt and between' as they move across space and time in the transition from one social status to another.

DNs are a fascinating example of liminality. They consistently change their physical and social state, and remote work norms and institutional functions remain in intense flux after the pandemic (Newbold et al., 2021). Remote work is normalizing, but firms and employers still struggle to manage norms within a virtual workplace (Wang, Liu, Qing, & Parker, 2020). Whether or not the worker is in a formal profession with strict behavioural expectations and institutional conventions (Alvesson & Sandberg, 2012), their worker identity and labour norms are bound to shift following the first phase of the pandemic. Many companies have shifted management practices, workplace norms, scheduling expectations, and even positions in this transition period (Behrens & Pekarek, 2023). Liminality is, thus, a relevant lens through which to analyze evolving worker identities.

Previous research has chiefly characterized worker identity as a stable, unchanging state (Abbott, 1988). However, transformations in worker identity have been studied in the contexts of gradual socialization (Pratt et al., 2006), new technologies (Nelson & Irwin, 2014), or aspirations for new professional opportunities (Kreiner & Sheep, 2009). Recently, attention has focused on the constant changes workers must undergo to keep up in a fast-paced, insecure labour market (Healy et al., 2017). First, scholars denoted how professional ambitions galvanize identity evolution; workers hoping to advance emulate the characteristics of higher-ranking colleagues, such as in the case of management training programs (Ibarra, 1999) or medical students choosing specializations (Pratt et al., 2006). Literature also delineated how abandoning undesirable job traits (Kreiner & Sheep, 2009) and collective social agreement (Goodrick & Reay, 2010) changes worker identities. These studies maintain that people change worker identities to align with their self-image. The pursuit of meaningful work shapes one's worker identity (Iatridis et al., 2021), especially for professionals who believe their work to be 'more important' than that of others (Lair et al., 2008). However, these studies assume that the pursuit of meaning can solely be derived from a job. They fail to address how prioritizing meaning in a worker's personal life – such as in the case of digital nomads – changes worker identity.

Now that we have a clear picture of how worker identity has been conceptualized, it is vital to note that very little is known about DNs' worker identities. In the past, others have investigated the discipline practices and popular careers among DNs (Cook, 2020), their reliance on gig work (Sutherland, 2017), and the utility of coworking hostels in separating their social and work lives (Chevtaeva, 2021). Many DNs have increased professional responsibilities: freelancers or business owners are responsible for acquiring clients and income (Reichenberger, 2018). DNs have learned to anchor their career identities without an organizational structure (Heuser & Reintjes, 2019). Freedom, association with the DN community, and self-determination of time use are crucial to DN worker identities. However, no literature has investigated how DNs' dynamic lives transform their worker identities. Thus, liminality is a relevant lens through which to analyze their evolving worker identities. Little research has been done on DNs' worker identity and its relation to location independence despite the striking results from the private sector. When Airbnb announced that their employees could live and work anywhere, their careers page was viewed over 800,000 times (Tan, 2022). In February 2021, Spotify announced its WFA model. Fast forward to today, and quit rates are down 15% compared to the same quarter in 2019 (Nawrat, 2022).

Nevertheless, when Apple forced its staff back to its offices, approximately 56% of its employees said they planned to leave (Berger, 2022). People are more committed than ever to the ability to work remotely: millions say they would find another job if forced to return to the office (Barrero et al., 2021; Kings College London, 2022). DNs undoubtedly fit within this transformation, but it is unknown in what ways they value their location independence and in what ways it defines their worker identity. This is important to understand. I, thus, investigate how location independence defines DN relational and socio-personal identities and how worker identity is affected as a result.

Relational Identity

It is relevant to analyze DNs' identities within the context of their changing social circles. Why? Because the literature shows the effects of interpersonal relationships on one's identity, development, and professional performance (Brewer & Gardner, 1996; Burke & Stets, 2009; Merton, 1957). We form our identities on three levels: individual, interpersonal, and collective. These are incredibly intertwined, and our self-esteem originates from our values, motivations, and success in fulfilling interpersonal roles. Relational identity is the self-image we derive from interpersonal relationships (Brewer & Gardner, 1996).

Understanding relational identities means understanding the formation and fulfilment of social roles. Social roles are 'sets of behavioural expectations associated with given positions in the social structure' (Ebaugh, 1988, p. 18). Role theory suggests that one's identity is based on the role one is expected to fill in a network and how successful one is in fulfilling those behavioural norms (Merton, 1957). For example, people define themselves through their relationships within the workplace. One's relational role changes based on those in the interaction. For example, a subordinate will define themselves differently from a supervisor than a coworker (Katz & Kahn, 1978). Role identity could include acting out the expectation of their respective roles, taking control of the resources that the role could normatively possess, or managing the diverse relationships and interactions between the various role partners (Hogg & Ridgeway, 2003; Stets & Burke, 2003).

At a higher level, Sluss and Ashford (2007) defined 'relational identity' as the expectations and implications of a role relationship. One's role identity may be 'the goals, values, beliefs, norms, interaction styles, and time horizons associated with the role', but their relational identity refers to the elements salient within a normative relationship. Different norms and signalling responsibilities may be associated with various roles within a given workplace. For example, an intern may be permitted to wear more casual clothes than a manager but would also be expected to work more hours to prove commitment. Still, it is established that social interactions transmute one's identity within an organization (Hatch & Schultz, 1997).

People are also expected to fulfil roles in social networks and morph their self-identification around their relations to others. Relationships serve the purpose of dictating one's role within a social organization and validating one's self-image (Burke & Stets, 2009). In his 'Theory of the Self', James (1890) proposed that people have 'multiple selves' corresponding to the different social roles in different relationships. This invokes the concept of 'identity salience' (Stryker 1968, 2002), which implies one may activate a specific identity within a particular relational context. People change their salient identities depending on the people around them.

This literature makes the critical assumption that relational identities are formed within more or less stable, albeit diverse, social circles, because of a static workplace, school, or social network. However, DNs are constantly permuting their social circles and reinventing their social personas in new environments. Flowerdew and Wang (2015) consider identity as 'social positions that individuals assume as they interact with others within communities by following certain rules and conventions'. Reed and Thomas (2019) showed how HR professionals shifting socio-professional networks cause changes in one's worker identity. Since DN communities are changing consistently, it is essential to consider how their social roles change.

The central focus of this paper is the cyclical influence between socio-personal, relational, and worker identities among DNs. The symbiotic dynamic between our relational and social identities has been studied at length, with academics finding that our relationships shape our worldview (Reid & Deaux, 1996) and our partisan affiliations. One's social circles impact career performance (Muller & Peres, 2019; Verbeke & Wuyts, 2007) and professional knowledge diffusion (Zheng et al., 2019). Workplace relationships define people's identity (Sluss & Ashford, 2007). DNs' social circles are constantly changing, either because they themselves travel regularly or their communities are composed of transient workers. This dynamic has not been investigated. To understand how DNs make professional decisions, form ambitions, and see the role of work in their lives, one must understand how their peers influence them.

Social and Personal Identity

The academic conversation on social and personal identity is comprehensive and stretches back over a century (James, 1890). Contemporarily, Social Identity Theory dictates who one is as coming from one's perceived membership in a social group, the characteristics of those within the group, and the activities and behaviours congruent with this social membership (Brown, 2000). Social self-categorization refers to one placing oneself within a pre-established social group, such as race, gender, or profession, and validation refers to an individual's acceptance within that group by its other members, or lack thereof (Hogg & Abrams, 1996). There has been extensive academic discourse separating and weaving together the concepts of personal and social identity. In the case of my study, they are incredibly interdependent, in that one's social environment shapes one's personal identity, and one's personal identity determines one's social circles. While social identity refers to one's belonging to a social category, personal identity refers to who one is, one's aspirations, values, and world views (Teschl & Derobert, 2008). Social identity is defined as group memberships and one's emotions attached to this membership (Tajfel, 1979), and personal identity is one's differentiation and integration 'not in relation to a community and its culture but to the self and its projects' (Hewitt, 1989).

While seemingly separate, Vignoles's analysis of the interconnectedness of social and personal factors in identity formation is particularly important for DNs (Vignoles, 2018). He explored the interdependence of social and personal definitions of identity, determining that one's social environment continually changes one's personal identity and an evolving personal self-image changes one's social circles. This study seeks to build upon his findings, addressing how DNs define and redefine themselves while living a transitive lifestyle and how this affects their worker identities.

However, although our circumstances and characteristics determine who we are, Wright would argue, 'People have considerable agency over the construction of their identities' (Wright et al., 2012, p. 1455). Those sharing this perspective often refer to 'identity work' as 'the range of activities individuals engage in to create, present, and sustain personal identities that are congruent with and supportive of the self-concept' (Snow & Anderson, 1987). Wright et al. explained how a people's moral prioritization of tackling climate change created and altered momentum for sustainability initiatives. This is an example of individuals pursuing identity work that aligns with their moral self-concept. Individuals' identity work may change societies and social structures (Giorgi & Palmisano, 2017; Wright et al., 2012). Vignoles builds upon this conclusion by highlighting how the separation of social and personal identity construction is often misleading and unhelpful, as it dismisses ways in which one shapes the other. He said, 'the processes by which individuals regulate their personal identities are inextricably linked to practices by which societies and groups regulate their members' (Vignoles, 2017, p. 308).

For DNs, it is interesting to consider the activities and behaviours that formulate their identity-shaping work because of their freedom of circumstance. Detached from many relational and material responsibilities, as well as a geographic tether (Sutherland & Jarrahi, 2017), DNs engage in travel and adventure activities according to their passions and interests (Muller, 2016). As people tend to engage in identity work more during periods of tension and change, it follows to question how often and profoundly DNs are reevaluating who they are (Beech, 2012). Juffermans considers the processes of identity work specifically for digital media entrepreneurs but does not focus on the symbiotic impacts of personal and relational identity transitions on worker identity (2020). Thus, it is essential to ask what elements of identity construction – societally predetermined, relational, or personal – most define them and their worker identities.

To understand what shapes DN's worker identities, one must investigate how they are impacted by (a) new remote work norms, fluctuating workplaces, and evolving attitudes towards work; (b) consistently rotating social networks; and (c) reevaluations of personal identity definers. Flux in all these categories, and the interrelationship between them, is what ultimately defines DN identity.

Over 56 countries have changed their visa programs and tax laws to attract these workers. Gentrification is rapidly accelerating in DN hubs, such as Mexico City, Canggu, and Medellin, and attracting global attention (Linthucum, 2022). Knowing what DNs value and how they define themselves provides useful insights to inform actions by governments and private actors alike, such as taxation and migratory policies to implement for DNs and remote work products to create based off DN needs.

METHODOLOGY

In order to fully understand the way DNs identified themselves and what motivated them, this study was conducted using community-based ethnography, in which I was able to seamlessly embed myself into the environment. Alongside participant observation, data were gathered through 50 individual interviews with DNs. Importantly, the 50 interview subjects were a sample of convenience; the sites I visited were chosen because I could conduct research there. They were not controlled for demographic composition. However, the interviews provide compelling insights into the decision making and values of subjects; a more quantitative study would likely fail to capture the core values of the new nomadic workforce. Qualitative research allows for the exploration of rationale and motivation behind actions, rather than simply what actions themselves were (Rahman, 2016). As DN research is still limited, understanding foundational concepts is important to motivate future quantitative studies.

Eligible study subjects were defined as DNs as in the Introduction: subjects were (a) working digitally and with the support of ICTs (Sutherland & Jarrahi, 2017); (b) working while nomadic, without one permanent 'home base' (Muller, 2016); and (c) were in pursuit of adventure, global, or new cultural experiences (Nash et al., 2018).

Participant research was conducted at multiple locations in Mexico. DN ethnography has been conducted in variety of international sites such as Portugal, Thailand (Cook, 2020), and Indonesia (Woldoff & Litchfield, 2021), but never in Mexico. Given its proximity to the United States, Mexico is an important destination for American DNs. Mexico is the fastest-growing DN hub by NomadList, a crowd-sourced remote work database that aggregates data based on 178,577 check-ins by remote workers. NomadList describes the internet reliability, monthly cost of living, population makeup, and best restaurants, accommodation, and coworking spaces in each DN hub city; essentially, it is a holy grail guide for hundreds of thousands of DNs. In 2017–2021, Nomad List found Playa del Carmen grew 225% in remote worker popularity, and Mexico City grew 179% (Nomad List, 2022).

I conducted research at seven locations of the international cowork hostel chain, Selina. With 163 locations worldwide, Selina has established itself as a global 'digital nomad hostel', promising upscale amenities, weekly events, trendy decor, and most importantly, full office space with stable internet. It carries high recognition among digital nomads. Selina's website describes their cowork program as such:

> Breathe life into your work from home routine and join digital nomads, creators, and entrepreneurs at Selina CoWork. Complete with high-speed WiFi and inspiring design, refresh your thinking and tap into a brand new level of productivity as you travel. Blending beautifully designed accommodation with coworking, recreation, wellness, and local experiences, Selina is custom-built for today's nomadic traveler, providing guests with a global infrastructure to travel and work abroad seamlessly. (Selina, 2023)

While there are other cowork offices and hostels within Mexico, Selina was selected for its reputation in attracting travellers who require remote work infrastructure. Immersive living within Selina hostels enabled direct access to the target demographic. I remained in each location for about one week, which allowed me to connect with long- and short-stay nomads.

The locations studied were Mexico City, Sayulita, Guadalajara, Puerto Escondido, Oaxaca City, Isla Mujeres, and Playa del Carmen. The sites varied in setting (e.g. beaches, mountains, cities). Conducting interviews through Selina allowed consistency of cowork sites and replicability within environments. Fig. 5.1a–d shows the consistent décor and set up of cowork spaces across various subject spots Selina gave me access to the offices and facilitated logistics for participant observation. The study was advertised at each location. Most subjects were recruited through interactions in cowork offices, restaurants, and common spaces. Participants were not compensated. The design and interview protocol were approved by Stanford University's Institutional Review Board.

In accordance with the IRB Human Subject Protocol, I took extensive measures to protect anonymity and protect confidential information. For example, subject demographic data were catalogued with a numeral system, in which their

(a) Meeting pods in Selina Guadalajara cowork office

(b) Selina Puerto Escondido cowork "hot desks"

(c) Hostel and event advertising in Selina Guadalajara

(d) Selina Isla Mujeres cowork "hot desks"

Fig. 5.1. Selina Cowork Offices at Different Study Sites.

identifiable characteristics were kept separate from interview data, under an encrypted sheet. Their interview audio recordings and transcripts were encrypted and kept separate as well.

Interviews were conducted between June and August 2022 in offices or common spaces in Selina hostels and followed a semi-structured approach. The interview protocol included key questions about DN productivity, motivation, valuation of work, personal and professional relationships, travel plans, and employment information. Leading questions were avoided and generally aimed to spur an anecdote. If subjects fell silent after a short answer, I allotted several seconds before moving on to ensure they fully expressed a thought. Interviews were conducted mostly in English, with a few in Spanish, lasting approximately 1 hour. All interviews were audio recorded and transcribed verbatim, using the software Otter, and reanalyzed for accuracy.

The data corpus consists of 50 interview transcripts and corresponding interview notes for each subject. Each transcript was read twice, and the audio was analyzed to capture social and auditory cues missed by the text analysis. I also examined primary source field notes describing social dynamics, interactions within cowork spaces, and personal experiences. To analyze the primary data, I used the Gioia approach to inductively extract central themes from interview responses, which then aggregated to broader perspectives on DNs' identities. This methodology presents a systematic analysis of qualitative research by identifying informant anecdotes as 'First-order codes' saturated from interviews and, as a researcher, assigning 'Second-order codes' to broader themes under which they fit (Gioia et al., 2012). The combination of self-reported informant evidence atop academically grounded dimensions allows rigorous, creative, and theory-based conclusions to emerge.

The Gioia approach was a well-suited methodology for this study for two reasons. It was developed to add rigour to the development of social theories. Inductive social research extrapolates a theory based on observations, while deductive research tests an existing hypothesis through data collection. As mentioned in the literature review, there is very limited academic research on digital nomadism, there are no existing theories to test. Instead, data must be gathered first; subsequently, theories must be developed from observing arising patterns. The Gioia methodology introduces consistency and structure to analyzing these patterns, allowing future researchers to base their studies on rigid modelling rather than loosely associated observations.

The theoretical coding for my findings is found in Fig. 5.2. I began by reading in-depth interviews and compiled quotes that mentioned similar keywords and descriptors of identity. For example, DNs mentioned they feel pressure to produce quality work to prevent employers from questioning their productivity while they travel, and how little political affiliation arises in hostel conversations. Once I found 10 or more mentions of an element such as these, I established them as a first-order condition. Evidentiary examples for first-order codes are illustrated in Fig. 5.3.

By determining how these recurring elements were related, I formulated DNs' identities. I determined how they may be related (Gioia & Chittipeddi, 1991). The second-order conditions showed the DNs' identities are composed of relational,

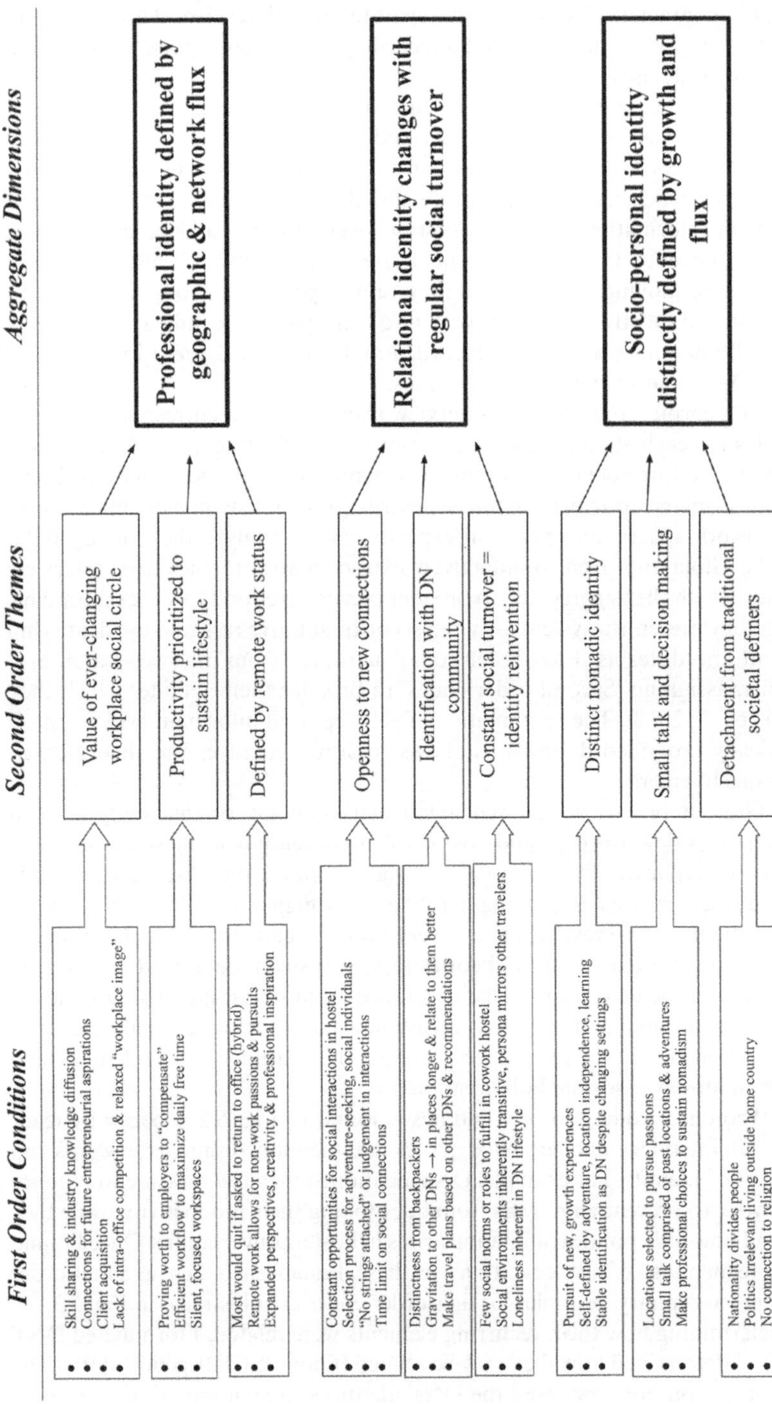

Fig. 5.2. Interview Coding Structure According to Gioia Methodology.

First Order Conditions	*Evidentiary Examples*
Skill sharing & industry knowledge diffusion	*"Some people might ask someone else for some marketing suggestions or ideas. I think the most ideas might be shared when [Selina] has talks organized and people share skills or present on specific subjects."* – Stephan, 29 year old South African programmer in Puerto Escondido
Connections for future entrepreneurial aspirations	*"Nomads are incredibly startup-oriented because they inherently think outside of the norms of society. If I am looking to start a business, I am going to want the most creative, determined, experienced partners I can find. I want to work with people who have seen the world and have diverse perspectives, not people that have only worked in an office their whole career"* – Raul, 35 year old Colombian CSM in Oaxaca City
Client acquisition	*"[As a graphic designer], I meet a lot of my clients in coworking spaces. People are very open about their work and there is high demand for good designers. It may be less stable, but I have access to so many clients traveling I wouldn't if I was in one place"* – Andres, 22 year old Mexican graphic designer in Mexico City
Lack of intra-office competition & relaxed "workplace image"	*"I am free to dress how I like. I am always in shorts, and flip flops, compared to when I was in an office and had to dress in a proper way. That changed when I started traveling, because who do I have to impress? I'll get promoted if I do good work, not based on my appearance."* – Alejandro, 43 year-old Mexican software engineer
Proving worth to employers to "compensate" for traveling	*"I want to be able to show my company that I can do the work. It doesn't matter if I'm here or there. I am going to perform. It is a privilege to be able to travel and work at the same time and I don't want to risk this arrangement. I want to keep living this lifestyle. I do not want my boss to think I am not working"* – Javier, 30 year old Colombian software engineer in Playa del Carmen
Efficient workflow to maximize daily free time	*"If I want to watch the sunset tonight, or go to yoga in the evening, or go to the beach with friends, I need to finish the work I have. Otherwise, I can't go. It's pretty simple. I am trying to finish as fast as I can."* – Anesha, 23 year old American marketing coordinator in Sayulita.
Silent, focused workspaces	*"Within the cowork, there is not a culture of talking about what you do or just chatting. If you are sitting on your laptop, people won't disturb you because you're in a flow state. Everyone is working so you feel pressure to be productive too. I use the cowork to get my tasks done so that I can actually go and do other things"* – Caroline 25 year old American CSM
Most would quit if asked to return to office (hybrid)	*"I'm already getting paid a lot. It just wouldn't be worth my time to go back. 20k or 30k is not going to upgrade anything in my lifestyle at all. The next upgrade is going to be 250k but that's out of [my employers'] price range. Some people in my role see the next big upgrade as working for Google or the big tech companies. However, I did not want to risk giving up the freedom that I have with this job."* – Nick, 33 year old American product manager in Sayulita
Remote work allows for non-work passions & pursuits	*"If I am not subject to my employer, it allows me to relocate to a new place for a passion. For instance, if I want to live at some location for six months while I get my [pilot] license, I can still have my corporate job"* – Fernando, 29 year old Mexican data analyst
Expanded perspectives, creativity & professional inspiration	*"When you travel this much, you see so many beautiful things. You meet so many beautiful people with so many amazing minds and ideas. At some point you start growing, professionally and personally. Being a graphic designer, I'm really influenced by what surrounds me."* – Andres, 22 year old Mexican graphic designer in Mexico City

Fig. 5.3. Interview Evidence for First-order Conditions.

professional, and socio-personal transformation. My core theory of identity evolution originated from a sketch of how these three elements of identity influence each other cyclically through the second-order dimensions. The final version of this cyclical figure can be found on page 33 (Fig. 5.8).

Beyond interview quotes, I attempted to integrate the hostel cowork environment. I produced in-depth notes on my observations and my experience working and living in Selina. These described topics of conversation that arose at the social areas (e.g. bar, common areas, pool), the social dynamics between the subjects I interviewed, the way they made plans for the future, their work schedules and habits, how they spent free time, and more.

Positionality. My study is based equally on participant observations and subject data. I was immersed in the research sites. I shared office facilities with subjects, slept in the same dorms, shared meals, and attended social events with subjects. From this unique position, I formed social bonds with subjects and engaged in non-interview conversations to elaborate on study topics.

As a privileged insider, I had access to participants' private information. Subjects exposed personal motivators, veiled professional ambitions, and ongoing anxieties, and revealed social dynamics within the hostel that would be inaccessible to an outside observer. I was accepted into the DN community in these hostels as a 21-year-old bilingual college student with extensive remote work and backpacking experience. People trusted me, which allowed in-depth and unencumbered participants observational access to subjects.

Sample

Employment types varied by full-time, independent contractor, freelancer, and business owner. Patterns quickly emerged in the interviews, including a commitment to location independence, valuation of work flexibility, and detachment from social and physical obligations.

This sample was intentionally selected from within Selina communities, as Selina attracts highly motivated remote workers requiring consistent internet connection and reliable amenities to ensure productive work. As described in the Methodology section, NomadList is an important platform widely used in the DN community to plan where to travel to, stay, and work. For each site of my study, NomadList recommends Selina as a top cowork office, representing its reputation among DNs. As Selina is more expensive than other hostels, in exchange for higher-quality amenities and WiFi connection, subjects were selected to be more established remote workers who needed to prioritize their careers.

Of the 50 interview subjects, 32 were men (64%) and 18 were women (36%) (Fig. 5.4a–f). The gender imbalance can be explained: more men than women travel alone, as hostels are safer for men and more accessible. This is representative of the clear gender skew found by NomadList statistics. Nomads were 80% male and 20% female ($N = 16{,}635$) (Nomad List, 2022). In addition, as a young woman, I might have attracted more male subjects than female.

The average age was 31.6 ($SD = 8.32$ years). The youngest was 22, and the oldest was 61. Subjects had been travelling for an average of 16.88 months; however,

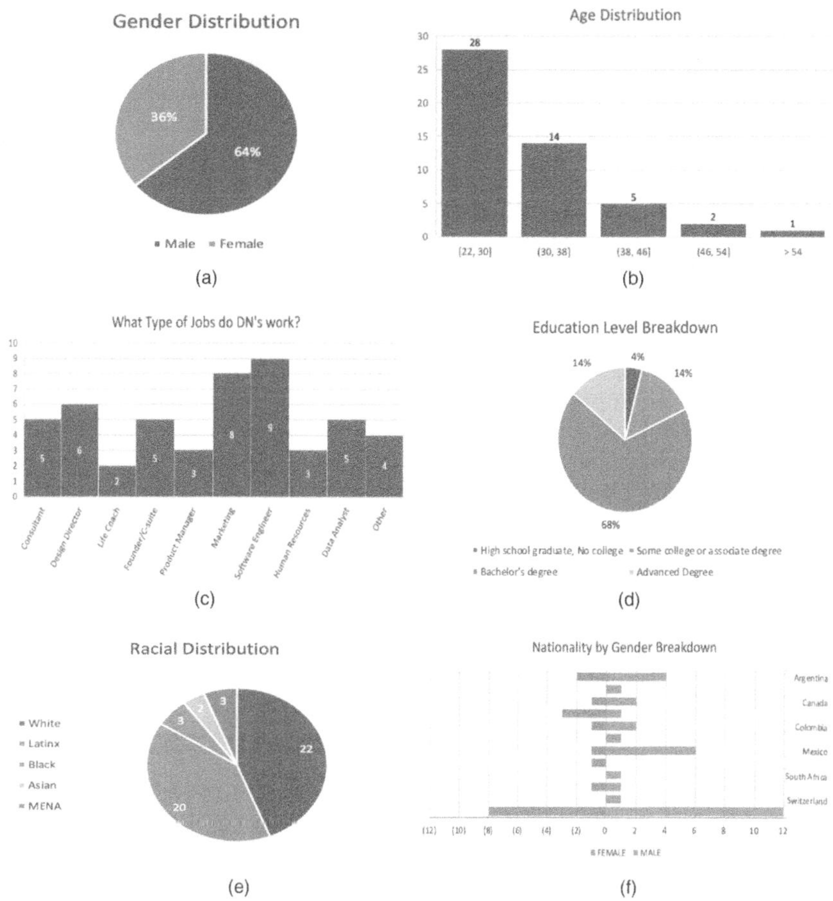

Fig. 5.4. Sample Skewed Towards US College-educated Men Aged 21–35.

the standard deviation of travel duration was 24.02 months. This implies that subjects had been travelling for a short time (1–3 months) or a much longer period (2+ years). About 42% had been travelling for six months or less, and only 18% had been travelling for more than two years. Subjects generally started before the pandemic or directly after first-phase pandemic travel restrictions began to lift, in the second half of 2021 and beginning of 2022.

DNs primarily cited convenience and affordability in choosing Mexico as a destination. Of the participants, 68% of subjects had a bachelor's degree, and 14% had a graduate degree. High levels of education accompany high salaries. Subjects reported an average income of \$93,450 (SD = \$102,972). Again, income was approximated and may have been overestimated, though the study requested an exact number. Only 14% earn less than \$15,000 per year, while 32% earn more than \$100,000 a year. For reference, the average annual salary in Mexico is

$19,915 (World Salaries, 2022). This presents an immensely important future area of research: impending gentrification of Mexico and other digital nomad havens. Knowledge workers tend to be high-earning, white collar workers in their home country. Thus, their arrival represents an influx of Western income with which locals cannot compete. Since DNs seek integration into local culture, they do not remain in tourist enclaves, such as resorts. Thus, they directly compete with locals in trendy neighbourhoods.

With few exceptions, subjects were primarily from North and South America. This may be due to affordability, convenience, and time zone requirements. About 40% were from the United States, 14% were from Mexico, and 12% were from Argentina. Many Latin American subjects worked as contractors and freelancers with US companies, earning salaries in dollars.

All subjects were knowledge workers. Several Americans were travelling without their employers' knowledge. They had diverse roles in various industries, such as software technology, professional services, and telecommunications. Notably, these professions have high-turnover rates (Petrone, 2018), and many others work as contractors with inherent job instability.

FINDINGS

The logistical, relational, and socio-personal flux that shapes DN worker identities is best exemplified through subjects' stories, especially through Andres experience. His story echoes important concepts translated in each of my interviews but is presented as an anecdotal through-line.

Andres' Story

I sat across from Andres in the open-plan office in Selina Mexico City. The walls were exposed brick, dotted with gold, industrial light fixtures and burgundy velvet couches. The office was empty. People had finished work and headed out to explore the city. As I began to shuffle through my questions for the first interview nervously, the 22-year-old graphic designer patted my hand and said, 'Relax, there's no rush' as he began to tell me about becoming a digital nomad.

Andres Became Enamoured With the Charm of Mexico City

Originally from Queretaro, Andres was working an unfulfilling administrative job remotely during the pandemic. He had always wanted to travel, and so he trained for a commercial pilots license in early 2021 to make this dream a reality. However, after a few months, he realized being a pilot was not what he was looking for. Andres decided to simply travel through his own country and arrived first at Selina Mexico City and fell in love with the city. The Selina location is right in the historic centre of the city, three blocks from the Palacio de Bellas Artes, as seen in Fig. 5.5. Pretty soon, he knew the city well and began giving tours to friends he met at the hostel. He told me of the immediate inspiration he felt in

Fig. 5.5. Palacio Bellas Artes, a Famous Art Museum, Is a 5 Minute Walk from Selina CDMX.

meeting DNs who had come from all over the world to see his country, and he began to design posters to advertise his tours. One day, he was sitting in the cowork office photoshopping an advertisement when he was approached by a pair of British founders he had met at the bar the previous day. They loved his work and told Andres they would pay him triple their normal rate for an urgent design they needed.

'This is how I began in graphic design. The jobs came out of the desire for the lifestyle. I want to travel, and I need to find jobs that allow me to do this'. Soon, he was creating designs for dozens of clients, most of whom he met through the hostel. Andres also gained professional inspiration from the travelling-working environment.

> As a graphic designer, my work is much better when I am traveling. I have met so many beautiful people, from different countries and with such different perspectives from mine. If you're always sitting in the same white box, you only think of the white box, right? Traveling forces me to think of new ideas and new solutions, especially because design is everywhere.

Andres told me of how his social and professional circle exploded upon becoming a DN, and how his professional value was augmented as a result.

He met friends from Spain and Brazil, Jews and Buddhists, programmers and attorneys, and digital marketers.

> In coworks, you create this impressive network and become more valuable for whoever you work for. Let's say my boss tells me he needs an accountant for a new project, or a really good data analyst to work on a huge problem, I can be like 'I know a guy I met in Tulum!' If you come to me and say you need someone to do 3D dynamic graphics, I think of three people immediately. At the end of the day, who adds more to a company: a person with a network like mine, or someone who only knows the people working in his office building, on the same projects as him?

Andres changed the most as a result of the friendships he formed. While travelling, he met one of his best friends who suggested that he get scuba certified in Cozumel, an island in the Caribbean. A content creator friend would subsidize the costs with his photography. Without work requiring him to be in one place, Andres agreed immediately. He spent weeks cultivating a new identity as a diver, exploring reefs and discovering dream-like underwater scenes. On the island, his network of travelling workers grew. With new people came new perspectives and new clients.

> As a digital nomad, we are always growing. We're not attached to anything, not even a past version of who we were. If I lose my job, I'll find another opportunity, a better one. If I lose my friends, I know I'm going to go to another country and make new ones. If I lose my relationship, I know I will meet someone else who's even more amazing somewhere else. It's a big world out there and we know everything changes.

Andres' professional persona, relational networks, and personal identity underwent rapid and dramatic changes. One may read his story and be tempted to see it as a singular case study of transformation. Yet, a significant majority of subjects identified this cyclical transformation within their own lives. Sydney, a 32-year-old design director from New York, stated clearly:

> I travel alone. I don't know anyone when I go places. It kind of forced me to be more outside of my box, which is cool. It also actually kind of plays into my work role too. I've become bolder now in my personal life, which has made me bolder now in my professional life. Before traveling, I did not have the voice to call things out in an office environment. I'm more managerial than I've ever been. I'm very point blank, whereas before, I was more focused on keeping the peace. It's a lot different now.

As mirrored in most of the interviews, Sydney's statement that she 'became bolder in her personal life and bolder in her professional life' captures the cyclical changes my subjects undergo. DNs regularly change who they are, their relationships, their skills, and how they spend their time. DNs do not simply undergo changes as they travel; they seek them out. They are defined by perpetual flux, and their existence is driven by frequent change to their professional, relational, and social identity. This is exemplified in my findings.

In the following section, I will describe the subtle details of a DN's worker, relational, and social identities. My findings demonstrate that these elements are clearly intertwined. A change in one causes a change in the rest, resulting in a state of constant identity evolution.

Worker Identities

DN worker identities are changing as a result of their ever-permuting network, skill sets, objectives and physical spaces. Subjects changed cities and hostels with different frequencies, with some DNs moving every two weeks and others every six months. It is important to note that throughout my interviews, digital nomads often referred to themselves as 'professionals' and referenced their 'professional identities', in terms of their varied careers, rather than formal professions with the associated norms, history, and institutions. To avoid confusion throughout this paper, I only refer to 'professional identity' when discussing said formal professions, and rather I centre my discussion around 'worker identity', a more broad and more appropriate term. However, when they refer to themselves as professionals, I have kept their language within the given quote.

Unlike traditional backpackers, who work odd jobs and volunteer gigs, DNs are defined by distinct career trajectories. Their jobs give them the ability to live comfortably, sustainable lives through their travels but also imbue them with a sense of purpose. This section outlines how DNs' worker identities are primarily defined by a prioritization of productivity, the non-negotiability of location independence, and an ever-changing workplace.

Some may be tempted to dismiss DNs as unreliable workers, more concerned with catching a wave than completing quality work on time. However, every DN I interviewed insisted on the importance of productivity and professionalism to their identity. Most subjects had set deliverables they needed to complete in a workday, regardless of the hours it took; thus, subjects were motivated to work efficiently to maximize their free time.

> If I want to watch the sunset tonight, or go to yoga in the evening, or go to the beach with friends, I need to finish the work I have. Otherwise, I can't go. It's pretty simple. I am trying to finish as fast as I can. (Anesha, a 23-year-old American marketing coordinator in Sayulita)

Anesha's job allows her the financial and locational freedom to work while travelling. To keep this job, she needs to deliver high-quality work on time. Productivity also a rises from a desire to prove themselves to their employers or clients. One should not read these passages to assume that quality of work does not matter; other DNs clearly state that delivering quality work is also essential. Because of the novelty and uncertainty of this new work arrangement, DNs do not want to risk losing a job that provides them with this freedom.

> I want to be able to show my company that I can do the work. It doesn't matter if I'm here or there. I am going to perform. It is a privilege to be able to travel and work at the same time and I don't want to risk this arrangement. I want to keep living this lifestyle. I do not want my boss to think I am not working. (Javier, a 30-year-old Colombian software engineer in Playa del Carmen)

> I think I have a fear of not being taken seriously, by my boss, by my coworkers. A lot of them are getting married, buying a house, having kids, and I am just here jumping from place to place. I want them to respect me. (Fernando, a 29-year-old Mexican data analyst)

There was a common theme among subjects that they tried to increase their productivity because they felt the need to 'compensate' for the fact they were travelling to their employers. Their desire to 'be taken seriously' is emblematic of their self-identification with their occupation. As Javier noted, he 'wants to keep living this lifestyle'; this goes beyond wanting to surf in his free time. He desires sustainability of his nomadism and feels pressure to augment his performance at work so as not to risk his remote job. In other words, DNs' jobs, and their performance in their roles, are important to how they see themselves and wish to be perceived.

While professionalism is essential to their identities, their specific job is not fixed. Many subjects expressed openness to switch jobs or even learn new skills for an entirely new career, especially if their remote status was threatened. To understand how much location independence mattered, subjects were asked: 'If your company were to return to a hybrid mode, how much of a salary raise (as a percentage of current salary) would you need to consider a return?'

A staggering 70% said they would not consider a return to office, no matter the pay raise. According to 35 DNs, freedom is worth more than any raise. This indicates a poignant distinction between how economists have traditionally conceptualized the trade-off between labour and leisure time (Kool & Botvinick, 2014).

> I would quit my job tomorrow if they told me that I had to come back. My priority is to travel. I can get another remote job in one week. (Sydney, 32-year-old American design manager in Mexico City)

> I'm already getting paid a lot. It just wouldn't be worth my time to go back. 20k or 30k is not going to upgrade anything in my lifestyle at all. The next upgrade is going to be 250k but that's out of [my employers'] price range. Some people in my role see the next big upgrade as working for Google or the big tech companies. However, I did not want to risk giving up the freedom that I have with this job. (Nick, 33-year-old American product manager in Sayulita)

Nick highlights that neither a financial upgrade nor a promotion to a high-status company would outweigh the advantages of being a DN. While they want jobs that give them direction and purpose, the main element they value in a job is the remote status that allows them to have a transitory lifestyle.

What is so valuable about remote status for the professional objectives of DNs? Why would they forgo security, community, and professional advancement in pursut of this lifestyle? Primarily, subjects cite being happier, more inspired, and more balanced while they travel. They are also concerned with network and professional enrichment. Thus, meeting highly skilled nomadic workers is a valuable lifestyle feature.

Cowork hostels, such as Selina, attract DNs through their amenities and promise of stable internet, but DNs look for workspaces to meet one another. They are attracted to the prospect of an ever-changing professional network. At any given time, one was equally likely to find a software engineer building a complex security algorithm, or a digital marketer implementing a Google Ads campaign, or a graphic designer creating 3D images to sell as NFTs. By virtue of working and living in the Selina space, DNs get access to highly specialized individuals and their diverse skill sets. A constantly changing network means freelancers can access unique client pools, and employees enrich their skills in ways a traditional office could not offer.

> [As a graphic designer], I meet a lot of my clients in coworking spaces. People are very open about their work and there is high demand for good designers. It may be less stable, but I have access to so many clients traveling I wouldn't if I was in one place. (Andres, a 22-year-old Mexican graphic designer in Mexico City)

> When you stay in one place, your perspective is limited. Companies are looking for people that know how to work remotely, and while you travel, you feel that there is opportunity. The people I meet at Selina are worth way more than a 20% raise. I know that if I want to start a company later on, I can message you and you'll be down to chat. (Raul, a 35-year-old Colombian CSM in Oaxaca City)

The benefit of an impermanent office lies in the people they meet, as Raul notes. Because DN's networks are far-reaching, they are always playing the role of mediator between parties looking for a connection. While DNs connect through Selina, surprisingly, they did not network within the physical cowork space. While DNs wanted to be around other professionals to keep them accountable, they did not necessarily want to interact with them during the workday. The cowork was a dedicated and focused space to work silently and individually and established a clear separation between socializing and work, with few interactions to distract.

> Within the cowork, there is not a culture of talking about what you do or just chatting. If you are sitting on your laptop, people won't disturb you because you're in a flow state. Everyone is working so you feel pressure to be productive too. I use the cowork to get my tasks done so that I can actually go and do other things. (Caroline 25-year-old American CSM)

Outside of the physical cowork office, however, skill sharing and networking are commonplace within DN communities, such as Selina. This can be attributed to the lack of a competitive culture within hostel coworks. People work fewer hours than in a traditional office, and DNs generally work on separate projects or companies. Time that, in a traditional office setting, would be dedicated to mentoring junior employees, allows for skill sharing and building connections among DNs. In Playa del Carmen, I witnessed a data analyst helping a freelance journalist understand the reach of her articles through her website's metrics. Suddenly, this journalist had acquired new knowledge that enhanced her ability to do her job. Every new connection may lead to a new skill or a job opportunity. The growth of their networks actively changes their worker identity, as it changes their professional network, their role, and their knowledge and skill sets (Fitzgerald, 2020).

The value of an ever-changing professional network also lies in the potential for new business partners. Subjects also tended to gravitate towards entrepreneurship. Many DNs work in high-demand, high-turnover careers, such as data analysts and programmers, and know the value of their skills in their competitive labour market. Some 22% of interviewees owned their own businesses, and another 30% were freelancers or independent contractors. While the other 48% were full-time employees, three of four subjects said they had entrepreneurial aspirations. They wanted to work for themselves or create passive income sources, such as e-commerce or real estate.

> I want to find a way to make this more sustainable. Working for a company, they can fire you whenever they want, especially as a contractor. If I continue doing this, I want my own business, my own income. (Javier, a 30-year-old Colombian Software Engineer in Playa del Carmen)

It was unsurprising that Javier noted the importance of financial autonomy to DNs. However, he highlights a challenging element of their professional lives: employment instability. Many were navigating uncertain norms in travelling and working concurrently – not necessarily breaking the rules but stretching them.

However, job instability is something many of them faced in their home countries as well. In an increasingly unstable labour market, a highly mobile, highly competitive workforce faces global competition and diminishing social benefits (Amman, Carpenter, & Neff, 2015). As described in 'Surviving the New Economy', many workers welcome risk in pursuit of an element of satisfaction or personal growth (Amman et al., 2015). This notion was salient in my interviews; DNs understand they can lose their jobs, but for many, this instability is similar to their home countries. According to the findings of this paper, all those pursuing this lifestyle accept risk as a part of their professional reality. For this reason, many gravitate towards financial independence, like Javier.

On this subject, Raul continued:

> Nomads are incredibly startup-oriented because they inherently think outside of the norms of society. If I am looking to start a business, I am going to want the most creative, determined, experienced partners I can find. I want to work with people who have seen the world and have diverse perspectives, not people that have only worked in an office their whole career.

The DN community attracts creative, entrepreneurial individuals. Raul said, when he decides to start a business, he wants to work with DNs due to their innovative and self-starter attitudes. For many nomads, building a network of DN professionals is an investment in their future as entrepreneurs.

A fascinating dynamic arose among coworkers who work in the same physical office as professionals who are not in the same role or company. As they are not competing for jobs, projects, or promotions, DNs exhibited a degree of openness with each other. Unlike a regular office dynamic, with set social hierarchies and norms, DNs can have a more relaxed and authentic workplace identity. Alejandro, a software engineer in Sayulita, explained how he felt much less pressure to maintain a professional image in the office.

> I am free to dress how I like. I am always in shorts, and flip flops, compared to when I was in an office and had to dress in a proper way. That changed when I started traveling, because who do I have to impress? I'll get promoted if I do good work, not based on my appearance. (Alejandro, 43-year-old Mexican software engineer)

This attitude was common among subjects, who paid little attention to their physical image among the cowork, dressing how they liked and generally avoiding social interactions. The norms differed in different coworks. For example, people tended to have more casual conversations within bigger coworks, such as Mexico City, as the office space was bigger than Sayulita, where sound was carried easily. In Puerto Escondido, many DNs opted to come to the office barefoot and slip out for a midday surf. No one really judged each other for how they decided to show up. This is an interesting issue that warrants further investigation.

The lack of fixed norms and the inherent temporariness of the cowork space means people have little to lose by representing themselves authentically in the office and creating 'office friendships' that are distinctly not intra-company relationships, with all the strings attached. I recall working in the Guadalajara office with the two subjects I interviewed. James, an Australian HR manager, was on a call with his coworkers, and on the pad of paper next to him scribbling, 'This girl is annoying the living daylights out of me', and slid it to Nahuel, an Argentinian product manager, as he tried to swallow his laughter while reviewing his code on his own work call. These light-hearted interactions were common among cowork friendships, without the intent of creating drama within Selina or distracting one another. Selina gossip differs from inter-office gossip, which could lead to sabotage, inefficiency, and issues within company dynamics; Selina 'coworkers' are not intra-company coworkers, who collaborate on projects and experience interpersonal office dynamics.

DNs do not have a distinct workplace 'role' to play within the Selina office; thus, their workplace identity changes as quickly and often as they change the offices. DNs form close relationships with each other, leading to light-hearted office dynamics, skill sharing, and often entrepreneurial connections. Since they are highly motivated and self-accountable professionals, they enter workspaces with clear objectives for their workday; thus, the offices themselves serve to allow workers to achieve personalized, silent, efficient workflows.

Overall, DN worker identities are shaped by frequent changes in physical workplaces, social/professional networks, office norms and roles, and career ambitions. They prioritize productivity and efficiency to sustain their lifestyles. Logistical flux – namely location independence – matters greatly to DN worker identity.

Relational Identities

Since DNs are always changing their physical environment, they have very high social turnover. As such, their relational identity – how they define themselves with relation to others – consistently changes (Brown, 2019). In most stable social environments, people act within expectations of their roles. One's 'role identity' according to IT, is defined by managing behaviours and social image to fit with a role, taking advantage of resources that the role could normatively possess, or mediating relationships between individuals with different roles (Hogg & Ridgeway, 2003; Stets & Burke, 2009). There are usually certain social expectations of people within a social network. However, because of the inherent transitivity of their social environment, DNs uniquely have no fixed social or professional roles to fill. The people surrounding them constantly change, meaning they have few obligations to the strangers they share a hostel with, and only loose social expectations are placed upon them. Goffman (1956) proposed that individuals perform theatrical performances to match those they share space with, and identity originates from these collective performances. In DN spaces, social performances are less oriented around rigid role expectations.

The inherent transitivity of their social situation means people represent themselves more authentically. There is nothing to gain from playing a certain social role.

> I feel so much more social here [in hostels] because there's just less pressure. If I get along with someone, great, and if I don't like someone, that's fine, I never have to see them again. It feels like people are just more open. (Daniella, 40-year-old data science manager in Puerto Escondido)

Openness to new connections was a recurring theme in interviews. It originated from a combination of factors. A selection bias should be noted: as they are incredibly social environments, hostels might attract more social individuals than DNs who choose to travel through Airbnb. DNs tend to travel alone, so making new friends is vital for social support and community. Thus, opportunities to make friends occur throughout the day, at breakfast in the shared kitchen, during morning yoga, or at social events.

As Daniella explains, people have little to lose because if they do not get along with someone, they 'never have to see them again'. DNs referred to the 'time crunch' as the need to take advantage of the short time they were in one place; there was a 'now or never' attitude to make friends. This makes them more willing to be vulnerable and share their past experiences as travellers. They often dole out advice on which were good for internet stability, thrilling activities, and unique experiences. Consider the openness necessary to get 50 people to explain to a stranger the difficulties of travelling, family background, value systems, professional journeys, and the most intimate elements of their identity. I had hundreds more informal conversations. That would never happen in New York or San Francisco office building. DNs must build trust and connections quickly to battle the loneliness and chaos of solo travel.

Still, social burnout is a prevalent theme that accompanies digital nomadism. People come to hostels to find connection, but loneliness is common. This was mentioned in essentially every interview. Individuals would cite the exhaustion they would feel in making connections they knew were transient. People are open to new connections, but travellers live with the knowledge they have to say goodbye several weeks later. I experienced this first hand, as I had been travelling and staying in hostels for nine weeks, though only for 7–14 days at a time. By the end of the research trip, I was exhausted when trying to socialize and was missing friends from past locations. This plagued subjects, but loneliness was acknowledged as the price to pay for this lifestyle.

> I think there's a sense of loneliness digital nomads share. You meet a lot of people, very interesting people, but most of them are transitive. They're just around for a week or two. It is a lonely lifestyle, especially if you travel by yourself. This lifestyle is not for everyone. You have to really want it. But it's about you getting to know more of the world and understanding new cultures and new people, and doing it right now because you're young. And yes, sometimes it's lonely and it's sad, but loneliness is not forever. (Fernando, 29-year-old data specialist in Puerto Escondido)

Across all locations, DNs tended to form closer relationships with each other, rather than with travellers who stayed for a few days at a time. This makes sense. DNs usually stayed in one place for several weeks and got to know each other. The social separation was not rigid. DNs did interact with travellers, but they gravitated to other working professionals. Daniella explained:

> I stayed in a Selina that was all backpackers – a non-stop, crazy party – and then went to another one which was super quiet and super chill. I really liked it better because I met a bunch of other people who are a little bit older. They were all working full time.

When I asked her why she liked being with other digital nomads better, she cited being able to relate more closely to other workers, in terms of sustainability and work constraints.

> Digital nomads tend to stay in one place longer. I mean, it's really fun to meet someone and go party with them for like two nights, but then they leave and you're just having the same conversation with people over and over again, versus if you're in the same place with somebody for an entire month, you get to know them better and can actually build a community.

These DN social groups were vital for the sustainability of their lifestyle. I often observed DNs making plans to travel to a new location together, often to hold on to a sense of community or belonging for longer. Subjects always arrived at a place with loose or non-existent plans for their next destination. DNs made residential and travel decisions, based on friends they would meet and recommendations of fellow travellers. A group in Playa del Carmen had known each other for three weeks and had travelled to Isla Mujeres together to work there for a week. It was common to see DNs discussing which locations in Mexico, Guatemala, and Colombia had the best attractions, DN social life, and working conditions. Many would make plans to continue onwards together.

While their immediate social circles are always changing, DNs are part of a greater interconnected social network with many overlapping nodes. This was vividly exemplified through social media, especially Instagram, a casual but widely used way to stay in contact. DNs use the 'mutual connections' feature to see what followers they have in common and find social overlap. Importantly, their immediate social circles constantly change as they move from place to place, but they are part of a more highly connected network.

As it is normal for people to emulate the goals and perspectives of those around them, so do DNs inherently become more and more like their peers in coworking hostels the longer they travel. As people travel with diverse perspectives and goals, DNs' identities change differently and unexpectedly. The changes in their social networks cause DNs to explore places, passions, and value systems only galvanized by new connections. This relational flux changes DN's professional networks, skills, and aspirations as they regularly meet new people who inspire them. Their worker identity evolved as a result.

Social and Personal Identities

As DNs tend to emulate the objectives and interests of the people they meet, their socio-personal identities are always changing. Personal identities are actively constructed; people can shape their identity to who they believe to be and what they care about (Luckman, 2008). Meanwhile, social identities refer to one's belonging to a social group, and their feelings towards their membership (Vignoles, 2018). Personal and social identity are conjoined in this section, as Vignoles argues, identity formation resulting from psychological (internal) definers of identity are inextricably linked to sociocultural (external) definers. In the case of DNs, it is most fascinating to discover whether personal or social elements are more important in the self-definition of identity.

DNs' personal identities were exemplified by what they talked about and how they made choices. Their small talk would focus on the places they had travelled to and the things they had done rather than on work or politics or nationality. People's conversations often skipped the banter about work stress or current events or who they knew in common. They went straight into talking about inspiring experiences or unique locations they have travelled to.

There was even a recurring joke about 'travel small talk' referring to the recounting of destinations DNs had visited and what they had done in each place.

It was customary for people to begin to describe the countries they had visited thus far, the challenges of travelling, and often finding mutual connections they made on the road. This led DNs to describe what had brought them to each place and allowed them to, within minutes of meeting a new person, share the passions and identity-forming activities they had been pursuing in recent months.

DNs defined themselves by the hobbies and interests that brought them to new cities and that they had picked up along the way. As noted in the literature review, socio-personal identities are defined by one's membership in social groups and one's personal values and interests. DNs are defined more by personal interests since belonging to fixed groups is not as important to them.

> Everyone that I meet, we're all here for the same purposes and for the same reasons. It's almost surreal how relatable someone is to you and you guys don't even come from the same place or upbringing. We connect over where we are now, rather than where we come from. (Georgia, 40-year-old American research instructor)

Until now, my findings have been based on my observations, experiences, and critical analysis of interviews. The following section provides DNs' own self-definition of their identities. It is intuitive that nomadic individuals would have weaker ties to social organizations, but the results were overwhelming. People are traditionally defined by their origin and their belief systems. Subjects were asked to identify the most and least important definers of their identity (Fig. 5.6): 92% of subjects said national identity was the least defining quality. They cited nationality as 'inauthentic' ('Anesha', Subject 0216), 'not something you choose about yourself' ('Fernando', Subject 0429). Several described themselves as 'a child of the world' (Subjects 0216, 0217, 0748, 0105, 0107).

> Countries put in separation if we are from different religions or political or nations. But [nomads] are not from just one country. We are not from one religion. We are not reflected by politicians. We are just people who want to travel around the world and work and be ourselves. (Nahuel, 26-year-old Argentine product manager in Guadalajara)

> I don't see why nationality has to identify us. We are all citizens of the world. A lot of the time, nationalities can keep you tied to one place, and it generates rivalries and separations. (Leon, 29-year-old Swiss data analyst in Isla Mujeres)

Ninety-four percent of subjects indicated that political affiliation defined their identity least, and 98% valued religion last. It is fascinating to consider what impact this ideological detachment may have on DN professional impact and migratory decisions in the future.

> I don't want to deal with politics. I don't want to vote for people that I think are idiots, especially in a country where I'm not living. I don't want to have to worry about what other people's decisions affect my life. (James, 23-year-old Australian HR manager in Guadalajara)

The implication of these findings is that DNs living and working outside of their home country feel that political decisions do not affect them. Political and national detachment could undoubtedly impact their work, if they lack a sense of responsibility for the ethical and social ramifications of their work. This is an

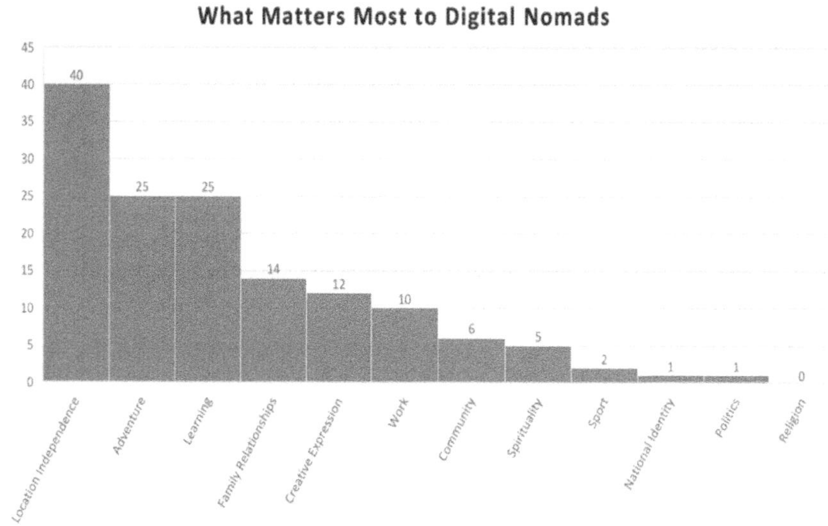

Fig. 5.6. Location Independence, Adventure and Learning Define Nomads' Identities Most, While They Cast Off Nationality, Politics and Religion.

important realization. Knowledge workers who work or consult for major companies and financial institutions, write software, and design ads the public sees, feel detached from their work's social and political ramifications.

If subjects are detached from institutions that have defined people for generations, how do they define themselves? For most, travelling and location independence was their identity. Callie, a 24-year-old Canadian videographer, said, 'I identify most with the nationality of a nomad'. A majority (80%) cited 'location independence' as their biggest identifier. In essence, they defined themselves as nomads above all else.

> Location independence doesn't mean I always want to travel always, it means I want to have the independence of whether I travel or not, or if I move or not. Or if I stay in an apartment, but I always have that independence and that freedom. (Enrique, 35-year-old Argentine data analyst in Isla Mujeres)

Professional location independence allowed subjects to design their lives around their passions and goals. Yet, DN's interests and passions change as they move from place to place. Ben, an American marketing director for a startup, explained, while sipping a cappuccino and watching the waves crash, how Puerto Escondido's legendary surf brought him to this town.

> Down here, I just do what I want, and I work around that. Yesterday, there was really good surf and I surfed three times, and worked from 8pm to midnight to make up for it. [Surf] is the reason I am here. I think I probably take advantage of the fact that nobody's watching me, but I make sure emails are answered. And my job gets done.

People also pursued the lifestyle to focus on goals of personal enrichment. Georgia shared her weight-loss journey with me. She became a DN and changed her social circle and work routine to make healthy living a larger part of who she was.

> I have not been as productive workwise as I would like to have been here, but I also lost 13 pounds. That's a win for me. My main goal in coming to Mexico is to be healthier overall. I have been trying to lose weight for years, but my 9-5 kept getting in the way. I needed a change. (Georgia, 40-year-old American research instructor in Sayulita)

Fig. 5.7a–d shows some attractive elements of various Selina locations. When not attached to a location for the sake of a job, DNs describe new opportunities to define themselves.

> If I am not subject to my employer, it allows me to relocate to a new place for a passion. For instance, if I want to live at some location for six months while I get my [pilot] license, I can still have my corporate job. (Fernando, 29-year-old Mexican Data Analyst)

(a) The famous Zicatela surf break pictured from the roof of Selina Puerto Escondido

(b) Selina Isla Mujeres has an on-site scuba diving shop opposite their cowork office

(c) The yoga studio in Selina Sayulita overlooks the ocean. They hold classes daily.

(d) La Guelaguetza, the indigenous cultural celebration of Oaxaca, in 2022.

Fig. 5.7. What Attracts Digital Nomads to Their Respective Locations?

DNs' identities transmute beyond work, politics, nationality, and traditional attachments, and when asked the biggest definers of their identity, they defined themselves primarily by 'location independence', 'adventure', and 'learning'. This exemplifies how DNs define themselves actively by seeking change. Location independence implies an allowance for geographic change, with the objective of seeking new experiences. Adventure refers to seeking new experiences out of their comfort zone, and subjects described the uptake of new hobbies and skills as them seeking adventure. Learning constitutes the pursuit of new skills or knowledge, and changing of one's identity inherently accompanies learning. DNs define their personal identity not by static characteristics but by dynamic growth processes and changes to their persona.

All subjects had reasons for coming to Mexico and breaking away from their routine. Leon is a Swiss data analyst, but he was in Isla Mujeres to learn scuba diving. Anesha described her desire to balance yoga and physical exercise with her marketing job, and picked Selina for its focus on wellness. Nahuel is an Argentine product manager by day, but he came to Guadalajara to organize parties and DJ by night. Raul is a Colombian client success manager, but he planned July to attend the Oaxacan festival of Guelaguetza. When I was in Oaxaca, I actually ran into Alberto, a 37-year-old Honduran-American product designer who I had interviewed in Mexico City. He had planned to stay in Mexico City for several more weeks, but had met a friend at the hostel who was planning to go to Guelaguetza, and so he changed his plans to experience it. This highlights an important element of DN decision making; small talk turns into people making residential choices based on conversations with others, whose desires, plans, and experiences inspire them to go to a new place. A single conversation can inspire one to move to a new city for a month and may lead them to a new hobby that will define their identity differently.

Social identity is constructed through physical and psychological categorizations – being in the same space and time and being a member of the same social classification. DNs' social identities are changing because their physical group is changing. People cycle through, but the psychological belonging to the category of 'DN' or 'working traveler' remains the same, giving it a distinctness and objectivity while remaining in flux (Reicher, 2011; Turner, 1982). In essence, DNs define their personal identity by ongoing evolution of passions, beliefs, and goals. This, in turn, characterizes their worker identity by this intentional flux.

A Digital Nomad's Identity in Flux

In investigating the research question, 'How does the logistical, socio-personal, and relational flux experienced by digital nomads shape their worker identity?', this study finds that a DN's identity is not just changing regularly; its inherent state of flux actively defines it. Most people usually seek stability in at least one identity category (e.g. professional, relational, or socio-personal), originating from our need to belong (Allen, Gray, Baumeister, & Leary 2021). DNs are distinct, not only because each of those identities are in flux, but also because DNs consciously seek that flux. When one category changes, other identity elements change as well, creating a cyclical feedback loop. Let's revisit the case of Andres.

Andres' main objective was to travel. He underwent significant changes to his worker, relational, and socio-personal identity to achieve this. His work role transformed from an administrator to a pilot, then to a graphic designer. His professional network expanded to include people from different backgrounds with diverse skill sets; thus, his skillset grew. He told me how a friend introduced him to designing NFTs and listing them online. This example highlights how a digital nomad's worker identity morphs as a consequence of the diversity of talent and culture they are surrounded with; for Andres, this lifestyle also sparked a new entrepreneurial idea.

> I was inspired by my conversations with nomads to create a company to connect freelance designers with digital nomad founders. I want to build this marketplace to connect people in the way I have been connected throughout my career.

His professional network and skillset changed due to his changing social network. It should be noted that change in Andres' DN life was initiated by his arriving at a new hostel, with a brand-new social circle; then his professional relationships changed as a result.

> I have noticed this pattern in travelers – we're all really friendly and looking for new connections. I could literally go right now to the bar and end up being friends with the person I sit next to by the end of the night. On a daily basis, you meet at least five or six new people. Just imagine what that does for your professional network. You are always meeting friends or clients or potential collaborators or future girlfriends, and you can be whoever you want.

As relational networks changed for Andres, he could represent himself more authentically because there was no pre-established social role for him to play among the new people he met. He found himself behaving more like an extrovert and mediator than he had prior to travelling without fear of judgement.

One best friend Andres met at Selina persuaded him to become a scuba diver. He described how diving became his whole life; it was all he talked and thought about. For several months, his personal identity revolved around diving, and so did his social network. As he met new people diving in Cozumel, his professional network expanded even more, and he took on projects he never would have worked on had he not gone to the island.

This is my core finding: when digital nomads change social networks, they also change their worker and personal identities. When their personal identities change as they pursue new interests in new places, their social circles change again, which then causes them to gain new professional skills, grow entrepreneurial ambitions, and grow their professional network. Because digital nomads live in perpetual relational and situational flux, their worker identities are constantly changing, either because they acquire new jobs, entrepreneurial goals, connections, skills, or professional knowledge.

The dynamic cycle in DN identity is illustrated in detail in Fig. 5.8. It details the mechanisms by which a shift in one element of identity inevitably causes a shift in at least one other, leading to further changes in the next.

Fig. 5.8 contains two congruent cycles; one can begin at one node and follow the cycle in either direction; of note, one node can influence the two to either side. Moving clockwise from worker identity (centre top), one follows how the

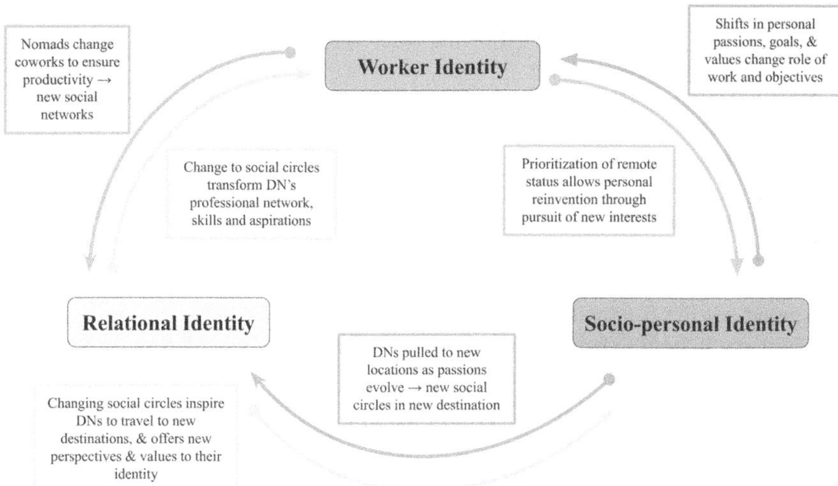

Fig. 5.8. The Cyclical Evolution of Digital Nomads' Identities.

prioritization of remote status enables digital nomads to develop their socio-personal identity in accordance with new passions. As their personal identities change (lower right), nomads travel to new places to pursue interests and thus find new social circles (lower left). This change in their social network cultivates new professional connections, skills, and perspectives on work. Moving counterclockwise from worker identity, one can see how DNs change workplaces to enforce productive habits, again exposing them to new social environments. As they meet new people, DNs are inspired to discover new places and absorb novel perspectives to their socio-personal identity. As their personal values and goals change, so too will their career persona and professional goals, to align with shifting personal goals. This is an ongoing cycle DNs expect, pursue, and embrace in their travels.

Andres' story illustrates this cycle; he sought a shift in his relational identity, changing his worker and social identities. This constant iteration of self is what he sought in the beginning of his travels.

> In Queretaro, I was caught up in the same circles, doing the same thing every day. I felt like I hadn't changed in years. This is really why I started traveling, to grow.

It should also be noted that these shifts do not happen accidentally; DNs actively seek these changes in their identity. They will have one conversation that inspires them to learn to surf in Puerto Escondido, or get to know the crypto community in Tulum, or learn Oaxacan cooking. This geographic change will fundamentally shift how they spend their time, thus changing the people in their social circle and, ultimately, their professional network. One may be tempted to view Andres' story as an isolated example of this evolutionary cycle, but identity evolution was observed in every interview for all DN nomads in the dataset.

Importantly, identity evolution does not always follow the same pattern: A shift can occur in any category first, but the interconnectedness of each categorical shift initiates a feedback cycle.

Nick began as a DN, staying in rented apartments. As a consequence of working alone, his productivity began to decline. He thus sought Selina as an office space which helped keep himself accountable. His workplace network, schedule, and environment changed his worker identity. The change in his coworker network in Selina was accompanied by a new social network, and the chance to reinvent himself socially. The friends he formed within the hostel inspired him to take up surfing, and he travelled to Sayulita to pursue this new passion. Surfing consumed his life for weeks. He became friends with the local surfing community and spent hours surfing each morning. His social and relational identities changed due to seeking a different workplace.

DNs are not only freelancers or entry-level employees. Consider the case of Omar, a 37-year-old American tech company founder and CEO. Omar kindly sat down with me, despite not sleeping all night as he coordinated urgent product improvements while a techno party raged in the hostel. He worked from Selina for the stable Wi-Fi, but stability is not always guaranteed.

> Imagine that your job is to deliver a service or fix a problem, and your internet goes down and you suddenly can't. It's like you are operating a restaurant and you don't have the ingredients.

Even though for many DNs, this work style is not the most stable or convenient, they refuse to give it up. Omar has been a DN since 2009. I asked him what made the regular troubles worth it over a traditional office with consistent Wi-Fi and better focus.

> I like change, I like changing environments. I like to learn from different cultures. I like to meet people I wouldn't have met at home. I am inspired a lot of the time by the people I meet in coworks and Mexicans I meet wherever I go. I think traveling makes me a better CEO, because I am better under stress and can work with very different people.

A DNs' identity is not just constantly changing but rather actively defined by its inherent and purposeful state of flux. The people working as DNs and the companies hiring them see their identity evolution as a feature and not a bug. DNs are always seeking interesting people and experiences to absorb the values, skills, and objectives of those they meet, which profoundly shapes who they are. This process causes DNs to constantly grow into more adaptable, creative professionals and more open-minded, fulfilled individuals.

DISCUSSION

This paper presents three significant and novel contributions to the literature on the sociology of work and to the growing academic discourse on digital nomadism.

First, the study provides a detailed image of a DN's professional life and situates their worker identity in the literature on liminality (Reed & Thomas, 2019). Traditionally, working professionals were tied to a specific geographic area to maintain high-paying careers (Florida, 2010). This study shows DNs reject this constraint, and instead documents how their worker identity revolves around their nomadism. Their worker identities exist in a state of purposeful liminality, as described by Beech (2010); they are constantly between skill sets, knowledge pools, professional networks, and career opportunities. This state of perpetual flux is one they actively seek, and they either pursue or tolerate instability in their worker identity for the advantages offered by permanent travelling. The constant professional liminality of DNs can be seen as a permanent state of reinvention, as seen in other professional contexts such as in consulting or marketing roles (Czarniawska & Mazza, 2003; Loacker & Sullivan, 2016). DNs are a distinct and relatively novel subset of the workforce not previously defined by liminality. DNs self-identify with an ever-growing professional network, a changing skill set, and constant exposure to new professional opportunities. Regular changes in DNs' lifestyles and locations imply regular changes to their work environments, office social circles, and outlooks on the role of work in their life. Compiling these factors yields a new type of worker identity whereby regular changes to worker identity define DNs. The ability to travel and work concurrently is extremely important to who they are, and as a result, DN's sacrifice promotions and pay raises, and are even willing to switch jobs, to maintain their ability to be nomadic. This aligns with research showing workers' high valuation of remote arrangements (Barrero et al., 2021; Mas & Pallais, 2017). However, DNs' identity centres on location independence; accordingly, most DNs reject offers to return to office work, no matter the monetary sacrifice. This follows Reay and Hinings findings that individuals do not uptake work practices that do not fit with their identity (2009).

Second, I describe the role dynamics, or lack thereof, within cowork spaces and DN hostels at large, and how these dynamics shape their worker identities. While DN cowork space has been studied (Nash et al., 2020), the social dynamics and their role in defining DNs' identity within them have not been contextualized within social role theory. For the most part, role theory and literature on workplace identity is focused on relationships within stable environments (Stets & Burke, 2000). A DNs' workplace identity (Agostini, 2004) is in flux because the offices from which they worked are inherently impermanent, along with the norms and dynamics within each space. DNs regularly face a new, clean social slate; thus, there is simply not enough time to establish and enforce 'behavioral expectations associated with given positions in a social structure' (Ebaugh, 1988, p. 18). Analyzing DN relationships within inherently transitive spaces offers a novel perspective to understand how impermanent office norms and relationships can influence a worker's professional outlook and ambitions. DNs tend to display striking social openness, enabling consistent growth of their professional network, skills, and knowledge. This study provides a detailed account of DNs' cowork dynamics that is missing from the literature and shines a light into how worker identities form in transitive workplaces, outside organizational roles. Remarkably, many definitions of worker identity simply do not apply to DNs who work outside of a physical company office. For instance, because the remote workers at Selina never worked at the same firm, digital nomads did not dictate their daily workplace interactions according to hierarchies and advantageous dynamics (Kahn & Katz, 1978). As DNs do not physically work amongst their company peers, nomads lack strict workplace roles; in fact, DNs cited an ability to represent themselves authentically within the cowork space, including the ability to wear the clothes they want, avoid social interactions or abstain from makeup and even shoes. As a result, there are no set expectations of how nomads in the cowork 'should' interact, or hierarchical nuances one may find within a 'normal' office, regardless of their rank or prestige. Digital nomads thus deviate from defining their worker identity by any fixed workplace norms, specifically because they do not have a rigid workplace role to fill. This paper is the first to focus on cowork workplace dynamics for digital nomads, positing insights that extend into discussions on changing workplaces. Working from a company office is increasingly uncommon as work transforms, and corporations like Meta and Chevron are rapidly selling office real estate (McLean, 2022). As more workers opt to work from office spaces they do not share with intra-company coworkers, analyzing workplace identity in unconventional workplaces will have added importance for studying the future of work and worker identity.

Third, I present a novel framework of the cycle driving the evolution of DNs' identities (Fig. 5.8). While past studies individually identified the flux in social circles, professional goals and perspectives, or personal identity work, this paper proposes a cyclical mechanism by which interrelated factors drive identity evolution among DNs. DNs prioritize travel because they seek change and aspire to grow. As such, they make decisions supportive of their self-concept. They define themselves above all, by their embrace of location independence, adventure, and desire to learn. Each of these traits is inherently defined by change. As DNs pursue new activities and interests, their physical and relational situations change. Most DNs are unwilling to give up the ability to pursue new desires in new places, unbridled by geographic constraints; thus, the majority reject offers to return to office, no matter the monetary sacrifice. Unlike past studies, I describe in detail how the regular changes in physical environments shift DNs social circles, which changes their professional network makeup and the skillsets and knowledge bases they are exposed to. The change in social circles changes the activities and definers discussed in DNs social environments, which inevitably leads to changes in their personal objectives and definers. The desire to pursue new personal projects or interests galvanize DNs to travel to new locations, meet new people, which then reshapes their worker identities. As workers, DNs reap ample personal and professional benefits from this ever-changing state; accordingly DNs define their worker identities by the benefits reaped and sacrificed needed to preserve their remote work status. While past studies have either identified the impacts of changing social circles on worker identities, or on personal self-image, or have related changing personal self-image to worker identity, this study contributes a novel mechanism linking all three elements of identity in a cyclical feedback loop. Understanding this mechanism for the dynamic evolution of DNs' self-image provides an important picture of these workers, what they care about, and how they make decisions. This information will be important as this labour trend grows and continues to influence the globe.

This study has strengths and limitations. Ethnographic research is a powerful tool for understanding people's motivations and decision-making processes, but it has limited control over sample makeup. Here, interviews were conducted from a convenience sample; subjects tended to be younger, male, and extroverted. In future research, it would be beneficial to analyze identity formation in a larger subject pool and to control for career, age, race, and nationality. This study focused on the symbiosis among socio-personal, relational, and worker identities within the cowork spaces. In future studies, it would be fascinating to explore the transitions of intra-company remote work relationships for DNs. This study documented DNs business-owning aspirations, but further study is required to understand when and why DNs decide to undertake entrepreneurship and how this decision is shaped by the people they meet while travelling.

Further investigation is needed into the growing markets for products, technology patents, and infrastructures to support digital nomadism. As more people replace a physical office with a cowork desk, the techno-tourism industry is likely to grow rapidly. Selina, the setting for this study, raised $395 million from four investment rounds. The company launched its IPO in late 2022 and aimed for a $1.2 billion valuation (O'Neill, 2022). Scholars should pay close attention to the infrastructure that supports nomads, as it is becoming a multi-billion dollar industry that is expected to see strong growth.

This study provides an in-depth overview of DNs' institutional identities, or lack thereof. In a future study, it would be fruitful to analyze how workplace norms vary among different cowork spaces, as discussed on page 24. Additionally, DNs loosen their ties to their nationality, political affiliation, and organized religion. But how does political and nationalistic detachment impact the work done by DNs? If, for example, a software engineer has little understanding of the risk of political radicalization posed by a product algorithm they designed, is a moral objection to the work less likely that with a worker living in their home country? If people cannot feel the socio-political impacts of their work, will their professional decisions be shaped solely by their own gain or personal circumstance? These questions are already salient in the business ethics field (Dempsey, 2015; Smith & Dubbink, 2011) and can yield fruitful future work. It is important to understand these factors and how DN status may change the ethical and political relationship of DNs with their work.

This research offers a relevant and fascinating perspective on the future of organizational structures. DNs make extensive efforts to prioritize detachment to pursue travel (Andino-Frydman, 2022). The world is already bearing witness to the massive impacts of digital nomadism on remote work policies, tax structures, and visa programs for remote workers. What is the global and local impact of having more people with the ability to define themselves by their passions, as opposed to hierarchical work dynamics and static definitions of social membership? How will young people make choices about their lives, and how will these decisions affect global migration and labour trends?

The remote work revolution is undeniable and more people are prioritizing travel now than in any past generation. As such, digital nomadism is expected to keep growing and evolving. Governments and private actors alike have capitalized upon the popularization of digital nomadism. Now, there is ample opportunity in academia to explore this exciting research area and build upon the novel findings in this paper.

DEDICATION

Writing this paper has been an incredible labour of love. It has been the most intellectually challenging and stimulating thing I have ever done, especially as it felt semi-autobiographical. As I travelled between study sites, I felt myself changing just as I saw my subjects evolve. I became more patient, curious, and excited about all life has to offer. I would leave each place with a new passion to pursue or country I wanted to visit, and I owe all of this to my wonderful subjects. Thank you for inspiring me and explaining with vulnerability and openness why you have chosen to pursue the path less taken.

I am incredibly indebted to my parents, Judith Frydman and Raul Andino, my friends, and my mentors who encouraged and supported me in digging deep into my countless research questions. I want to thank Emilia Diaz, Chloe Shrager, and Natalie Milan in particular for the hours spent on FaceTime on unstable jungle wifi as we talked through these complex concepts. Thank you to the RSW Editors for your thoughtful feedback throughout the editing process and to my advisors, Nick Bloom and Gabe Wolfenstein, at Stanford University, for your patient guidance in the last year. I could not have done this without you.

I hope you enjoy the story I tell through this research, and it inspires you to think a bit differently about the nature of work and how we ought to structure our lives in this new age. The world is changing and we must pay attention to how we change with it.

Thank you,
Alma Andino-Frydman

REFERENCES

Abbott, A. (1988). The system of professions. https://doi.org/10.7208/chicago/9780226189666.001.0001.

Agostino, J. (2004). *Workplace identity*. Thesis, Swinburne Research Bank.

Albert, S., & Whetten, D. (1985). Organizational identity. *Research in Organizational Behavior*, *7*, 263–295.

Allen, K.-A., Gray, D. L. L., Baumeister, R. F., & Leary, M. R. (2021). The need to belong: A deep dive into the origins, implications, and future of a foundational construct. *Educational Psychology Review*, *34*(2), 1133–1156. https://doi.org/10.1007/s10648-021-09633-6

Alvesson, M., Ashcraft, K. L., & Thomas, R. (2008). Identity matters: Reflections on the construction of identity scholarship in organization studies. *Organization*, *15*(1), 5–28. https://doi.org/10.1177/1350508407084426

Alvesson, M., & Sandberg, J. (2012). Has management studies lost its way? Ideas for more imaginative and innovative research. *Journal of Management Studies*, *50*(1), 128–152. https://doi.org/10.1111/j.1467-6486.2012.01070.x

Amman, J., Carpenter, T., & Neff, G. (2015). *Surviving the new economy*. London: Routledge.

Andino-Frydman, A. (2022). *Work and pleasure; investigating the rise of digital nomads in Mexico*. Stanford Institute for Economic Policy Research. https://doi.org/https://siepr.stanford.edu/publications/working-paper/work-and-pleasure-investigating-rise-digital-nomads-mexico

Barbour, J. B., & Lammers, J. C. (2015). Measuring professional identity: A review of the literature and a multilevel confirmatory factor analysis of professional identity constructs. *Journal of Professions and Organization, 2*(1), 38–60. https://doi.org/10.1093/jpo/jou009

Barrero, J. M., Bloom, N., & Davis, S. J. (2021a). Let me work from home, or I will find another job. *SSRN Electronic Journal*. https://doi.org/10.2139/ssrn.3890988

Barrero, J. M., Bloom, N., & Davis, S. J. (2021b). Why working from home will stick. *National Bureau of Economic Research*. https://doi.org/10.3386/w28731.

Beech, N. (2010). Liminality and the practices of identity reconstruction. *Human Relations, 64*(2), 285–302. https://doi.org/10.1177/0018726710371235

Behrens, M., & Pekarek, A. (2022). Delivering the goods? German industrial relations institutions during the COVID-19 crisis. *Industrial Relations: A Journal of Economy and Society, 62*(2), 126–144.

Beijaard, D., Meijer, P. C., & Verloop, N. (2004). Reconsidering research on teachers' professional identity. *Teaching and Teacher Education, 20*(2), 107–128. https://doi.org/10.1016/j.tate.2003.07.001

Berger, C. (2022). Just weeks after returning to the office, many Apple workers are unhappy and ready to quit. *Fortune*. Retrieved from https://fortune.com/2022/05/02/apple-workers-unhappy-return-to-the-office-hybrid-work-pandemic/. Accessed on March 31, 2023.

Biskup, M. J., Kaplan, S., Bradley-Geist, J. C., & Membere, A. A. (2019). Just how miserable is work? A meta-analysis comparing work and non-work affect. *Plos One, 14*(3). https://doi.org/10.1371/journal.pone.0212594

Brewer, M. B., & Gardner, W. (1996). Who is this 'we'? Levels of collective identity and self representations. *Journal of Personality and Social Psychology, 71*(1), 83–93. https://doi.org/10.1037/0022-3514.71.1.83

Brown, A. D. (2014). Identities and identity work in organizations. *International Journal of Management Reviews, 17*(1), 20–40. https://doi.org/10.1111/ijmr.12035

Brown, A. D. (2018). Identities in organization studies. *Organization Studies, 40*(1), 7–22. https://doi.org/10.1177/0170840618765014

Brown, R. (2000). Social identity theory: Past achievements, current problems and future challenges. *European Journal of Social Psychology, 30*(6), 745–778. https://doi.org/10.1002/1099-0992(200011/12)30:6<745::aid-ejsp24>3.0.co;2-o

Burke, P. J., & Stets, J. E. (2009). *Identity theory*. Oxford University Press. https://doi.org/10.1093/acprof:oso/9780195388275.001.0001

Chevtaeva, E., & Denizci-Guillet, B. (2021). Digital Nomads' lifestyles and coworkation. *Journal of Destination Marketing & Management, 21*, 100633. https://doi.org/10.1016/j.jdmm.2021.100633

Chreim, S., Williams, B. E., & Hinings, C. R. (2007). Interlevel influences on the reconstruction of professional role identity. *Academy of Management Journal, 50*(6), 1515–1539. https://doi.org/10.5465/amj.2007.28226248

Cook, D. (2020). The freedom trap: Digital nomads and the use of disciplining practices to manage work/leisure boundaries. *Information Technology & Tourism, 22*(3), 355–390. https://doi.org/10.1007/s40558-020-00172-4

Czarniawska, B., & Mazza, C. (2003). Consulting as a liminal space. *Human Relations, 56*(3), 267–290. https://doi.org/10.1177/00187267030560036l2

Dempsey, J. (2015). Moral responsibility, shared values, and corporate culture. *Business Ethics Quarterly, 25*(3), 319–340. Retrieved from http://www.jstor.org/stable/43695063

Dutton, J. E., Dukerich, J. M., & Harquail, C. V. (1994). Organizational images and member identification. *Administrative Science Quarterly, 39*(2), 239–263. https://doi.org/10.2307/2393235

Ebaugh, H. R. (1988). *Becoming an ex: The process of role exit* (p. 18). University of Chicago Press. https://doi.org/10.7208/chicago/9780226160535.001.0001

Elliott, J. (2022). What is a digital nomad? Ehat to know about a work and travel lifestyle. Retrieved from https://www.uschamber.com/co/grow/thrive/what-is-a-digital-nomad#:~:text=Digital%20nomads%20are%20remote%20workers,opportunity%20millions%20of%20Americans%20choose. Accessed on April 3, 2023.

Florida, R. (2010). *The geography of high-paying jobs*. The Atlantic. Retrieved from https://www.theatlantic.com/business/archive/2010/08/the-geography-of-high-paying-jobs/60918/. Accessed on March 31, 2023.

Gioia, D. A., & Chittipeddi, K. (1991). Sensemaking and sensegiving in strategic change initiation. *Strategic Management Journal, 12*(6), 433–448. https://doi.org/10.1002/smj.4250120604

Gioia, D. A., Corley, K. G., & Hamilton, A. L. (2012) Seeking qualitative rigor in inductive research. *Organizational Research Methods, 16*(1), 15–31. https://doi.org/10.1177/1094428112452151

Giorgi, S., & Palmisano, S. (2017). Sober intoxication: Institutional contradictions and identity work in the everyday life of four religious communities in Italy. *Organization Studies, 38*(6), 795–819. https://doi.org/10.1177/0170840616685355

Goffman, E. (1956). *The presentation of self in everyday life*. London: Penguin Classics.

Goodrick, E., & Reay, T. (2010). Florence nightingale endures: Legitimizing a new professional role identity. *Journal of Management Studies, 47*(1), 55–84. https://doi.org/10.1111/j.1467-6486.2009.00860.x

Hatch, M. J., & Schultz, M. (2002). The dynamics of organizational identity. *Human Relations, 55*(8), 989–1018. https://doi.org/10.1177/0018726702055008181

Healy, J., Nicholson, D., & Pekarek, A. (2017). Should we take the gig economy seriously? *Labour & Industry: A Journal of the Social and Economic Relations of Work, 27*(3), 232–248.

Hewitt, J. P. (1989). *Dilemmas of the American self*. Philadelphia, PA: Temple University Press.

Hochschild, A. R. (2018). The time bind: When work becomes home and home becomes work. *Inequality in the 21st Century*, 359–362. https://doi.org/10.4324/9780429499821-63

Hogg, M., & Ridgeway, C. (2003). Social identity: Sociological and social psychological perspectives. *Social Psychology Quarterly, 66*(2). https://doi.org/10.4135/9781446263471.

Hogg, M. A., & Abrams, D. (1996). *Social identifications: A social psychology of intergroup relations and group processes*. London: Routledge.

Iatridis, K., Gond, J.-P., & Kesidou, E. (2021). How meaningfulness and professional identity interact in emerging professions: The case of corporate social responsibility consultants. *Organization Studies, 43*(9), 1401–1423. https://doi.org/10.1177/01708406211035506

Ibarra, H. (1999). Provisional selves: Experimenting with image and identity in professional adaptation. *Administrative Science Quarterly, 44*(4), 764–791. https://doi.org/10.2307/2667055

James, W. (1890). The consciousness of self. Essay. In *The principles of psychology in two volumes* (p. 319). New York, NY: Holt.

Jo Hatch, M., & Schultz, M. (1997). Relations between organizational culture, identity and image. *European Journal of Marketing, 31*(5/6), 356–365. https://doi.org/10.1108/eb060636

Katz, D., & Kahn, R. L. (1978). *The social psychology of organizations* (2nd ed.). New York, NY: Wiley.

Kings College London. (2022). A quarter of employees would rather quit than be forced back to the office. Retrieved from https://phys.org/news/2022-09-quarter-employees-office.html. Accessed on March 31, 2023.

Kofodimos, J. R. (2004). *Balancing act: How managers can integrate successful careers and fulfilling personal lives*. Washington, DC: UMI Books on Demand.

Kool, W., & Botvinick, M. (2014). A labor/leisure tradeoff in cognitive control. *Motivation Science, 1*(S), 3–18. https://doi.org/10.1037/2333-8113.1.S.3

Kreiner, G., & Sheep, M. (2009). Growing pains and gains: Framing identity dynamics as opportunities for identity growth. *Exploring Positive Identities and Organizations*, 47–70. https://doi.org/10.4324/9780203879245-10

Lair, D. J., Shenoy, S., McClellan, J. G., & McGuire, T. (2008). The politics of meaning/ful work. *Management Communication Quarterly, 22*(1), 172–180. https://doi.org/10.1177/0893318908318263

Leary, M. R., Tangney, J. P., Stets, J., & Burke, P. (2005). A sociological approach to self and identity. Essay. In *Handbook of self and identity* (pp. 128–129). New York, NY: Guilford Press.

Lewis, S. (2003). The integration of paid work and the rest of life. Is post-industrial work the new leisure? *Leisure Studies, 22*(4), 343–345. https://doi.org/10.1080/02614360310001594131

Linthicum, K. (2022). Californians and other Americans are flooding Mexico City. Some locals want them to go home. *Los Angeles Times*. Retrieved from https://www.latimes.com/world-nation/story/2022-07-27/americans-are-flooding-mexico-city-some-mexicans-want-them-to-go-home. Accessed on March 31, 2023.

Loacker, B., & Sullivan, K. R. (2016). The liminality of branding. *Marketing Theory, 16*(3), 361–382. https://doi.org/10.1177/1470593116636661

LSE Department of Management. (2017). Social entrepreneurs beware: Don't ignore culture, ethics and behavioral norms. *LinkedIn*. Retrieved from https://www.linkedin.com/pulse/social-entrepreneurs-beware-dont-ignore-culture-norms-management/. Accessed on April 3, 2023.

Luckmann, T. (2008). On social interaction and the communicative construction of personal identity, knowledge and reality. *Organization Studies*, *29*(2), 277–290. https://doi.org/10.1177/0170840607087260

Makimoto, T., & Manners, D. (1997). *Digital Nomad*. London: John Wiley & Sons.

Mas, A., & Pallais, A. (2017). Valuing alternative work arrangements. *American Economic Review*, *107*(12), 3722–3759. https://doi.org/10.1257/aer.20161500

MBO Partners. (2023). *2022 Digital nomads report shows 131% growth since 2019*. MBO Partners. Retrieved from https://www.mbopartners.com/state-of-independence/digital-nomads/. Accessed on April 3, 2023.

McLean, T. (2022). Bay area company selling HQ, encouraging employees to move to Texas. *SFGATE*. Retrieved from https://www.sfgate.com/bayarea/article/chevron-selling-bay-area-headquarters-17268695.php. Accessed on March 31, 2023.

Merton, R. K. (1957). *Social theory and social structure; Toward the codification of theory and research*. Glencoe, IL: Free Press.

Mikkola, L., & Valo, M. (2020). Workplace relationships. Essay. In L. Mikkola & M. Valo (Eds.), *Workplace communication*. (pp. 3–4) New York, NY: Routledge.

Muller, E., & Peres, R. (2019). The effect of social networks structure on innovation performance: A review and directions for research. *International Journal of Research in Marketing*, *36*(1), 3–19. https://doi.org/10.1016/j.ijresmar.2018.05.003

Nash, (Evyn) C., Jarrahi, M. H., & Sutherland, W. (2020). Nomadic work and location independence: The role of space in shaping the work of digital nomads. *Human Behavior and Emerging Technologies*, *3*(2), 271–282. https://doi.org/10.1002/hbe2.234

Nash, C., Jarrahi, M. H., Sutherland, W., & Phillips, G. (2018). Digital Nomads beyond the Buzzword: Defining digital nomadic work and use of digital technologies. *Transforming Digital Worlds*, 207–217. https://doi.org/10.1007/978-3-319-78105-1_25

Nawrat, A. (2022). *WFA drives down attrition at Spotify*. UNLEASH. Retrieved from http://unleash.ai/future-of-work/wfa-drives-down-attrition-at-spotify/. Accessed on March 31, 2023.

Nelson, A. J., & Irwin, J. (2014). 'Defining what we do—All over again': Occupational identity, technological change, and the librarian/internet-search relationship. *Academy of Management Journal*, *57*(3), 892–928. https://doi.org/10.5465/amj.2012.0201

Newbold, J. W., Rudnicka, A., Cook, D., Cecchinato, M. E., Gould, S. J. J., & Cox, A. L. (2021). The new normals of work: A framework for understanding responses to disruptions created by new futures of work. *Human–Computer Interaction*, *37*(6), 508–531. https://doi.org/10.1080/07370024.2021.1982391

Nomad List. (2022). Fastest growing remote work hubs of 2022. Retrieved June 1, 2022, from https://nomadlist.com/fastest-growing-remote-work-hubs

O'Neill, S. (2022). Selina aims to go public at $1.2 billion valuation via Blank Check deal. *Skift*. Retrieved from https://skift.com/2021/12/02/selina-aims-to-go-public-at-1-2-billion-valuation-via-blank-check-deal/. Accessed on March 31, 2023.

Petrone, P. (2018). See the industries with the highest turnover (and why it's so high). *LinkedIn*. Retrieved from https://www.linkedin.com/business/learning/blog/learner-engagement/see-the-industries-with-the-highest-turnover-and-why-it-s-so-high. Accessed on March 31, 2023.

Pratt, M. G., Rockmann, K. W., & Kaufmann, J. B. (2006). Constructing professional identity: The role of work and identity learning cycles in the customization of identity among medical residents. *Academy of Management Journal*, *49*(2), 235–262. https://doi.org/10.5465/amj.2006.20786060

Rahman, M. S. (2016). The advantages and disadvantages of using qualitative and quantitative approaches and methods in language 'Testing and assessment' research: A literature review. *Journal of Education and Learning*, *6*(1), 102. https://doi.org/10.5539/jel.v6n1p102

Reay, T., Goodrick, E., Waldorff, S. B., & Casebeer, A. (2017). Getting leopards to change their spots: Co-creating a new professional role identity. *Academy of Management Journal*, *60*(3), 1043–1070. https://doi.org/10.5465/amj.2014.0802

Reay, T., & Hinings, C. R. (2009). Managing the rivalry of competing institutional logics. *Organization Studies*, *30*(6), 629–652. https://doi.org/10.1177/0170840609104803

Reed, C., & Thomas, R. (2019). Embracing indeterminacy: On being a liminal professional. *British Journal of Management*, *32*(1), 219–234. https://doi.org/10.1111/1467-8551.12385

Reichenberger, I. (2021). Digital Nomads – Drifters 2.0? *ATLAS annual conference*. https://doi.org/10.26686/wgtn.13946708

Reid, A., & Deaux, K. (1996). Relationship between social and personal identities: Segregation or integration. *Journal of Personality and Social Psychology*, *71*(6), 1084–1091. https://doi.org/10.1037/0022-3514.71.6.1084

Rodgers, C. (2008). The development of the personal self and professional identity in learning to teach. Essay. In K. Scott (Ed.), *Handbook of research on teacher education* (Vol. 3, p. 733). London: Taylor & Francis Group.

Schauster, E., Ferrucci, P., Tandoc, E., & Walker, T. (2021). Advertising primed: How professional identity affects moral reasoning. *Journal of Business Ethics*, *171*, 175–187. https://doi.org/10.1007/s10551-020-04429-0

Selina. (2023). Our story – How it all started. Retrieved from https://whatis.selina.com/. Accessed on March 31, 2023.

Sennett, R. (2007). *The culture of new capitalism*. Brantford, ON: W. Ross MacDonald School Resource Services Library.

Sias, P. M. (2005). Workplace relationship quality and employee information experiences. *Communication Studies*, *56*(4), 375–395. Retrieved from https://www.tandfonline.com/doi/abs/10.1080/10510970500319450

Sluss, D. M., & Ashforth, B. E. (2007). Relational identity and identification: Defining ourselves through work relationships. *Academy of Management Review*, *32*(1), 9–32. https://doi.org/10.5465/amr.2007.23463672

Smith, J., & Dubbink, W. (2011). Understanding the role of moral principles in business ethics: A Kantian perspective. *Business Ethics Quarterly*, *21*(2), 205–231. Retrieved from http://www.jstor.org/stable/41304427

Snow, D. A., & Anderson, L. (1987). Identity work among the homeless: The verbal construction and avowal of personal identities. *American Journal of Sociology*, *92*(6), 1336–1371. https://doi.org/10.1086/228668

Stets, J. E., & Serpe, R. T. (2013). Identity theory. In J. DeLamater & A. Ward (Eds.), *Handbook of Social Psychology*. Dordrecht: Springer. https://doi.org/10.1007/978-94-007-6772-0_2

Stryker, S. (1968). Identity salience and role performance: The relevance of symbolic interaction theory for family research. *Journal of Marriage and the Family*, *30*(4), 558. https://doi.org/10.2307/349494

Stryker, S., & Burke, P. J. (2000). The past, present, and future of an identity theory. *Social Psychology Quarterly*, *63*(4), 284. https://doi.org/10.2307/2695840

Sutherland, W., & Jarrahi, M. H. (2017). The gig economy and information infrastructure. *Proceedings of the ACM on Human-Computer Interaction*, *1*(CSCW), 1–24. https://doi.org/10.1145/3134732

Tajfel, H. (1979). Individuals and groups in social psychology*. *British Journal of Social and Clinical Psychology*, *18*(2), 183–190. https://doi.org/10.1111/j.2044-8260.1979.tb00324.x

Tan, H. (2022). Airbnb said more than 800,000 people flocked to its careers page after it announced that employees could live and work anywhere. *Business Insider*. Retrieved from https://www.businessinsider.com/airbnbs-careers-page-viewed-800k-times-work-from-anywhere-benefit-2022-5. Accessed on March 31, 2023.

Teschl, M., & Derobert, L. (2008). Does identity matter? On the relevance of identity and interaction for capabilities. *The Capability Approach*, 125–156. https://doi.org/10.1017/cbo9780511492587.006

Thompson, B. Y. (2021). Seeking same: Digital nomads seek community. In *Digital Nomads living on the margins: Remote-Working Laptop Entrepreneurs in the gig economy* (pp. 81–90). https://doi.org/10.1108/978-1-80071-545-520211007

Thornton, P. H., Ocasio, W., & Lounsbury, M. (2013). *The institutional logics perspective: A new approach to culture, structure, and process*. Oxford: Oxford University Press.

Trede, F., Macklin, R., & Bridges, D. (2012). Professional identity development: A review of the higher education literature. *Studies in Higher Education*, *37*(3), 365–384. https://doi.org/10.1080/03075079.2010.521237

Twenge, J. M., Sherman, R. A., Exline, J. J., & Grubbs, J. B. (2016). Declines in American adults' religious participation and beliefs, 1972–2014. *SAGE Open*, *6*(1), 215824401663813. https://doi.org/10.1177/2158244016638133

Valencia, M. (2023). 54 Digital nomad visas offered by countries in 2023. *Traveling Lifestyle*. Retrieved from https://www.travelinglifestyle.net/countries-offering-digital-nomad-visas-and-residency/#Colombia. Accessed on April 3, 2023.

Vallas, S. P., & Cummins, E. R. (2015). Personal branding and identity norms in the popular business press: Enterprise culture in an age of precarity. *Organization Studies*, *36*(3), 293–319. https://doi.org/10.1177/0170840614563741

Vaughn, K. (2018). You will spend 90,000 hours of your lifetime at work. Are you happy? *Medium*. Retrieved from https://kassandravaughn.medium.com/you-will-spend-90-000-hours-of-your-lifetime-at-work-are-you-happy-5a2b5b0120ff. Accessed on March 31, 2023.

Verbeke, W., & Wuyts, S. (2007). Moving in social circles—Social circle membership and performance implications. *Journal of Organizational Behavior*, *28*(4), 357–379. https://doi.org/10.1002/job.423

Vignoles, V. L. (2018). Identity: Personal and social. In *The Oxford handbook of personality and social psychology* (pp. 288–316). https://doi.org/10.1093/oxfordhb/9780190224837.013.12

Walsh, K., & Gordon, J. R. (2008). Creating an individual work identity. *Human Resource Management Review*, *18*(1), 46–61.

Wang, B., Liu, Y., Qian, J., & Parker, S. K. (2020). Achieving effective remote working during the COVID-19 pandemic: A work design perspective. *Applied Psychology*, *70*(1), 16–59. https://doi.org/10.1111/apps.12290

Woldoff, R. A., & Litchfield, R. C. (2021). Digital Nomads. https://doi.org/10.1093/oso/9780190931780.001.0001.

World Salaries. (2022). Average salary in Mexico for 2022. Retrieved June 31, 2022, from https://worldsalaries.com/average-salary-in-mexico/

Wright, C., Nyberg, D., & Grant, D. (2012). 'Hippies on the third floor': Climate change, narrative identity and the micro-politics of corporate environmentalism. *Organization Studies*, *33*(11), 1451–75. https://doi.org/10.1177/0170840612463316

Ybema, S., Beech, N., & Ellis, N. (2011). Transitional and perpetual liminality: An identity practice perspective. *Anthropology Southern Africa*, *34*(1–2), 21–29. https://doi.org/10.1080/23323256.2011.11500005

Zhang, W. (2022). Political disengagement among youth: A comparison between 2011 and 2020. *Frontiers in Psychology*, *13*. https://doi.org/10.3389/fpsyg.2022.809432

Zheng, X., Yin, H., & Li, Z. (2018). Exploring the relationships among instructional leadership, professional learning communities and teacher self-efficacy in China. *Educational Management Administration & Leadership*, *47*(6), 843–859. https://doi.org/10.1177/1741143218764176

CHAPTER 6

THE GREAT REALIZATION: ONLINE FREELANCERS AND THE MEANING OF FLEXIBILITY

Michael Dunn[a], Isabel Munoz[b], Clea O'Neil[a] and Steve Sawyer[b]

[a]*Skidmore College, Saratoga Springs, NY, USA*
[b]*Syracuse University, Syracuse, NY, USA*

ABSTRACT

In this chapter, we theorize about online freelancers' approaches to work flexibility. Drawing from an ongoing digital ethnography of US-based online freelancers pursuing work on digital platforms, our data question the common conceptualizations around the flexibility of online freelancing. We posit that the flexibility of where to work, not when to work, is the most important attribute of their work arrangement. Our data show (1) the online freelancers in our study prefer the stability and sustainability of full-time work over freelancing when both are offered as remote options; (2) full-time remote employment increases these workers' freelancing control / flexibility; (3) these workers keep freelance work options open even as they transition to more permanent full-time work arrangements. We discuss how these findings relate to workplace culture shifts and what this means for contemporary working arrangements. Our insights contribute to the discourses on knowledge-based gig work and for what it means to study individuals online.

Keywords: Digital ethnography; flexibility; platforms; gig economy; future of work; non-standard work arrangement

Ethnographies of Work
Research in the Sociology of Work, Volume 35, 139–156

ISSN: 0277-2833/doi:10.1108/S0277-283320230000035006

In this chapter, we focus attention on online freelancers and their pursuit of work flexibility. To do this, we draw on data from an ongoing digital ethnography of online freelancers in the United States that now involves 95 participants, 187 interviews, 200 survey responses, and substantial trace and secondary data collection across the first 46 months of this study. Beginning in 2019, we have been following online freelancers as they have navigated from pre-COVID times through the turbulence of a pandemic and now into the current 'great resignation'. We have observed that while the workers have claimed that the flexibility of when to work was the most important attribute for their work, it turns out that the flexibility of where they work is most important. These insights contribute to the thematic issue's call to ethnographically advance the discourses on knowledge-based gig work and online platforms.

Flexibility has been an issue explored in work scholarship, across multiple intellectual spaces, for many decades (e.g. Allen, Johnson, Kiburz, & Shockey, 2013; Brozovic, 2018; Smith, 1997; Wood, 1989). Bal and Izak (2021) analyzed nearly 50 years of literature in workplace flexibility, including 262 of the most important publications in the topic and summarized the four lenses through which flexibility has been examined across the different disciplines: (1) organizational flexibility (e.g. Schreyögg & Sydow, 2010); (2) flexibility in worker behaviour (e.g. Beltrán-Martín, Roca-Puig, Escrig-Tena, & Bou-Llusar, 2008; Wright & Snell, 1998); (3) flexible kinds of work (e.g. contractual status, Wilson, Brown, & Cregan, 2008); and (4) workplace flexibility (e.g. Hill et al., 2008). The increase in workplace flexibility has been identified as beneficial because it promotes employee productivity and satisfaction (Glass & Finley, 2002).

The current issues surrounding flexibility have come front and centre with the increases in non-standard work arrangements. Prioritization of work-life balance often drives workers to secure a flexible arrangement that fits their personal priorities, including childcare (White & Maniam, 2020). Gig work platforms allow for increased flexibility, but additional labour is often necessary to combat the restraints of the digital platform itself (Lehdonvirta, 2018). An increase of non-standard work arrangements suggests that the definition of flexibility is continually evolving. Indeed, 'flexibility' is recognized as one of the major shifts in the future of work and workplaces (Kossek, Gettings, & Misra, 2021).

While the desire for flexibility predates the COVID-19 era, the COVID-19 pandemic has accelerated the pace of flexible work arrangements. Indeed, firms have been turning to flexible structures and specifically the platform economy to increase business flexibility and agility. Flexible workers enable firms to quickly and efficiently scale human resources up and down to meet changes in the market (Davis, 2016). Workers have also been increasingly `more willing to embark on flexible or non-standard work arrangements, which has also accelerated through the pandemic (Managing Flexible Work Arrangements, 2022; Saad & Wigert, 2021; Thier, 2022). In 2021 alone, 47.4 million workers in the United States voluntarily left their jobs (Tappe & CNN Business, 2022), representing over a quarter of the total workforce (Andrew, 2022). In tandem – seemingly due in part to the COVID-19 pandemic – the work landscape has brought a greater focus on (and greater dependence on) remote work, with estimates that almost 70% of full-time 'white collar' workers are working remotely in some capacity (Saad & Wigert, 2021). Many scholars and pundits believe the trend will continue in perpetuity (Gibbons, 2022; Kambouris, 2021). This suggests flexible work arrangements are likely to be an increasingly common aspect of many futures of work.

One type of independent worker, online freelancers, has always worked remotely, increasingly securing these temporary jobs or gigs via online labour platforms like Upwork, Toptal, and many other similar sites. Online freelance work differs in at least three ways from the food delivery, ride-sharing, and home-renting gigs that get substantial scholarly and public attention. First, online freelancing tends to be performed independent of place (Kalleberg & Dunn, 2016). Second, online freelancing requires cognitive labour, leveraging both the worker's experience and mastery of a body of knowledge, such as architecture, graphic design, or legal writing (Gandini, 2019). Third, online freelance work typically requires sustained interaction between a worker and an employer (Sutherland, Jarrahi, Dunn, & Nelson, 2020). These differences noted, online freelance work is similar to other gig-, or project-, based-work in that there is little commitment between employer and worker beyond the specifics of the project's contract: it is explicitly temporary work (Howcroft & Bergvall-Kåreborn, 2019; Wood, Graham, Lehdonvirta, & Hjorth, 2019).

Because online freelance work is secured and completed remotely, workers are susceptible to greater competition in the online labour market, as the easy access to online platforms reduces barriers for other workers to enter and compete (Dunn, 2017). And, online labour markets have few of the workplace protections afforded to full-time workers, particularly in the United States (ILO Organization, 2016; Mckay, Pollack, & Fitzpayne, 2019).

The online labour markets in which freelancers seek jobs rely on online labour platforms like Upwork and Fiverr. These online labour platforms serve as intermediaries, standing between employers and workers. As such, they are market-makers, exerting control over the ways in which employers present their jobs; the ways in which workers present themselves online, seek and complete work; and how these parties resolve differences. Given their powerful role and positionality, Vallas and Schor (2020) argue that these online labor platforms are 'permissive potentates': providing a set of generative mechanisms that give platform owners the ability to establish the ways in which their online presence and the market they mediate will operate. For the workers, one of the reasons online labour platforms, and the online labour markets they intermediate, have become so important is the flexibility afforded by the gigs (Dunn, Munoz, & Sawyer, 2021; Kuek et al., 2015; Munoz, Dunn, & Sawyer, 2022). Simultaneously, digital platforms have emerged as a key technological form enabling and constraining work flexibility (Rani & Furrer, 2021).

The platform economy literature has focused on several different axes of flexibility. Some argue flexibility is about freedom for the workers to optimize their resources (time and other assets) (Burtch, Carnahan, & Greenwood, 2018). Others have cited hours worked and workplace location (Woodcock & Graham, 2019). And, some see flexibility as multidimensional (Berg, Furrer, Harmon, Rani, & Silberman, 2018; Churchill & Craig, 2019). The flexibility most commonly associated with this work arrangement is that of flexibility to decide when to work, schedule flexibility (e.g. Chen, Chevalier, Rossi, & Oehlsen, 2019; Johns & Gratton, 2013; Katsnelson & Oberholzer-Gee, 2021; Kuek et al., 2015; Malone, 2004; Sundararajan, 2017; Wheatley, 2017; Wu, Zhang, Li, & Liu, 2019). Scholars have identified various potential advantages to flexible scheduling, such as allowing paid work to be combined with life circumstances that prevent otherwise regular work and a reduction in tensions related to work-family conflicts (Jarrahi, Sawyer, & Erickson, 2021). Furthermore, several large-scale consumer surveys have found that the general public's perception of flexibility in the gig economy is about scheduling flexibility (Atske, 2021; Healy, Pekarek, & Vromen, 2020).

Perhaps, the biggest proponents of schedule flexibility as a hallmark of gig work are the platforms themselves (Warren, 2021). Platforms, by asserting schedule flexibility as a core benefit, also distance themselves from the ongoing debate on worker classification. Without the promise of flexible scheduling, platforms would have a more difficult time asserting the current legal status of online freelance workers as independent contractors. Warren (2021) frames the 'positive sell of flexibility to worker(s)' by the platforms to the workers as '... one to achieve better work-life balance' (p. 529).

Indeed, online freelancers, much like other workers, have multiple and diverse work preferences and motivations that bring them to this work arrangement. Warren (2021) asserts that for online freelance workers these factors are centred on temporal (time) and monetary (money) dimensions. Our research has led us to the conclusion that while workers might have different motivations and preferences, they have explicitly selected a more precarious work arrangement in exchange for the flexibility it affords. And, as we have explored career strategies and motivations, schedule flexibility was a central attribute (Dunn, Stephany, Sawyer, Munoz, Raheja, 2021; Munoz et al., 2022; Sawyer, Dunn, Munoz, Stephany, & Raheja, 2020; Sawyer, Dunn, Rancy et al., 2020).

More recently, we have witnessed an empirical shift in the career strategies of these workers. We argue this is being fuelled, in part, by the greater availability of remote work options in the traditional workplace. We have seen many of the workers we have been following in our digital ethnography who had chosen online freelancing for the 'flexibility' it affords, leaving for what can be argued as less 'flexible' work arrangements. While, the workers participating in our study claimed that the flexibility of when to work was the most important attribute for their work, when presented with an opportunity for a remote position in a more traditional work arrangement (with less flexibility of when to work) that was seen as a more attractive option.

FOLLOWING ONLINE FREELANCERS OVER TIME: DIGITAL ETHNOGRAPHY OF CAREER PATHS

The data and interim analyses reported below come from an ongoing study where we are following US-based online freelancers to better understand their career paths, working strategies and approaches to work. This means we are studying an online phenomena; therefore, we have designed the study around the principles of digital ethnography (Burrell, 2009; Góralska, 2020; Murthy, 2008; Ritter, 2021). For us this means that direct and sustained contact with the participants as they are situated in their social world is happening on and through digital mediation (e.g. Ritter, 2021). Being 'there' means being online with participants – to the extent that we are given access and are welcomed. Our approach also emphasizes that sustained engagement online will be episodic.

Current approaches to digital ethnography reflect 25 years of development and now encompass multiple techniques and principles (Pink et al., 2015). And, while the sociological and anthropological interests in digital technologies have been a subject of study for many decades, digitally located fieldwork continues to draw criticism despite clear evidence of the robustness and rigour of this approach (Ito, 1996; Nardi, 1996). For us, this means that digital ethnography we practice unfolds differently than the lived experiences of many non-digital ethnographers. This also means we must be particularly attentive to be reflexive and open to unorthodox arrangements (per Pink et al., 2015).

Our data collection is based on a panel design and involves four separate but interrelated efforts: interviews, surveys, field notes, and secondary trace data. We gather data using all four at each round of data collection. In each round, data collection is framed by the interview. The topics and questions on the interview are supported by a short survey that is designed to collect quantifiable data such as hours worked, gender, family and household arrangements, etc. (see Table 6.1 for an overview of themes for survey and interview questions). The secondary data collection – such as reviewing worker's Upwork profiles, LinkedIn presence and other sources that they suggest for us – is done at the same time as the interview. And, the field notes are used as a means to reflect on the data effort, what is learned in the doing of these data collection efforts, and to highlight salient points.

In particular, our approach to digital ethnography centres on interviews using ethnographic techniques, per (Spradley, 2016). Spradley's approach to interviewing centres on the primacy of the participant's knowledge that is embedded in the norms, language patterns and learned cultures that may not be evident to the interviewer. As such, the roles of words, the importance of open-ended discourse, accommodating the non-linearity of these interviews relative to topics (e.g. using probes and careful listening), and the attention to the participant's 'positionality' or location in their larger social systems are critical considerations in designing the interview (see Table 6.1).

We use Slack[1] as a shared digital repository of field notes used by all research staff, so the source and location of our data is online, to allow shared access by all research team members. The field notes and surveys are all designed to complement the interviews. We also collect trace data from these worker's online presences (e.g. LinkedIn) – when allowed – and pursue sustained engagement with the participants between interviews and across the multiple years and rounds of data collection.

Table 6.1. Themes for Survey and Interview Questions.[a]

Data Collection	Themes for Survey	Themes for Interview Questions
Round 1 – 75 Surveys – 67 Interviews	(1) Work arrangements and experience overview (2) Upwork efforts, benefits, and satisfaction (3) Value of education and experience (4) Demographics (Gender, age, education, etc.)	(1) Overview of work and the role of freelancing (2) Labour market strategy (3) Efforts for securing work and pay fairness (4) Organizing for work (5) Challenges in freelancing (6) Closing questions and interest in future participation
Round 2 – 71 Surveys – 69 Interviews	(1) Work arrangements and satisfaction (2) Freelance efforts and financial security (3) Freelance branding and LinkedIn	(1) Household arrangements and work-life balance (2) Reviewing changes to work arrangements (3) Pricing and bidding strategies (4) Online identity and social media branding (5) Networks and community building (6) Closing questions and interest in future participation
Round 3 – 54 Surveys – 50 Interviews	(1) Work arrangements, satisfaction, and predictability (2) Freelance efforts and financial security (3) Work set up, pricing arrangements and Upwork features	(1) Reviewing changes to work arrangements (2) Experiences with the platform/ features (3) Organizing for work (4) Networks and community building (5) Closing questions and interest in future participation

This table provides an overview of the data collection efforts and themes. It shows the number of complete surveys and interviews per round, and while most participants complete both the interview and survey for the project, a few of the participants only completed the survey or only the interview portion, which means the number of survey and interview participants are not the same.

The recruitment and data collection efforts reflect our panel-based approach. As such, we are collecting data from the same participants across time. To wit, data collection for Round 1 ran from November 2019 to May 2020 with 75 original participants. Data collection for Round 2 ran from November 2020 to August 2021. During this round, we lost 24 participants but added 20 Black, Latinx, and multiracial workers to diversify our sample. Doing so allowed us to pursue new research questions related to racial differences in worker experience, reflecting what we were learning from the first round of the panel study. Recruitment and data collection for Round 3 ran from November 2021 to May 2022. Across these, we have now interacted with 95 unique US-based online freelancers, most twice, and many thrice (with 75 participants who were included since the first round and the 20 new workers added in Round 2, see Table 6.3). In each round of data collection, we had some drop off among participants, losing a total of 24 after Round 1 and 17 more after Round 2, meaning that there were times that only some respondents provided their views.

This combination of data sources, and our attention to situating the online freelancer in their larger social world as part of the study, reflects the realities that online work focuses attention on the networks of relations, sociotechnical interdependencies of work, digital technologies, and platform-mediated online interactions. These realities are exactly why digital approaches to ethnographic scholarship are popular and useful.

Most currently published research on flexibility does not employ a digital ethnographic approach. Instead, much of this prior research investigates in-person freelance and platform labour at a specific moment in time. These studies draw on smaller samples, limited by job type, age, or location. The digital nature of our research allows for the longitudinal study of online freelancers who live in different locations, have different skill/education levels, pursue different occupations, and complete a variety of jobs. Without digital research techniques, it would prove extremely difficult to follow such a large number of non-homogeneous freelancers, let alone over the course of multiple years. The digital ethnographic approach our study utilizes allows for entirely remote interactions with freelancers, emulating the type of correspondence that online freelancers have with clients. Freelancers are classified into one of three groups based on the types of services they provide on Upwork[2]: administrative, technology, and creative jobs (see Table 6.2).

The interview and survey data were analyzed independently and then together, leveraging both grounded analysis and guidance from the extant literature. We used thematic analysis to find patterns and common themes within the interview data. Initially, transcripts were individually reviewed, and reports on common patterns were developed. Themes and supporting data were posted to a group channel and discussed during weekly research meetings to develop a shared understanding. The analyses were done using the text analysis software DeDoose, with interview transcripts serving as the corpus for this analysis. Field notes served to clarify transcripts and to seed our research discussions. Both *a priori* constructs (such as occupation and experience) and themes that emerged from the ground-up coding (e.g. flexibility) were coded. The survey and trace data were the sources of the descriptive statistics presented in Table 6.3.

Table 6.2. Freelancer Occupational Categorization.

Freelancer Categories	Job Examples
Administrative	Data entry, virtual assistant, transcription
Technology	Data science, software engineering, information security & compliance
Creative	Blog writing, graphic design, photography

Table 6.3. Freelancer Sample Characteristics and Total Survey Participants.[a]

		Round 1 November 2019–May 2020	Round 2 November 2020–March 2021	Round 3 November 2021–May 2022
Total participants (survey and/or interview)		(75 total)	(71 total)	(54 total)
Gender	Female	47 (63%)	39 (55%)	27 (50%)
	Male	27 (36%)	32 (45%)	27 (50%)
	N/A	1 (1%)	–	–
Job classification	Administrative	32 (43%)	29 (41%)	21 (39%)
	Technology	12 (16%)	12 (17%)	12 (22%)
	Creative	31 (41%)	30 (42%)	21 (39%)
Education	No college degree	8 (11%)	9 (13%)	5 (9%)
	Associates	3 (4%)	4 (6%)	4 (7%)
	Bachelors	33 (44%)	31 (44%)	23 (43%)
	Postgraduate degree	30 (40%)	27 (38%)	22 (41%)
	N/A	1 (1%)	–	–
Have children	Yes	36 (48%)	34 (48%)	25 (46%)
	No	39 (52%)	37 (52%)	29 (54%)
Marital status	Never married	21 (28%)	22 (31%)	18 (33%)
	Married	47 (63%)	42 (59%)	31 (57%)
	Divorced/separated	5 (7%)	7 (10%)	5 (9%)
	Widowed	1 (1%)	–	–
	N/A	1 (1%)	–	–
Race/Ethnicity	White (Non-Hispanic)	45 (60%)	34 (48%)	24 (44%)
	Black/African American	11 (15%)	14 (20%)	10 (19%)
	Asian	5 (7%)	5 (7%)	4 (7%)
	Multiracial, More than one race	7 (9%)	6 (8%)	6 (11%)
	Hispanic	3 (4%)	10 (14%)	8 (15%)
	Other race	3 (4%)	2 (3%)	2 (4%)
	N/A	1 (1%)	–	–

This table highlights demographics from the survey participants. Due to the design of the panel study, participants in the study have participated for one, two or all three of the data collection rounds. The number of interview participants is not included in this table, see Table 1 for total number of interview participants.

EVIDENCE: FLEXIBILITY'S DIFFERENT MEANINGS

We focus on what flexibility means to the workers we have been following, drawing on interviews, surveys, field notes, and secondary data. These data make clear the primary reason the online freelancers we are following pursue this form of work is the perceived flexibility it affords. These data also show that the flexibility these workers seek varies across several dimensions, including scheduling flexibility (control over when to work), task flexibility (control over the projects to work on), and spatial/location flexibility (control over where to work). Most of the workers we spoke to highlighted the importance of schedule flexibility and the ability to work when they wanted. Many also mentioned the importance of this flexibility to accommodate their caregiving responsibilities (e.g. P01, P02, P06, P09, P15, P16, P18, P19, P23, P24, P26, P27, P28, P33, P46, P47, P52, P62, P64).

> The flexibility is excellent. I think that's the primary reason I was using [Upwork] ... My son was in preschool at that time ... It serves a purpose. (P28, Marketing Research)

> I have the flexibility. I love it ... If my son is sick, then I can stay home with him and get work done while he's sleeping. (P02, Legal Analyst)

> I love the flexibility ... it was great to be flexible, take care of other people in my family. Even though I had given up most of the work, I was still doing some things. (P18, Tutor)

> I have a young son. I'm not too far from DC, so the DC attorney life was kind of a rat race for me. I was gone a minimum 60 hours a week from my family every single week, traveling a lot. My son was struggling in school and there were all kinds of different effects on my home life that I wasn't OK with, and now I'm able to make, essentially, the same amount of money .... (P01, Data analyst)

The flexibility to work independent of a predefined schedule and location was important for (1) those who find it challenging to secure work based on where they live (P06, P15); (2) those dealing with life transitions or other personal circumstances, such as illnesses or recovery (P10, P18); and (3) those pursuing specific lifestyle choices such as traveling (P18, P41, P63) and other non-standard arrangements, like seasonal farming (P13), working from a sailboat (P40), and those working across multiple locations (P24, P63).

> Some of my gig work can be done when I'm out of the house, which doesn't happen quite as much anymore. The other benefit of gig work is when I was going through cancer treatment and spent a lot of time in doctors' offices .... I could work around cancer treatments. (P18, Tutoring)

> I have a lot of family in Mexico, and I have a place to stay and it's very cheap, so I spend a large part of the year there. But my official place of residence is New York, so, moving back and forth, as long as I have my laptop with me, and as long as I have a place with an internet connection and relative quiet, I can always apportion a six-hour block of time when necessary to do some work. And fundamentally, that's the office, you know ... And that's pretty mobile and modular and so on. (P63, Writer/Editor)

More themes emerged from the analysis and we report on three in this chapter: (1) the online freelancers whom we are following seem to prefer the stability and sustainability of full-time work over freelancing when both are offered as remote options; (2) full-time remote employment increases these worker's freelancing control and flexibility; and (3) these workers keep freelance work options open even as they transition to more permanent full-time work arrangements. Each of these findings are discussed below.

STABILITY OVER FLEXIBILITY: WORKERS PREFER FREELANCING UNTIL SECURING FULL-TIME REMOTE WORK

Because we have been able to gather data over time, we have the ability to gain insights into how these online freelance workers navigate changing career opportunities. In our latest round (Round 3) of interviews and data collection, participants made clear to us that their need for spatial flexibility (of where to work) was exacerbated at the height of the COVID-19 pandemic. At that time, life circumstances led individuals to re-think their priorities in life, with many highlighting changes in how they viewed their careers and the need for more flexible working arrangements in order to better accommodate these priorities. One participant highlights this heightened awareness and importance of spatial flexibility, stating:

> The urgency to have options to work remote is greater … I think Covid has highlighted the importance of having options to generate money without needing to leave the home, and ultimately offer more flexibility. (P51, CAD, Drafter)

Data show that worker preferences and career arrangements have changed over the three years of the study (2019–2022). There is a decrease in the number of participants who report solely relying on income from freelancing. In our Round 1 survey (2019–2020), 40 out of 75 (53%) of the freelancers in our sample reported freelancing as their primary source of work. A year later, in our Round 2 survey (2020–2021), 20 out of 71 (28%) workers reported working solely as a freelancer. And, in our latest survey, Round 3 (2021–2022), eight out of 54 (15%) workers reported working solely as a freelancer. Insights from the interviews also reflect the change in preference away from freelancing. This change appears to stem primarily from workers seeking more employment stability (e.g. P06, P07, P66, P48) and due to an increased availability of remote work opportunities (e.g. P20, P37).

> Upwork used to be my full-time job, but I now use Upwork on a part-time basis to kind of supplement other things I'm doing. It's funny, because I was actually freelancing for a while, and now I work part-time at a coffee shop. So I can still freelance, but I just needed more income, and I've just found that at least with the work I'm doing, it's really hard just with the recession. (P07, Freelance Writer)

> I'm extremely lucky right now … I'm in a situation where I don't have to leave home and I still have full employment. In fact, they offered to convert me just recently from contractor to full-time status, so it's actually getting better for me in terms of stability of employment. This will probably mean, however, that there's going to be less freelancing in the future. (P66, Graphic Designer)

> My freelance work was going really well and everything. Sometime over the summer, a full-time position just landed in my lap. I took it in the fall, the end of September. But one of the conditions for that position that I negotiated into my contract was that I could continue doing my freelance work as long as there were no conflicts of interest and time capacity, the ability to do the work. (P37, Urban Planner)

Data show that many of the workers we have been following prefer the stability of traditional full-time work over freelancing (part or full-time) when both options are available remotely. This is the case for online freelancers who indicated that freelancing was their primary source of income or secondary source of income. Over the course of 2021–2022, 16 out of 50 workers (32%) interviewed in Round 3 had transitioned to new full-time employment, with all but one transitioning to a remote work arrangement.

While previous rounds of data collection made clear participants embraced the schedule flexibility of when to work, our latest round of data also makes clear that full-time remote options afford workers the spatial flexibility they seek while also providing work and income stability. Many workers have indicated that this balance is important to them. When faced with losing some schedule flexibility in exchange for more stable work arrangements with spatial flexibility, it was a calculation worth taking. Workers prefer full-time remote arrangements as they are able to access worker protections and benefits that full-time employment affords, such as health care and paid leave, which are unavailable to most freelancers (due to independent contractor status).

> My full time job is remote as well so I'm working from home either way. Probably I would have considered Upwork more if I had to go to work [physically]. Before the pandemic, less employers offered remote jobs. That's why I was working mostly on Upwork. But now since a lot of employers, a lot of companies, are offering remote jobs, full time jobs, I prefer that. Because it's more stable, and income is stable and you get paid leaves and all kinds of benefits of the full-time job that Upwork doesn't provide. (P48, Accountant)

> Back in 2019 when I started freelancing [remote work] was not something that most employers offered in traditional positions so I went to freelancing and to Upwork. However, of course, due to the pandemic a lot more employers are interested in offering either hybrid or fully remote opportunities. So once that taboo was kinda gone, especially in 2021, I was able to find a full-time position that offered fully remote, and of course offered more stable pay and also health benefits as well so that's what I transitioned into. (P41, Copy Editor)

> So now that I have a [full-time remote] job that is more promising, I feel more secure now, and I have benefits with the other job, too. That's something I didn't have when I was working with Upwork. I did enjoy the flexibility when I was a freelancer, but now that I have goals, I have more bills to pay, I actually appreciate that a company hired me. (P12, Virtual Assistant)

KEEPING OPTIONS OPEN: SITUATIONAL ARRANGEMENTS IN THE CONTEMPORARY WORKFORCE

Finally, even as we saw these workers' preferences about freelancing change, with some transitioning from freelancing to full-time employment, these workers did not leave freelancing. The online freelancers we are following who transitioned to full-time work kept their Upwork profile available as a back-up or alternative option. It was common for these workers to keep their Upwork profiles visible while taking on few-to-no projects. Some of the participants who transitioned to full-time traditional employment relied on clients reaching out to them with work opportunities. Both approaches make clear that continuing relationships with freelance clients lessens the risk these workers may feel as they transition to full-time work: freelancing is an alternative path as needed.

> My career changed, so now I mostly work my full-time job, and I put Upwork aside. I'm open to offers. I don't seek clients, but I'm open to clients to find me and offer me some gigs. Also, I prefer doing fixed-budget tasks in Upwork more than hourly work, because currently my full-time job is taking pretty much all of my time. (P48, Accountant, Has full-time (FT) work and Upwork provides extra income)

> I'm not letting go of Upwork work or of freelancing, but I actually feel more secure now than when I was working as a contractor within Upwork. (P12, Virtual Assistant, Has FT work and Upwork provides extra income)

> I may be able to exert some extra time at certain points in my life and other points in time. If life gets a little too busy, I might not be able to dive into it as much, but I do think it's something I could see myself doing, because it's kind of at my will when I want to work and how much I want to work, so that's really quite convenient. (P20, Administrative Data Entry, Has FT work and Upwork provides extra income)

Some of the workers we are following keep their Upwork accounts open in case they will need to return to freelancing in the future. For these workers, freelancing currently feels too unstable. When financial stability becomes more important than the flexibility of freelancing, many workers choose to secure traditional part- or full-time work. For several workers, traditional employment may not be their ideal working arrangement, but instead a financial necessity. Some of these workers express interest in returning to freelance work in the future.

> With the cost of living as high as it is, without universal healthcare, being self-employed and having to pay the self-employment tax, isn't sustainable for the long-term. I think I will ultimately, once … [cuts out] … a physical job, not a remote job. That's my projection. I hope I'm wrong. If I could make this somehow enough for us, for example, maybe if I could have a physical job on the weekends and do freelance during the week, I would love to do that. But I can't get my hopes up too high. It may be the reverse in the end. It may be that I need to do freelance on the weekends as an additional source of income. We will see. (P39, Writer, Translator, Editor on Upwork and has another less-than-FT jobs)

> Upwork used to be my full-time job, but I now use Upwork on a part-time basis to kind of supplement other things I'm doing. It's funny, because I was actually freelancing for a while, and now I work part-time at a coffee shop. So I can still freelance, but I just needed more income, and I've just found that at least with the work I'm doing, it's really hard just with the recession … I'm planning on doing this for another few months, but this is definitely not long-term, sustainable, like freelancing was pre-Covid-19 for me. (P07, Writer on Upwork and also has part-time (PT) work and is looking for FT work)

> I just looked at it as supplemental anyway. It's not my main core competency; I look at it as a lead generation source, and for what it's worth, I want to be independent of any third party getting the clients, and I want to track my own clients, and I'm working on that. (P46, Analyst, has PT work and is looking for FT work)

DISCUSSION: FLEXIBILITY, WORK, AND THE FUTURE

As workers and organizations emerge from the lockdowns and pandemic-related changes of the past two years, it seems that remote work has moved from a discussion of possible futures to a common practice. Likewise, the increase in the availability of remote work has led workers to reconsider their career trajectories and working arrangements. This rethinking is evident in the significant number of voluntary separations recently, amounting to over 25% of the workforce (Tappe & CNN Business, 2022), and the steady rise of freelance and online employment options.

Indeed, it is now common for job ads to explicitly articulate if they are remote, in-person or some hybrid combination of these working arrangements (Anders, 2021). Our data make clear that online freelancers are aware of this when rethinking working arrangements. We also found that the online freelancers we have been following are picking alternate paths – trajectories that make sense to them. Furthermore, the diversity in motivation, career goals, skills, and occupations demonstrates the heterogeneity in the online labour market. Despite this heterogeneity, a common thread across these workers is the emphasis placed on the importance of flexibility.

For years, scholars, pundits, and workers have heralded 'flexibility', or the freedom to decide when to work, as the hallmark characteristic attracting workers to online freelancing (Chen, Chevalier, Rossi, & Oehlsen, 2019; Johns & Gratton, 2013; Katsnelson & Oberholzer-Gee, 2021; Kuek et al., 2015; Malone, 2004; Sundararajan, 2017; Wheatley, 2017; Wu et al., 2019). That is because this work offers '… a flexible working schedule [that] allows individuals to take better care of their families, continue to study, or start their own businesses while working and earning a salary' (Kuek et al., 2015).

Insights from our data challenge this view of flexibility – the freedom to decide when to work – as the hallmark characteristic attracting workers to freelancing. Our data show that being able to work remotely is particularly critical for individuals who have been choosing to pursue online freelance work. And while many of these workers note freelancing allows them to choose clients, projects, and schedules, data show that most individuals choose online freelancing based on the flexibility to choose where they will work. For example, many of the workers we have followed make clear their personal needs require them to seek a work-from-home arrangement, while others seek the ability to be able to work from anywhere as they travel. As such, the ability to work remotely is more important to them than task flexibility and scheduling flexibility.

Given that market forces dictate to a large extent what and how much work is available for online workers, freelancers tend to have less control over the clients and projects available at any given point in time. And, with work availability also varying by occupation, some workers are left to take on less than desirable jobs, pay, schedules, and clients (Gershon, 2011). This means that even as they have little control over these factors, online freelancers can control where they work. As such, flexibility is as much about the ability to choose where to work as it is the ability to search for and complete work whenever one wants. So when there is an opportunity for a more standard work arrangement that allows an online freelancer to work remotely, many opt for this more stable and sustainable option, even if they are afforded less flexibility about when to work.

We further note implications of an increased reliance on working remotely as part of standard work arrangements to the (1) future of work, (2) future full-time workers, and (3) online freelancers could be profound. First, in the past decade we have seen explosive growth in the online labour market. To this point, the global market for online labour has grown approximately 50% over the past three years, with an estimated 56 million online freelancers globally (Kässi & Lehdonvirta, 2018). These platform-mediated online labour markets provide opportunities for organizations to help absorb market shocks and for workers to find project-based (or gig) work (Gray & Suri, 2019; Kalleberg, 2003; Lehdonvirta, Kässi, Hjorth, Barnard, & Graham, 2019).

What does the increase in the availability of remote work mean to the future of online labour markets? The answer likely depends on if the online labour market is distinct or complementary. If the market is distinct, we would expect a smaller impact over long term. That is, as a distinct labour market, the fluctuation in the supply and demand in the primary labour market is mostly independent from the fluctuations in the online labour market. However, if the markets are complementary, changes in the primary labour market will have a more direct and long term impact. Our findings suggest that the online labour market and the traditional labour market are complementary in the United States, but, we see value in the further interrogation of this question (see also, Stephany, Dunn, Sawyer, & Lehdonvirta, 2020). We also see the potential of examining this question through other analytical perspectives. For example, given the geographic variation in economic structures, labour laws, and labour market attributes, the interactions between the traditional and online labour market may differ.

Second, we found that workers in our study who shifted to full-time remote work continue to freelance in some capacity. The freelancers whom we have been speaking with for years are choosing to keep their online profiles visible and available should a client want to inquire about their services. We see this as a strategic career move, beyond the clear financial possibilities. Keeping their profile active and visible means keeping their options open. Should their new arrangement fall through or the terms change in ways that no longer serve them, they're able to resume their freelancing activity as before. We also surmise that workers keep their profiles open because should they choose to close, delete, or deactivate their profile, they would lose all of their built up capital that is embedded into their profile on the platform. The capital includes their job ratings, job success score, client reviews, performance and activity badges, and other platform-driven metrics. Our respondents note high ratings, strong metrics, and great reviews from clients help them secure more projects and ask for higher wages. The value of these platform-specific measures, metrics, and scores disappear if a worker leaves the platform and deletes their profile: this social capital does not go with them. Thus, leaving their profile active means keeping their options open.

Finally, and perhaps paradoxically, it seems that online freelancers who keep their profile active even as they take on a more standard job have greater agency – despite the diminished flexibility of full-time remote work. With a stable income and benefits, workers who continue to freelance are better able to avoid taking on jobs, clients, or schedules which do not align as well with their needs. In particular, workers with remote full-time work feel they have the control to be more selective.

We found this increased control related to task flexibility. As workers have more stable income, they are more likely to pass up on work that is not aligned with their task preferences (e.g. P17, P34, P40, P58), including taking in consideration the project type, clients, and pay that is tied to a specific job, and the alignment with the freelancer's values and goals. So, while the work hasn't changed, the work is decidedly less precarious. And, while the control exerted by the platforms is well-documented (Howcroft & Bergvall-Kåreborn, 2019; Vallas & Schor, 2020), their employment situation moderates the platform's market-making control.

CONCLUSION

Looking forward, we offer two insights into navigating the future of work and reflect on the value of digital ethnography to provide insights unavailable via other means. Our first insight is that this approach to work continues to grow. This insight reflects the reality that as workers' and employers' expectations of employment continue to shift from careers to a greater focus on tasks rather than jobs, the demand for freelance workers will increase. Yet, many workers prefer the stability and the workplace protections afforded to full-time workers. As our findings show, online freelance workers will take remote full-time employment in lieu of freelancing, even if they have been committed to this path for some time. If organizations continue to seek independent workers, a sustainable arrangement needs to include social policies specifically focused on providing these workers with greater access to benefits and other workplace protections.

Second, we see the desire for remote work as one indicator that contemporary in-person workplace cultures are misaligned with the needs of twenty-first-century workers – and the neologism of 'the Great Resignation' serves as evidence of this misalignment. Our data make clear the workers we are following care deeply about the flexibility of choosing where they work (supporting Warren's, 2021 assertions). As our participants have noted, their choices for work arrangements were often made considering the broader context of life trajectories and finances while factoring in family needs and/or partners' interests. Our data also suggest online freelancer workers prize both flexibility (about when and where to do work) and stability (of work availability). Warren (2021) argues that current organizational strategies tend to focus too heavily on issues of time. Given what we are learning, it is no wonder that organizations pursuing a 'business as usual' strategy of in-person work as the path forward face increased difficulty in hiring and retaining experienced workers. If what we see from the online freelancers we have been following reflects a larger trend, then the Great Resignation reflects a great realization – that the flexibility of where to work is the most important attribute of their work arrangement.

Finally, we note that pursuing digital ethnography has positioned us to observe the long-term impacts of the great realization on our online freelancers. This approach requires investing in relationship-building, puts a premium on selecting participants to maximize insight, and is resource-intensive relative to both the researcher needs and the time scales. Without the patience to track change over time, in the situations where this work happens, we would not be able to explain change or see trajectories. For this reason, more field-based studies like this are needed so that we can learn more about the ways in which this and other possible futures of work are being realized.

NOTES

1. See https://slack.com, see also Ritter (2016) for his digital ethnography of Slack.
2. Upwork sometimes changes their job categories, so this provides us a means to compare over time.

REFERENCES

Allen, T., Johnson, R. C., Kiburz, K. M., & Shockley, K. M. (2013). Work-family conflict and flexible work arrangements: Deconstructing flexibility. *Personnel Psychology*, *66*(2), 345–376.

Anders, G. (2021). Employers catch on: remote job posts rise 357% as tech, media lead the way. Retrieved from https://www.linkedin.com/pulse/employers-catch-remote-job-posts-rise-457-tech-media-lead-anders/

Andrew, J. (2022). *The employee-employer disconnect that's fueling the Great Resignation*. Fast Company. Retrieved from https://www.fastcompany.com/90728005/the-employee-employer-disconnect-thats-fueling-the-great-resignation?partner=rss&utm_campaign=rss+fastcompany&utm_content=rss&utm_medium=feed&utm_source=rss

Atske, S. (2021). *The state of gig work in 2021*. Pew Research Center: Internet, Science & Tech. Retrieved from https://www.pewresearch.org/internet/2021/12/08/the-state-of-gig-work-in-2021/

Bal, P., & Izak, M. (2021). Paradigms of flexibility: A systematic review of research on workplace flexibility. *European Management Review*, *18*(1), 37–50. https://doi.org/10.1111/emre.12423

Beltrán-Martín, I., Roca-Puig, V., Escrig-Tena, A., & Bou-Llusar, J. C. (2008). Human resource flexibility as a mediating variable between high performance work systems and performance. *Journal of Management*, *34*(5), 1009–1044.

Berg, J., Furrer, M., Harmon, E., Rani, U., & Silberman, M. S. (2018). Digital labour platforms and the future of work. Towards decent work in the online world. Rapport de l'OIT. Retrieved from http://wtf.tw/text/digital_labour_platforms_and_the_future_of_work.pdf

Brozovic, D. (2018). Strategic flexibility: A review of the literature. *International Journal of Management Reviews*, *20*(1), 3–31.

Burrell, J. (2009). The field site as a network: A strategy for locating ethnographic research. *Field Methods*, *21*(2), 181–199. https://doi.org/10.1177/1525822X08329699

Burtch, G., Carnahan, S., & Greenwood, B. N. (2018). Can you gig it? An empirical examination of the gig economy and entrepreneurial activity. *Management Science*. https://doi.org/10.1287/mnsc.2017.2916

Chen, M. K., Chevalier, J. A., Rossi, P. E., & Oehlsen, E. (2019). The value of flexible work: Evidence from Uber drivers. *The Journal of Political Economy*, *127*(6), 2735–2794. https://doi.org/10.1086/702171

Churchill, B., & Craig, L. (2019). Gender in the gig economy: Men and women using digital platforms to secure work in Australia. *Journal of Sociology*, *55*(4), 741–761.

Davis, G. (2016). What might replace the modern corporation? Uberization and the web page enterprise. *Seattle University Law Review*, *39*(2), 501–515.

Dunn, M. (2017). Digital work: New opportunities or lost wages? *American Journal of Management*, *17*(4), 10–27.

Dunn, M., Munoz, I., & Sawyer, S. (2021). Gender differences and lost flexibility in online freelancing during the COVID-19 pandemic. *Frontiers in Sociology*, *6*, 738024. https://doi.org/10.3389/fsoc.2021.738024

Dunn, M., Stephany, F., Sawyer, S., Munoz, I., & Raheja, R. (2021). When motivation becomes desperation: Online freelancing during the Covid-19 pandemic. https://osf.io/preprints/socarxiv/67ptf/

Gandini, A. (2019). Labour process theory and the gig economy. *Human Relations*, *72*(6), 1039–1056. https://doi.org/10.1177/0018726718790002

Gershon, I. (2011). Neoliberal agency. *Current Anthropology*, *52*(4), 537–555. https://doi.org/10.1086/660866

Gibbons, S. (2022). Remote work is here to stay: How to keep your business secure. *Forbes Magazine*. Retrieved from https://www.forbes.com/sites/serenitygibbons/2022/03/08/remote-work-is-here-to-stay-how-to-keep-your-business-secure/

Glass, J. L., & Finley, A. (2002). Coverage and effectiveness of family-responsive workplace policies. *Human Resource Management Review*, *12*(3), 313–337. https://doi.org/10.1016/S1053-4822(02)00063-3

Góralska, M. (2020). Anthropology from home. *Anthropology in Action: Newsletter of the British Association for Social Anthropology in Policy and Practice (BASAPP)*, *27*(1), 46–52. https://doi.org/10.3167/aia.2020.270105

Gray, M., & Suri, S. (2019). *Ghost work: How to stop Silicon Valley from building a new global underclass*. Boston, MA: Houghton Mifflin Harcourt.

Healy, J., Pekarek, A., & Vromen, A. (2020). Sceptics or supporters? Consumers' views of work in the gig economy. *New Technology, Work and Employment*, *35*(1), 1–19. https://doi.org/10.1111/ntwe.12157

Howcroft, D., & Bergvall-Kåreborn, B. (2019). A typology of crowdwork platforms. *Work Employment and Society*, *33*(1), 21–38. https://doi.org/10.1177/0950017018760136

ILO Organization. (2016). *Non-standard employment around the world: Understanding challenges, shaping prospects*. Geneva: ILO Publications. Retrieved from https://www.ilo.org/global/publications/books/WCMS_534326/lang–en/index.htm

Ito, M. (1996). Theory, method, and design in anthropologies of the internet. *Social Science Computer Review*, *14*(1), 24–26. https://doi.org/10.1177/089443939601400107

Jarrahi, M. H., Sawyer, S., & Erickson, I. (2021). Digital assemblages, information infrastructures, and mobile knowledge work. *Journal of Information Technology Impact*, 026839622110509. https://doi.org/10.1177/02683962211050943

Jeffrey Hill, E., Grzywacz, J. G., Allen, S., Blanchard, V. L., Matz-Costa, C., Shulkin, S., & Pitt-Catsouphes, M. (2008). Defining and conceptualizing workplace flexibility. *Community, Work and Family*, *11*(2), 149–163.

Johns, T., & Gratton, L. (2013). The third wave of virtual work. *Harvard Business Review*, *91*(1), 66–73. Retrieved from https://dialnet.unirioja.es/servlet/articulo?codigo=4289550

Kalleberg, A. L. (2003). Flexible firms and labor market segmentation: Effects of workplace restructuring on jobs and workers. *Work and Occupations*, *30*(2), 154–175. https://doi.org/10.1177/0730888403251683

Kalleberg, A. L., & Dunn, M. (2016). Good jobs, bad jobs in the gig economy. *Perspectives on Work*, *20*(1–2).

Kambouris, A. (2021). Remote work is here to stay. It's time to update the way you lead. *Entrepreneur*. Retrieved from https://www.entrepreneur.com/article/395311

Kässi, O., & Lehdonvirta, V. (2018). Online labour index: Measuring the online gig economy for policy and research. *Technological Forecasting and Social Change*, *137*, 241–248. https://doi.org/10.1016/j.techfore.2018.07.056

Katsnelson, L., & Oberholzer-Gee, F. (2021). Being the boss: Gig workers' value of flexible work. Retrieved from https://www.hbs.edu/ris/Publication%20Files/21-124_4a28fd0c-e395-46ce-b621-2b32c3dd2fa0.pdf

Kossek, E. E., Gettings, P., & Misra, K. (2021). The future of flexibility at work. *Harvard Business Review*. Retrieved from https://hbr.org/2021/09/the-future-of-flexibility-at-work

Kuek, S. C., Paradi-Guilford, C., Fayomi, T., Imaizumi, S., Ipeirotis, P., Pina, P., & Singh, M. (2015). The global opportunity in online outsourcing. Retrieved from https://openknowledge.worldbank.org/handle/10986/22284

Lehdonvirta, V. (2018). Flexibility in the gig economy: Managing time on three online piecework platforms. *New Technology, Work and Employment*, *33*, 13–29. https://doi.org/10.1111/ntwe.12102

Lehdonvirta, V., Kässi, O., Hjorth, I., Barnard, H., & Graham, M. (2019). The global platform economy: A new offshoring institution enabling emerging-economy micro-providers. *Journal of Management*, *45*(2), 567–599. https://doi.org/10.1177/0149206318786781

Malone, T. W. (2004). *The future of work–How the new order of business will shape your organization, your management style, and your life*. Boston, MA: Harvard Business School Press.

Managing Flexible Work Arrangements. (2022). SHRM. Retrieved from https://www.shrm.org/resourcesandtools/tools-and-samples/toolkits/pages/managingflexibleworkarrangements.aspx. Accessed on June 17, 2022.

Mckay, C., Pollack, E., & Fitzpayne, A. (2019). *Automation and a changing economy*. The Aspen Institute. Retrieved from https://www.aspeninstitute.org/wp-content/uploads/2019/04/Automation-and-a-Changing-Economy_Policies-for-Shared-Prosperity_April-2019.pdf

Munoz, I., Dunn, M., & Sawyer, S. (2022). Flexibility, occupation and gender: insights from a panel study of online freelancers. *Information for a better world: Shaping the global future* (pp. 311–318). https://doi.org/10.1007/978-3-030-96957-8_27

Murthy, D. (2008). Digital ethnography: An examination of the use of new technologies for social research. *Sociology*, *42*(5), 837–855. https://doi.org/10.1177/0038038508094565

Nardi, B. A. (1996). Context and consciousness: Activity theory and human-computer interaction. Retrieved from https://books.google.ca/books?hl=en&lr=&id=JeqcgPlS2UAC&oi=fnd&pg=PR7&ots=e0dbWxC_Hu&sig=H_0r66H82Hjmoi-VMLbqf2VUYak

Pink, S., Horst, H., Postill, J., Hjorth, L., Lewis, T., & Tacchi, J. (2015). *Digital ethnography: Principles and practice*. London: SAGE Publications.

Rani, U., & Furrer, M. (2021). Digital labour platforms and new forms of flexible work in developing countries: Algorithmic management of work and workers. *Competition & Change*, *25*(2), 212–236. https://doi.org/10.1177/1024529420905187

Ritter, C. S. (2021). Rethinking digital ethnography: A qualitative approach to understanding interfaces. *Qualitative Research: QR*, 14687941211000540. https://doi.org/10.1177/14687941211000540

Saad, L., & Wigert, B. (2021). Remote work persisting and trending permanent. Retrieved from https://news.gallup.com/poll/355907/remote-work-persisting-trending-permanent.aspx

Sawyer, S., Dunn, M., Munoz, I., Stephany, F., & Raheja, R. (2020). *Freelancing online during the COVID-19 pandemic*. https://www.microsoft.com/en-us/research/publication/freelancing-online-during-the-covid-19-pandemic/

Sawyer, S., Dunn, M., Rancy, J. P., Munoz, I., Raheja, R., Vaccaro, G., Caruso, A., Weller, H., & Moffly, L. (2020). Freelancing and labor in the digital economy. *Microsoft new future of work symposium 2020*. Retrieved from https://www.microsoft.com/en-us/research/publication/freelancing-and-labor-in-the-digital-economy/

Schreyögg, G., & Sydow, J. (2010). Organizing for fluidity? Dilemmas of new organizational forms. *Organization Science*, *21*(6), 1251–1262.

Smith, V. (1997). New forms of work organization. *Annual Review of Sociology*, *23*, 315–339.

Spradley, J. P. (2016). *The ethnographic interview*. Waveland Press. Retrieved from https://play.google.com/store/books/details?id=KZ3lCwAAQBAJ

Stephany, F., Dunn, M., Sawyer, S., & Lehdonvirta, V. (2020), Distancing bonus or downscaling loss? The changing livelihood of us online workers in times of COVID-19. *Journal of Economic and Human Geography*, *111*, 561–573. https://doi.org/10.1111/tesg.12455

Sundararajan, A. (2017). *The sharing economy: The end of employment and the rise of crowd-based capitalism*. MIT Press. Retrieved from https://play.google.com/store/books/details?id=tg38DwAAQBAJ

Sutherland, W., Jarrahi, M. H., Dunn, M., & Nelson, S. B. (2020). Work precarity and gig literacies in online freelancing. *Work, Employment and Society*, *34*(3), 457–475. https://doi.org/10.1177/0950017019886511

Tappe, A., & CNN Business (2022). Where are all the workers? Here are four reasons behind the labor shortage. *CNN*. Retrieved from https://www.cnn.com/videos/business/2022/01/14/labor-shortage-economy-js-orig.cnn

Thier, J. (2022). 95% of knowledge workers want flexible hours more than hybrid work, and managers should pay attention. *Fortune*. Retrieved from https://fortune.com/2022/02/03/knowledge-workers-say-they-want-flexible-hours-more-than-hybrid-work/

Vallas, S., & Schor, J. B. (2020). What do platforms do? Understanding the gig economy. *Annual Review of Sociology*, *46*(1), 273–294. https://doi.org/10.1146/annurev-soc-121919-054857

Warren T. (2021). Work–life balance and gig work: 'Where are we now' and 'where to next' with the work–life balance agenda? *Journal of Industrial Relations*, *63*(4), 522–545. https://doi.org/10.1177/00221856211007161

Wheatley, D. (2017). Employee satisfaction and use of flexible working arrangements. *Work Employment and Society*, *31*(4), 567–585. https://doi.org/10.1177/0950017016631447

White, C., & Maniam, B. (2020). Flexible working arrangements, work-life balance, and working women. *Journal of Business and Accounting*, *13*(1), 59–73.

Wilson, K., Brown, M., & Cregan, C. (2008). Job quality and flexible practices: An investigation of employee perceptions. *The International Journal of Human Resource Management*, *19*(3), 473–486.

Wood, A. J., Graham, M., Lehdonvirta, V., & Hjorth, I. (2019). Good gig, bad gig: Autonomy and algorithmic control in the global gig economy. *Work Employment and Society*, *33*(1), 56–75. https://doi.org/10.1177/0950017018785616

Wood, S. (Ed.). (1989). *Transformation of work: Skill, flexibility and the labour process*. New York City, NY: HarperCollins.

Woodcock, J., & Graham, M. (2019). *The gig economy. A critical introduction*. Cambridge: Polity. Retrieved from http://acdc2007.free.fr/woodcock2020.pdf

Wright, P. M., & Snell, S. A. (1998). Toward a unifying framework for exploring fit and flexibility in strategic human resource management. *AMRO*, *23*(4), 756–772.

Wu, Q., Zhang, H., Li, Z., & Liu, K. (2019). Labor control in the gig economy: Evidence from Uber in China. *Indian Journal of Industrial Relations*, *61*(4), 574–596. https://doi.org/10.1177/0022185619854472

CHAPTER 7

WHAT HAPPENED? ETHNOGRAPHIC STORIES OF THE STRATEGIC ROAD NETWORK

Felicity Heathcote-Marcz[a] and Sideeq Mohammed[b]

[a]*CDS, Leeds, UK*
[b]*Kent Business School, Canterbury, UK*

ABSTRACT

Good ethnographic work produces stories. Stories are told to us by our interlocutors. We record them in our fieldnotes and read about them in archival or policy documents. We see and hear them occur around us, we participate in them, and they become a core part of our memories of the field. Given that 'telling stories is one of the fundamental things we do as human beings' (Falconi & Graber, 2019, p. 1), stories are perhaps the most crucial resource by which we as ethnographers make sense of a field, allowing us to translate what happened to others so that they might be able to vicariously travel through the fields which we studied.

Yet when we look at the ethnographies published in leading management and organization studies journals, stories are increasingly hidden from view. We argue in this short chapter, for a return to storytelling at the centre of the production of ethnography. We seek an opening of the closed world of academic storytelling to those audiences excluded from such networks, including those whom we ethnographers are writing about. We retell nine short stories from an ethnography of Traffic Officers and the breakdowns they encounter on the strategic road network. These vignettes form a non-linear narrative of some of the most emotive and embodied encounters in our fieldwork in transport and

Ethnographies of Work
Research in the Sociology of Work, Volume 35, 157–163

ISSN: 0277-2833/doi:10.1108/S0277-283320230000035007

mobility spaces between 2018 and 2019. We leave our readers to draw conclusions, implications, and linkages from these stories and offer an invitation to debate and conversation on the themes encountered therein.

Keywords: Ethnography; breakdown; mobility; transport; stories; organization studies

Stories are the stuff ethnography is made from. They are told to us by our interlocutors. We record them in our fieldnotes. We read about them in archival or policy documents. We see and hear them occur around us. We participate in them and they become a core part of our memories of the field. Given that 'telling stories is one of the fundamental things we do as human beings' (Falconi & Graber, 2019, p. 1), it should come as no surprise that stories are perhaps the most crucial resource by which we as ethnographers make sense of a field, constituting the core of our everyday practices and allowing us to undertake that crucial work of translating *what happened* to others so that they might be able to vicariously travel through the fields which we studied.

Yet when we look at the ethnographies published in leading management and organization studies journals, stories are increasingly hidden from view, buried behind the clawing miasma of a pervasive pseudo-positivism that asks us to define and describe our methods, to make generalizeable claims, and to 'theorize' in order to make a 'contribution'; as though ethnography were a clear cut science and not something closer to the practice of Benjamin's (2006) 'storyteller'. Stuck in an academy where doing ethnography at all feels like a coup (O'Doherty & Neyland, 2019), we are often complicit in reproducing the scorn and/or suspicion that the academy has for ethnographic work in our own writing and it is perhaps our guilt at this that has motivated us to try to write a different kind of chapter here; one that places ethnographic stories at the fore and refuses to demean them as insufficiently important to be told unless accompanied by the artifice of some theoretical gesture. We simply wish to share some stories without effacing the complexity of our field.

What follows are some fragments of stories from an ethnography of England's Strategic Road Network (SRN), that is – motorways and major A-roads. These vignettes form a non-linear narrative of some of the most emotive and embodied encounters in our fieldwork, studying the work of Traffic Officer's ethnographically on England's Strategic Road Network between 2018 and 2019 as part of a consultancy project.

END OF THE ROAD

First outstation visit. Sunrise is glaring at us. Hurts my eyes. We wait to be deployed and the shifts change, personal protective equipment (PPE) comes off and goes on.

> I'll never forget one fatal. A young woman. I stayed with her as she died. She kept telling me I don't want to die like this, am I going to die? What could I do? I waited for the emergency services and held her hand as she slipped away. A metal pillar had pierced her body in the crash.

PERSONAL PROTECTIVE EQUIPMENT

Lorry. Heart Attack. M6. Crashed into the barrier.

Our PPE is ok. It depends how fast you can put it on … the police have zips on their trouser pockets, proper combat trousers. Ours aren't so well made. Our torches, little torches, are not bright enough. Not fit for purpose.

The cameras on our vehicles were meant to protect us, but they're used to check on us.

The M6 incident was called in at 6.10am. Still ongoing at 3pm. That's a classic example of no one wanting to make a decision. No one wants to take the rap. It's frustrating getting a call that you only have 20 minutes left on your KPI [key performance indicator] to clear an incident, but there's nothing you can do. Fire or Ambulance or Police have decided to close the road, it's their scene. We have no control.

The foundations training is the most basic we've ever had it, down from 4 weeks to 2 weeks.

I think we should have the power to issue fines for non-compliance, like aggressive behaviour. People know we're not police. People know we can't do anything.

Disagreement between an on-road Traffic Officer (TO) and a Regional Operations Centre (ROC) operator.

You soon find out who's in charge on the road.

I think it's unsafe, I'm towing the vehicle ahead to the hard shoulder, please set signs and signals now.

I'm not sure what happens after the debrief. It's unclear if any lessons are being learned.

The outstation is draughty, but the tea is hot. The TOs talk to me about dynamic risk assessments (DRA) and work instructions (WIs).

Is there a conflict between the organization trying to roll out a 'just culture' when the Work Instructions are so prescriptive?

For example: a TO was dismissed for crossing the central reservation. But there were lane closures on both sides. I was told at a safety briefing that the BROC team (special Brexit contingency planning team) do this regularly.

Another example: I towed an elderly couple off the motorway to the services. The Work Instructions say I shouldn't have done this, but it was very hot, they were vulnerable. I had to make the judgement call.

There are always moral dilemmas.

TOs [Traffic Officers] shouldn't try to hide behind a DRA (dynamic risk assessment). A valid DRA should be justifiable in court.

They always criticize what you got wrong. The rest of the organization feels we are a poor relation.

ON THE ROAD

I watch as an Extinction Rebellion protestor pops up on the CCTV – they are attaching a political banner to the overhead bridge, so this is visible to the motorists below.

Mark takes me over to another call handler. He is speaking to a white van driver who has broken down in a precarious position away from a hard shoulder. He tells me he has seen people climb over barriers and cling on for dear life.

> People ring up family members and ask them to come [onto the motorway hard shoulder] and wait with them. This can be much more dangerous.
>
> One guy recently took his BBQ out on the hard shoulder on a nice Summer's day. Taking his life in his hands.
>
> Overheating is a common reason for breakdowns. TOs used to carry water so it was an easy fix. We're not allowed now. So stranded drivers wait a lot longer for recovery [to arrive with water for the engine].
>
> The dynamic hard shoulder is resource intensive. Needs human intervention to spot problems and set signs and signals. Would prefer all lane running [smart motorways]. It takes time to set red Xs too.
>
> Compliance is poor, there are incursions into roadworks, near misses with engineers. Most people ignore red Xs.

FIRST TO LAST

> The media always give the police the credit and us the blame. Or we're ignored, as if we weren't there, first on scene clearing the mess.
>
> Emergency services don't always include us in what's happening. We're not 'first responders', but trying to show we're not their enemy. The fire service are much better than they were but we could clear so much more with more dialogue, more cooperation.
>
> More should be pushed to the police. They should do more to lead and collaborate. Whoever is first on the scene, often us, takes on 'bronze command'. I'd expect a single crew TO to stop and make a scene safe, but they shouldn't take on bronze command.
>
> KPIs can be a source of tension between police and TOs. The police aren't under so much pressure to clear incidents and re-open the motorway.

CULTURE TROUBLE

Tina tells me about her shifts supporting a different team in the South which I had heard from several managers had some significant resourcing and cultural problems:

> They were f-ing and blinding, shouting across desks in the control room, and flinging cones down the verge on the road .... Culture breeds, if it's allowed to carry on.
>
> Some team members are still very misogynistic. I want to know I've got where I have on an equal footing, I had to work hard (female TO).
>
> It was months and months before we got the comms about what went wrong. Why John died [A Traffic Officer killed while on duty].

The ride out was sombre. Dark sky. Industrial landscape. TO spoke candidly that he had tired of the service.

> Civil servants in uniform, that's us. We were always bolted on. The business sees us as a tumour.

THE CUSTOMER JOURNEY

On the hard shoulder. Stopped foreign HGV with a tyre blow out. Driver has been waiting a long time in the cold. I ask in Google Translate 'Do you feel safe? Unsafe? OK?' They respond 'OK' with a thumbs up.

Interviews with disabled drivers. Some Motability vehicles. Physical and mental health issues.

> I stop and get out of my car every hour I'm driving. I have to or I'd find it too difficult to get out after long periods of not moving.

> The ideal thing would be a Traffic Officer trained in mental health issues.

> TOs are very nice people. They've helped me when I've broken down. Motorists refuse to move or do what they say. They need more powers from the police.

> People using the roads are customers of the Highways Agency. We should be treated like it.

> If I'm stuck in a traffic queue for hours my diabetes would be dangerous. I get dizzy and could collapse.

> The highways patrol saw me and rescued me when I broke down. Even gave me biscuits. I'll always remember that.

Two elderly women waiting on the hard shoulder. Warning light was flashing. We approach. They ask the TO is it safer to stop or keep going?

A man with learning difficulties has run out of fuel. His fiancée joins us on the hard shoulder to pick him up.

Abandoned vehicles. Stat removals. Suspicious circumstances. ROC operator tells me about dangerous driving behaviours.

> There was a fatality on the M6 2 months ago. He got pulled over for tired driving. He fell asleep and got hit. Some drivers have a mentality of I'll have a rest when I get there.

BREAKING THE RULES

The HGV driver we were now talking to at his passenger side door did not speak English, as I was told by several Traffic Officers was often the case with HGV drivers who broke down. The windscreen was badly cracked on the front passenger side. As me and the attending Traffic Officer observed this, he said:

> they don't maintain vehicles to UK standards – we see all sorts of shoddiness!

The Traffic Officer then tried to type what the HGV driver should do into a translation app as I watched from behind the hard shoulder barrier. The driver did not want to leave his vehicle and tried to get back into the cab. The Traffic Officer took the HGV keys out of the ignition when the driver was looking elsewhere and put them in his pocket.

> We shouldn't really do it but that would have been a big risk to let him back in there, in case he tried to drive off, that happens.

The HGV driver began arguing with his boss in Romanian on his mobile, and eventually the phone was passed to the Traffic Officer.

> No, I'm sorry, it has to be moved, the price is fixed for this size of vehicle if you don't have recovery (breakdown cover).

As this scene was unfolding, traffic continued to flash past us all at 70 or 80 mph. I would become used to the noise after several ride-outs, the blast of sound and fear that comes with every passing car. It dulls the senses over time.

A NEAR MISS

Tense room. Lots of tea and sympathy in the outstation after the incident.

> He just doesn't listen to me! I told him we didn't feel safe clearing it. They should be listening to us on scene, we should be making the decision to attend or not and he knows that!

Heavy goods vehicle (HGV) too close. Bulging muscles and tears. Signed off for the rest of the day.

> We don't know what we're going to find. One time, [another officer] and I attended a breakdown and two women pointed dirty needles at us. I'm ex-prison and he's ex police and fire so we know how to handle ourselves, but still.

Long list of near misses on the whiteboard. Not reported on the official system. No point apparently. Newspaper clipping on the wall 'most dangerous road in the UK'.

> [...] often we'll get there [to an incident] first, we have this triage role, we have to decide how serious injuries are, whether to call the police or fire or ambulance, and sometimes we get it wrong.

Team take turns manning a little tuck shop. Keeps spirits up.

> There should be more presence from the welfare van when we're stuck out in all weathers [at an incident]. Can be hours.

ON THE BARRIER

Parked in the TOV [Traffic Officer Vehicle] on a motorway bridge. The TO I was with was watching a man at the edge.

> They build up to it, slowly. It starts with watching the traffic. Then they might lean over the bridge to get a better look. Then they'll sit on the bridge and dangle their legs. Then they'll lean forward as far as they can while sitting on the bridge. Then, one day they'll just let go.

The man doesn't want to give his details. He's getting agitated as the TO tries to speak to him at the barrier and I watch.

> Running out of fuel might be the most common reason for breakdowns we see. We saw a big increase during the financial crisis and recession, people were winging it, not filling up and breakdown cover was the first thing to cut back on.

> TOs get lots of mental breakdowns, like people taking their clothes off, drunk, fighting with police. There was a man a while back who thought he was being hunted and Jesus would save him.
>
> If there's a breakdown in live lane, then the safety advice is to 'do what you think is safest'. This is so that if something happens, the organisation is not on the hook.

FOR ETHNOGRAPHIC STORIES

How should we tell ethnographic stories? How do we let people know what happened? Is it possible to still tell tales of the field in academic contexts without an explicit and functionalist dance of knowledge production politics?

In this short chapter, we sought to tell a few stories. To pass them on so that the reader might make sense of them. We presented them here as we remember them, not as completely formed tales that we report for analysis, but as fragments and snippets; segmentary passages that hold for us the experiences and vibrance of the field. They keep us with them, moving on a journey that is durative and bumpy, like accompanying a Traffic Officer on their shift patrolling England's motorways and A-roads. The power of a story speaks here, for us, in *the remembering* (see Rowlinson, Casey, Hansen, & Mills, 2014), in the way the partial connections of the stories open up a space for the world of the SRN to emerge again as something new.

We have sought this to be a departure from the forms and conventions of contemporary journal article-making. We would like to precipitate a productive discussion on storytelling and story-making in the praxis of ethnography. We would like to open up these stories from the boundaries of academic networks where they habitually reside; to stay with the trouble together … in collective thinking (Haraway, 2016) with a wider audience. We would like academic and practitioner colleagues who may be interested in this work to comprehend the ideas of our full paper, without having to spend time at unpaid labour sifting thousands of words. We would like to make our stories accessible to those we are writing about. We would like the voices of our interlocutors to be heard more loudly. We would like our memories and the stories of which we were a part to be valued rather than marginalized and hidden from view.

We believe by offering a short paper to this collection, that we may contribute to a parallel track of knowledge production, where stories made in ethnography can be taken seriously as an end in themselves.

REFERENCES

Benjamin, W. (2006). The storyteller: Reflections on the works of Nikolai Leskov. In D. Hale (Ed.), *The novel: An anthology of criticism and theory 1900–2000* (pp. 361–378). London: Blackwell Publishers.

Falconi, E. A., & Graber, K. E. (2019). Ethnographic approaches to storytelling as narrative practice. In E. A. Falconi & K. E. Graber (Eds.), *Storytelling as narrative practice* (pp. 1–24). London: Brill. https://doi.org/10.1163/9789004393936_002

Haraway, D. (2019). *Staying with the trouble*. Durham, NC: Duke University Press.

O'Doherty, D., & Neyland, D. (2019). The developments in ethnographic studies of organising: Towards objects of ignorance and objects of concern. *Organization*. https://doi.org/10.1177/1350508419836965

Rowlinson, M., Casey, A., Hansen, P. H., & Mills, A. J. (2014). Narratives and memory in organizations. *Organization*, *21*(4), 441–446. https://doi.org/10.1177/1350508414527256

CHAPTER 8

FEELING PRECARIOUS IN ETHNOGRAPHIC RESEARCH METHODS AND IN PERSONAL CIRCUMSTANCES: IDEAL TYPES AND REAL WORLD COMPLEXITY

Krzysztof Z. Jankowski

The University of Glasgow, Glasgow, UK

ABSTRACT

This chapter discusses the impact of the sociological imagination and ethnographic research methods on identifying the 'real' nature of conceptualized phenomena. The examination is done by comparing the researcher's experience of work-related precarity in ethnographic methods and in the researcher's personal circumstances immediately following the fieldwork. Such a juxtaposition shows what had been emphasized by ethnography and the effects of the researcher's social context on the concepts under study. In the case of fieldwork, many of the practical difficulties of precarious work were encountered. However, the context of being an ethnographer altered how work precarity was felt. In the personal circumstances that followed the fieldwork, precariousness was strongly felt in a more general manner. This occurred in a discrete event that involved multiple factors of employment, housing, institutions relied on, and personal relationships. Such differences between fieldwork and personal circumstances illuminate

Ethnographies of Work
Research in the Sociology of Work, Volume 35, 165–172

Published under exclusive licence by Emerald Publishing Limited
ISSN: 0277-2833/doi:10.1108/S0277-283320230000035008

on the tendency to isolate phenomena in fieldwork, which poses the risk of making ethnographic reality out of ideal types.

Keywords: Ethnography; insecurity; methodology; social theory; precarity; work

INTRODUCTION

Research on work insecurity has come to focus on the material and subjective aspects of precarity: a milieu of unpredictability and an associated sense of insecurity (Bourdieu, 1998; Campbell & Price, 2016; Waite, 2009; Worth, 2016). However, tracking the 'transmission' of precarity from structures of work to subjective experience has become contested (Campbell & Price, 2016). This arises from the myriad of possible insecure working conditions and the individual characteristics and social location of workers. For example, it may not be insecure hours but a lack of state and family support that 'makes' someone precarious (Antonucci, 2018). This raises questions as to the cause, form, and reality of precarity. To illuminate the role of work and social location in precarity, this chapter examines how two different conditions – ethnographic fieldwork and the personal circumstances immediately following – made the researcher feel precarious. Where in the fieldwork the precariousness of work was refracted by the researcher's position, in the largely non-work personal circumstances that followed the researcher felt precarious more intensely. Such a comparison illuminates whether ideal types may lead ethnographic fieldwork at the expense of the true complexity present.

Employment, economic, and political systems that do not guarantee an everyday sense of security have been investigated under the rubric of precarity by scholars as diverse as Pierre Bourdieu (1998) and Judith Butler (2015). One focus, so called precarious work – that is work which is '*uncertain*, *unstable*, and *insecure*' (Kalleberg & Vallas, 2017, p. 1) – is described as compounding with other structural factors like access to welfare to leave workers vulnerable (Vosko, 2010). Furthermore, approaches focusing on subjective themes have been developed by feminist geographers such as Waite (2009, p. 416) who describe a pervasive precarity that 'conjures life worlds that are inflected with uncertainty and instability'. As such, precarity is considered to involve both 'objective' or economic structural factors such as the terms of employment, and the subjective *feeling* of being precarious that results (Alberti, Bessa, Hardy, Trappmann, & Umney, 2018; Worth, 2016).

However, with such broad interpretations, locating precarity has become contested (Antonucci, 2018; Campbell & Price, 2016). If precarity is a pervasive condition, then it is unclear whether to locate it in particular persons, places, or times. This makes it difficult to equate feeling precarious in different structural positions, such as that of creative (Donald, Gertler, & Tyler, 2013) and care workers (Baines, Kent, & Kent, 2019) that face very different work insecurities. As such, a re-evaluation is taking place as to the extent and subjective nature of precarity. Campbell and Price (2016, p. 316) ask, 'To what extent is the precariousness of work transmitted to the worker?' In this question, the term 'transmission' invokes critical thought into how the unpredictability of insecure economic and employment structures is actually translated into a state of being or feeling precarious. To this end, Campbell and Price (2016) argue for a holistic view of positionality, taking into account the subject's social context: their social location in structures that constrain or enable action. To proceed, this chapter engages with these thoughts while examining feeling precarious in fieldwork and the personal circumstances that followed.

AN ETHNOGRAPHY OF NON-PERMANENT WORK

The researcher investigated precarious work using ethnographic methods. This involved moving to London and taking a variety of jobs. Initially, the researcher took on gig work through Handy to do gardening and cleaning, following this the researcher onboarded with a number of employment agencies. These agencies placed him in warehousing, manufacturing, and retail roles on term or zero hour contracts. This, however, only covers part of the experience, and much of the field work was spent looking for work and going through many unsuccessful applications. There were also more practical aspects to negotiate, like finding workplaces for the first time. The fieldwork period was a total of nine months from 2020 to 2021 during the height of the coronavirus pandemic and associated 'lockdown' policy. In total, the researcher worked for eight employers, through four agencies, on assignments lasting from two hours to eight weeks. The expectation was that through ethnographic methods the researcher would not only be able to learn about precarious work, but also how the conditions of precarious work translate into wider experiences of insecurity and the feeling of such.

Ethnographers always come into the field with personal and academic perspectives which colour how it is viewed and what conclusions are drawn from it (Lichterman, 2017). Whether one believes that ethnographic fieldwork produces a universal or a partial view, researchers need to consider their common-sense assumptions or social position that shape their research agenda, perspective, and field experience (Lichterman, 2017). The conceptual breadth of precarity only exacerbates such concerns. While the researcher held the view that feeling precarious would be a product of multiple factors, it was believed that employment would be the key one. This was an anecdotal belief, albeit supported by the observation that even the most open-ended frameworks to study precarity, such as precarization (Alberti et al., 2018) or feeling precarious (Worth, 2016), retain employment as the central pillar. In terms of position, the researcher was concerned his relatively privileged position may exclude him from certain sectors of precarious work, such as manufacturing or cleaning. The method therefore aimed to combine precarious employment with an extended fieldwork period of 10 months working in a number of different sectors although limited by where the researcher could get hired.

The biographical position of an ethnographer is important to understanding their experience in the field. I had worked similar precarious jobs at different times throughout my life in New Zealand and Hong Kong but never in the UK. However, COVID-19 made finding work more difficult than in the past. I was new to London and, in many ways, was arriving as if I had come from abroad for the first time. Precarious work has significant ethnic and language boundaries, too, and in some workplaces, I was the only white native English speaker.

WORKING PRECARITY

While many of the mechanical insecurities of precarious work were encountered, such as difficulties getting hired and poor working conditions, the translation of such into feeling precarious was affected by the financial and professional securities/vulnerabilities of being an ethnographer. While this can be seen as interference from social position, such as class and ethnicity, it may also be indicative of the concept of precarity functioning in actual circumstances.

The fieldwork involved many of the practical difficulties of insecure work. Initially, it was a challenge to understand the job market, decide where to apply, and conceive what jobs the researcher might have a chance to get. This was aggravated by the coronavirus pandemic which closed down the two key sectors the researcher had experience in: clerical and hospitality. Once the researcher got a reply to a job inquiry, there were subsequent difficulties in passing the requirements to actually get hired. Many potential jobs were lost part way through the application process due to some unexpected complication, such as requiring a UK national insurance number. There were further insecurities about working conditions, such as working night shifts, which the researcher struggled. When a job was found, it would suddenly end, and the process would begin again. This meant the researcher was contending with the insecurity of precarious work on a daily basis.

Such negotiations of precarious work, however, only 'transmitted' (Campbell & Price, 2016) precarity from work to life in terms of being an ethnographer. While the researcher rarely earned enough to cover his rent and living expenses, the realities of a PhD stipend, personal savings, and ongoing freelance work held prior to the fieldwork meant the feeling of precariousness was never present in the direst terms of finances. However, precarity is not just a matter of economics, there may be subjective insecurities of social position, narrative, or personal condition, too (Alberti et al., 2018; Worth, 2016). During the fieldwork, setbacks in finding work were felt as an insecurity of progress in research as an ethnographer, rather than as a worker. In these regard then, the researchers' position 'interfered' with feeling precarious as a precarious worker. However, rather than consider this as an exceptional circumstance, I suggest that being an ethnographer is a social context, of which precarious workers may have versions of themselves.

While the issue of being a PhD researcher could be a limitation of autoethnographic methods, I raise if it is indicative of the social context, of which any precarious workers' own context may be a key or even transformative factor. The mediating impact of being an ethnographer on the transmission of insecurities from work to life, in terms of protecting finances yet exposing one to an insecurity of research progress, raises questions about the presence of similar social contexts for all precarious workers. These contexts, that are going to tend to exist from job to job and be resistant to change, are likely to be common. While the working conditions of a given job may be precarious in the sense of poor conditions or insecurity, in terms of a fully rounded precarious individual or feeling precarious, then contextual factors are liable to interact to a significant degree, possibly even overcoming and transforming those conditions. This raises questions as to the universalism of purely work and welfare-related interpretations of precarity. While not every social context will affect insecurities, it will always be the medium through which precarity is manifest, such as in the case of the insecurity of research progress.

This raises the prospect that the commonly used terms – precarity, precarious worker, and, to some extent, feeling precarious – are ideal types and that the flaw in method and analysis was attempting to study and isolate these in the real world as such. While these concepts are typically interpreted broadly, in order to be identifiable, they are deployed on data in specific forms that are indicative of certain interpretations. When replicated and codified by others, the limited interpretations are transformed into ideal types. In reality, the author's inability to feel precarious as a worker was a case of the precarious worker ideal-type inter-reacting with the social context, in this case being an ethnographer. This raises two cautions: to what extent does the social context overwhelm the ideal-type into never occurring as predicted, and, how do we design ideal types to be valid and yet sensitive to such transformations of social context. In this case, much of the issue lies in the extension from work to life, where the precarious worker ideal type is likely to only be valid in the sphere of which it was developed: work. Therefore, the extension (or transmission) of work precarity into a wider boundary than it was initially devised is likely to lead to overextension and essentialization.

PERSONAL CIRCUMSTANCES: RETURNING TO GLASGOW

I now tack to the personal circumstances that immediately followed the fieldwork. After the fieldwork, the researcher moved back to Glasgow and needed to find a flat to live in for the medium term. However, a number of compounding factors came together that made this difficult, and it was at this point that the researcher felt precarious in a more general and personal sense.

In mid-2021, it was time to end the fieldwork and move back to Glasgow, a process that involved coordinating many moving parts. The research project had its own schedule that needed to be kept, and the researcher also needed to be back in time to teach in-person tutorials as a graduate teaching assistant. This was complicated by quite a number of personal and environmental factors. The rental and short-term let markets were being squeezed by both a greater than usual number of university students and the COP26 climate conference. Adding to this, the researcher's partner was moving from outside the UK to Glasgow with two pets, so a suitable home was needed by the time they arrived. Finally, there was the question of storing the researcher's possessions he did not bring on fieldwork. During the ethnography, these were kept in the researcher's university office; however, the university decided to reclaim the office. For these reasons, temporary accommodation could not be used and a medium- or long-term solution was needed by a certain date. Therefore, the researcher was facing a housing insecurity that drew on not just needing to move to Glasgow to start work but also personal relationships, holding onto possessions, and housing pets.

The practice of such a circumstance involved a frantic search for accommodation. Some property agents explicitly did not accept pets or students, or there was difficultly in having the researcher's income –consisting of a stipend and casual work – recognized. This fed into the feeling of precariousness during the search, that as two migrants with non-standard incomes and pets, we were, in a sense, at the bottom of the list. Applying for accommodation came to mirror that of the fieldwork job search: dedicating time every day, responding quickly to any agent, and extending the search wider and wider. Nonetheless, after two weeks of looking and having made 10 unsuccessful offers, it started to look like finding a property would be impossible. Meanwhile, news reports, social media posts, and anecdotes were filtering through about students leaving Glasgow due to not finding anywhere to live. The apparent impossibility of finding somewhere to live made the researcher feel precarious in a way that never occurred during the fieldwork. Furthermore, these concerns were amplified by concern over loved ones, storing possessions, and facing the prospect of beginning teaching while living in temporary accommodation. These concerns took on the pervasive quality often theorized of precarity (Ettlinger, 2007). The pervasiveness was not just that the insecurity could potentially impact many things in the researcher's life but also that the concerns entered the researcher's thoughts throughout every day.

The social context was largely the same as that during the fieldwork; however, there were now differences in its impact. As the research project was no longer a mediating factor, in some ways, my concerns were more 'basic' in that they regarded issues closer to day-to-day living. Where as during the fieldwork being a researcher was largely a shield against economic vulnerability, in moving to Glasgow that social context became a causal factor in driving the move itself. This causal role continued to have an impact through shaping the circumstances of the search – rent a hotel, move to another city, delay the move, or continue with the search as is, etc. The integral factor of social context brings it closer to precarity itself. The social context does not 'manifest', in the sense of a separate entity, nor can be considered to 'alter', ideal types of precarity of working and economic conditions, or the feelings of such. Instead, social context constitutes the make-up of precarity as an ongoing and multidimensional event that is of, and limited to, the particular vulnerabilities and protections that are constituting it through time. For example, the precariousness of moving to Glasgow was not just about the search for housing but had the dimensions of honouring relationships and storing possessions, among others, that shaped the boundary and form of the event. By this, I contend that social context is best thought of not as exacerbating or mitigating factors upon a concept, but that the relative conditions, vulnerabilities, and strengths of the event are precarious in the first place. This perspective suggests that there are likely to be many different 'types' of such events; however, if the ethnographer is too wedded to a conceptual schema, such as precarity, then they may not be identifiable.

Reflecting on this period, the nature of precarity as an 'event' suggests that it is difficult to isolate in research. Feeling precarious was not an unlimited phenomenon as it is sometimes portrayed (Ettlinger, 2007) but occurred in a discrete period of vulnerability with a beginning of moving to Glasgow, a middle of searching and feeling insecure, and an end. This event had no single, scientifically identifiable cause but was wholly multidimensional as it involved the task of assembling employment, housing, and personal relationships. Furthermore, its complicated existence was tied to fleeting processes and vulnerabilities. Nonetheless, there are cases of feeling precarious over long periods of time (Worth, 2016), and these could be explained as a series of overlapping and vulnerable operations and events. As an event, precarity is difficult to isolate in fieldwork, as rather than being an outcome of a single academic interest, such as insecure work, precarity is a time dense with fleeting, repeating, and elongated vulnerabilities. Precarity does linger psychologically though, looking back, feeling precarious exists as something that was moved through but may nonetheless occur again.

DISCUSSION AND CONCLUSION

In this chapter, I have juxtaposed fieldwork and personal circumstances to investigate the leanings that ethnographic methods introduce into knowledge creation about work. This has drawn out some key points. The first centres around the effect of being a researcher on feeling precarious due to uncertain work. Here the social context of the individual (Campbell & Price, 2016) has a mitigating and exacerbating role to play; however, this raises questions about being too guided by ideal types in field research. The examination of personal circumstances hones questions about the location of feeling precarious in relation to work. Instead of encountering a pervasive precariousness as a result of a social position, the researcher instead encountered a multidimensional event that is deemed precarious.

The juxtaposition of field work and personal circumstances illuminates how the sociological imagination, sociology literature, and the practicalities of ethnography reveal or obscure aspects of precarious work. The literature holds a developed notion of precarious work that focuses on the characteristics of a job, and this is often associated with the broader notions of being and feeling precarious (Alberti et al., 2018; Kalleberg, 2018). In this light, the precarity of the ethnography was mostly contained in the workplace. Here, the inability to predict was present in the pragmatic difficulties of non-permanent work, such as struggling to find and hold employment, working erratic hours, and working in bad conditions. While the practical uncertainties of work were soundly identified and experienced, the general precarious experience of such was not. From one perspective, this was because of a limitation in research methods that of being unable to completely shed one's researcher position and completely become a precarious worker. However, another possibility is raised that the sociological methods employed narrowed the perspective to one that unduly excluded the complexities of the environment and fully contextualized persons. The research design, in being centred on work out of both practical and theoretical concerns, was less open to the issues of friendships, housing, recreation, etc., that may play a factor and have their own relationships to work.

This discussion raises questions about the concepts which guide the study of work insecurity. In the case of this researcher, both precarious work and feeling precarious were not encountered in any pure form but always as a messy, mixed, and blurred formula that came close to transforming into something else. In the field work and personal circumstances examined in this chapter, structural insecurities of the social context were translated into feeling precarious in surprising ways. Therefore, a focused research effort into the mode and factors of the translation from social context to life is needed to advance the understanding of insecure work. Instead of being led by the ideal types into greater and greater nuanced understanding, these concepts instead need to be interrogated against the real world and the real lives of people. As such, while ideal types are appropriate for initiating and planning ethnographies, they need to be questioned during the fieldwork and data analysis. At that point, a different type of concept that is highly reactive to different circumstances may be more applicable.

REFERENCES

Alberti, G., Bessa, I., Hardy, K., Trappmann, V. & Umney, C. (2018). In, against and beyond precarity: Work in insecure times. *Work, Employment and Society*, *32*(3), 447–457.

Antonucci, L. (2018). Not all experiences of precarious work lead to precarity: The case study of young people at university and their welfare mixes. *Journal of Youth Studies*, *21*(7), 888–904.

Baines, D., Kent, P., & Kent, S. (2019). 'Off my own back': Precarity on the frontlines of care work. *Work, Employment and Society*, *33*(5), 877–887.

Bourdieu, P. (1998). *Acts of resistance: Against the new myths of our time*. New York, NY: Polity Press.

Butler, J. (2015). Foreword. In I. Lorey (Ed.), *State of insecurity: Government of the precarious* (pp. vii–x). London: Verso Books.

Campbell, I., & Price, R. (2016). Precarious work and precarious workers: Towards an improved conceptualisation. *The Economic and Labour Relations Review*, *27*(3), 314–332.

Donald, B., Gertler, M. S., & Tyler, P. (2013). Creatives after the crash. *Cambridge Journal of Regions, Economy and Society*, *6*, 3–21.

Ettlinger, N. (2007). Precarity unbound. *Alternatives*, *32*(3), 319–340.

Kalleberg, A. L. (2018). *Precarious lives: Job insecurity and well-being in rich democracies*. Cambridge: Polity Press.

Kalleberg, A. L., & Vallas, S. P. (2017). Probing precarious work: Theory, research, and politics. In A. Kalleberg & S. Vallas (Eds.), *Precarious work* (pp. 1–30). Bingley: Emerald Publishing Limited.

Lichterman, P. (2017). Interpretive reflexivity in ethnography. *Ethnography*, *18*(1), 35–45.

Vosko, L. F. (2010). *Managing the margins: Gender, citizenship, and the international regulation of precarious employment*. Oxford: Oxford University Press.

Waite, L. (2009). A place and space for a critical geography of precarity? *Geography Compass*, *3*(1), 412–433.

Worth, N. (2016). Feeling precarious: Millennial women and work. *Environment and Planning D: Society and Space*, *34*(4), 601–616.

CHAPTER 9

REVEALING ONESELF: WHEN DOING FIELDWORK WITH JOURNALISTS CHALLENGES YOUR IDENTITY WORK AS A RESEARCHER IN MANAGEMENT

Laurianne Terlinden

Louvain Research Institute in Management and Organisations, Université catholique de Louvain, Ottignies-Louvain-la-Neuve, Belgium

ABSTRACT

This personal reflection piece relates my experience of vulnerability as a researcher when doing ethnographic fieldwork with journalists. Drawing on my empirical and emotional experience, I show the way the encounters in the field made me feel vulnerable and challenged my identity as a researcher. The chapter also introduces the way my self-disclosure in various ways as a fellow imperfect human being – a.o. regarding motherhood – was an important way to build relationships with the research participants and gain their trust. By doing so, this reflective commentary seeks to contribute to a better understanding of the articulation between researcher identity, fieldwork, and vulnerability.

Keywords: Ethnography; emotional engagement; reflexivity; researcher identity; motherhood; vulnerability

Ethnographies of Work
Research in the Sociology of Work, Volume 35, 173–181

ISSN: 0277-2833/doi:10.1108/S0277-283320230000035009

> I arrive in the meeting room for the first face-to-face meeting with the journalists.
>
> I have been waiting for this moment for two years. For two years, my attempts to immerse myself in the department have been aborted, firstly for fear that my presence and my research would contribute to exacerbate the prevailing social instability – a fear expressed by the HR manager without consulting the management of the department concerned – and secondly because of the eruption of the global COVID-19 epidemic and its consequences in terms of forced distancing from the field.
>
> I enter the meeting room with a pounding heart, full of preconceived ideas about this meeting with the journalists. I try to reassure myself by going to see Ben, my key informant for this part of the field, who is also the facilitator of the meeting. He doesn't seem to make as much fuss about my presence as I do; he greets me quickly and cuts me short when I start a conversation by thanking him for introducing me to this project group. Then I go to say hello to the HR person I've met before, whose presence I find reassuring in this place. However, we are quickly interrupted by journalists.
>
> I feel disappointed and vulnerable. So, I take a seat, hidden behind a plexiglass panel at the end of the table, and try to remain unnoticed by looking focused behind my computer, waiting for the meeting to start. [Fieldnotes, 20 May 2021]

This chapter presents a personal reflective commentary, drawing upon my own experience of ethnographic encounters with journalists as a young, female PhD researcher in management. Drawing on my personal fieldnotes, I show how facing participants and their suspicious look on my status, my research field, and my approach in general – challenged my identity as a researcher. I argue that the researcher's self-disclosure in various ways as a fellow imperfect human being is an important way to build relationships with the research participants and gain their trust. This is done, for instance, not only through the use of offbeat humour but also through the sharing of more personal and sensitive situations encountered, in my case, in motherhood and parenthood.

In this reflective contribution, I, thus, address the personal, emotional, and identity dimensions of fieldwork. I argue that, beyond an opportunistic way to establish good relations with participants to acquire rich ethnographic data, this personal involvement deeply impacts one's identity, making it impossible to 'divorce [the] fieldwork self from [the] other self' (Coffey, 1999). By doing so, I intend to contribute to previous research (Bell, 1999; Coffey, 1999) showing the way field relations are used to socialize with research participants, the resulting strong interrelation between the self and the field, and how this leads researchers to engage in increased identity work, mediated by gender, parenthood, and other personal characteristics. Subsequently, I aim at equipping (future) ethnographers to help them face the discomfort that one can experience when entering the field and feeling subjected to power relations with participants. I hence wish to invite those experiencing these power relations to reflect on and share their own experience in order to diversify a literature that still mostly focuses on experiences of white, experienced male researchers, often presumed to be in a position of 'ethnographic authority' (see e.g. Van Maanen, 1995) towards research participants.

BACKGROUND

The research that forms the background of this chapter is ethnographic fieldwork in Mediabel, a public broadcasting organization where I studied managers' identity constructions (Alvesson & Willmott, 2002) in the context of an internal reorganization towards organizational 'agility'. Qualitative data were collected over a four-year period (between January 2019 and December 2022). I was present in the organization between one and three days a week, depending on the phase of my abductive research. During the course of the study, I undertook about 50 exploratory and semi-structured interviews with managers and journalists, observed some 200 hours of meetings, participated in corporate social events and, above all, had countless informal talks with workers and managers of the organization. All these were carefully documented in descriptive and reflexive fieldnotes. The fieldwork was conducted in French, translations of quotes and fieldnotes used in this chapter are mine. My physical immersion in the organization was interrupted several times; a first time in order to take a step back at university for intermediary data analysis and theorizing and a second time because of the COVID-19 crisis that broke out during the second year of my fieldwork and was directly followed by my maternity leave.

Accepting subjectivity in the production of knowledge – resulting from the researcher's interpretation of the meaning given by the individuals to the reality under study – implies considering knowledge as context-related, subjective and multiple, in the sense that it is a function of each person's interpretation (actors and researcher) of the same reality. In this chapter, I reflect on the importance of the intersubjective dimension in my experience of the field and in the restitution that I make of it. I seek to highlight the interpretations that individuals give to the studied social phenomena, as well as my own interpretations of it. Therefore, this intersubjective approach takes place at two levels. Firstly, at the level of the observed reality, where I seek to understand the interpretation that individuals make of their reality and, in particular, the identity issues that come into play. Secondly, at the level of my research approach *in se*, intersubjectivity is played out not only in the relationships I establish with individuals but also in the interpretation that I, as a researcher, make of this very interpretation given by the individuals I meet. It is this second part of the intersubjective approach concerning the encounters – particularly the emotional encounter – with the participants that I especially wish to explore in greater depth here.

The present reflection is, thus, based on the concept of identity work, seeking to show how a researcher's own identity is influenced by the encounters in the research field. This question of identity work is central to understand how qualitative researchers, and especially ethnographers, 'continuously [engage] in forming, repairing, maintaining, strengthening or revising the constructions that are productive of a precarious sense of coherence and distinctiveness' (Alvesson & Willmott, 2002, p. 626) while doing research. The encounters recounted here – that of a young female PhD researcher in management with a team of journalists from a public broadcasting company – may seem insignificant but proved to be key in my identity work as they implied the constant negotiation of meanings and knowledge between domains inside and outside the research context, in search for some consistence.

REGARDING THE INTEREST OF STUDYING THE RESEARCHER'S IDENTITY WORK IN RELATION TO FIELDWORK

As Alvesson and Svenningson (2011) show in their study of identity work, in a consultant–client relationship and insofar as identities are constructed, negotiated, and reproduced in social interactions, a consultant can only construct a positive identity since the client reflects back to him or her a positive image of themselves. The identity work of consultants, as the authors observe, is supported by the feeling of participating in a change within the organization by bringing knowledge and consistency to the organizational project. While in our ethnographic relationship, we are free from a monetized service relationship, the image of ourselves that the research participants send us back has a strong impact on our sense of legitimacy and, hence, on our identity work. The conviction of the relevance and usefulness – the performative aim being induced by this desire for recognition of the field – of the research in its own temporality is, therefore, central in the search for legitimacy and leads to increased identity work.

Often, this identity work does not stick to the identity as a researcher but also includes the implication of other sides of the personal identity. In my case, as I show later in this chapter, the imposed discretion that forms the researcher's academic identity slowly gave way to a greater affirmation of myself, as a subjective and imperfect being. My readings and exchanges with fellow ethnographers teach me to accept this developed proximity with the field by no longer trying to control my personal identity in the field, but by displaying it, while taking the necessary distance to understand this identity and the way it colours the field and the analysis I make of it. In this way, I strengthen my ethnographic and critical posture, in which reflexivity is central. The very writing of what follows is part of this identity work, putting words on both the process and the outcome of a changing vision of myself throughout the fieldwork and the encounters with journalists.

JOURNALISTS AS CHALLENGING AGENTS OF MY IDENTITY AS A RESEARCHER IN MANAGEMENT

The professional identity of journalists promoting qualitative reporter work and independence (Barros, 2018; Deuze, 2005) does not make them what some authors refer to in the literature as 'docile informants' (Coffey, 1999). Journalists have a specific relation ship with research and investigation. While the basis of the research work, such as collecting data, may seem similar to journalistic work, the intent behind it, its temporality, the way it is analyzed and the end result differ a lot. When our role as researchers is to understand social phenomena, journalists rather aim at informing their public about current and short-term phenomena. Not knowing in advance what we are going to find – especially in the abductive approach I mobilize – and whether it will be of any interest at all seems inconceivable to journalists. Journalists, on their side, quickly draw conclusions suggesting causality by analyzing elements 'on the fire'. This positioning, which I would roughly associate with a positivist approach to research, contrasts with my long-term approach characterized by an interpretative and critical epistemology. As a result, when journalists tend to analyze every situation they encounter, I experience this as a judgement of what I would have analyzed otherwise. But as public figures I watch on television or hear on the radio, I unconsciously give them all the more credit.

Apart from the differences of vision about what good research or investigation means, the actual field of my research also seemed to be problematic. As soon as I started to organize my fieldwork in the department, I was asked half-heartedly what a researcher in management was doing there, why I was not leaving the study of journalists to communication specialists. This seemed to imply that only a journalist can investigate and produce an informed analysis of journalists and of the media industry. I, thus, lacked the recognition of my status as a researcher in management towards this population who, as will be explained to me later, is very critical about management and all that is related to it.

> Historically, there is a little historical tension between the word journalist and the word manager (…) In the sense that the journalist sees himself as someone who is independent, who resists pressure, who doesn't fit into a mould, who has to go beyond the official discourse, whether it's union or managerial or whatever… This is the model we all have in mind. (Hervé, Manager, 30 years of experience as field journalist)

Finally, the profession of journalist remains mainly masculine. Despite a relative equity in the access to the profession, newsrooms are still very gendered, qualified as a 'media world of "testosterones"' (Le Cam, Libert, & Ménalque, 2021, p. 136). I had read several reports on discrimination towards women in the media industry and heard testimonies of women in the organization who suffered from moral and sexual harassment. Being a young, female researcher in this context did not help to give me confidence but rather strengthened my feeling of inferiority. While previous fieldwork experience with, among others, HR employees and managers had finally made me feel comfortable doing research in the organization, my status as a researcher in management being valued and recognized, meeting journalists, thus, put me in what I experienced as a vulnerable position.

Even though the fears that I had at the start proved to be partly wrong when I knew the journalists better, they were nevertheless partly confirmed in the interactions I had with them. Indeed, once contact and trust had been established, journalists opened up to me and also seemed interested in the analysis I could provide from a management perspective. However, I also faced uncomfortable situations where I felt personally targeted by some journalists' remarks or behaviours. During the department project meetings I attended at the start of my fieldwork with journalists, for instance, I occasionally received remarks that seemed hostile to me. For example, at the beginning of a meeting that I attended to analyze the participatory process within the project team in terms of power and authority, Ben, my key informant, told me referring to the juice offered at the buffet: 'Laurianne, you will be able to observe the effect of apple-ginger juice on decision-making'. A remark which, beyond the double meaning given the aphrodisiac effect attributed to ginger, seemed highly ironic to me in relation to the subject of my research and observations. My research was as futile as studying the effect of a juice on human interactions and could be reduced to the influence of A on B, which I believe is in opposition to my interpretative and critical approach. This remark made me feel uncomfortable but mostly angry; I felt the frustration rising in me although I refrained from commenting and remained professional – at least this is the way I perceived it at that time.

SELF-DISCLOSURE AS A GATEWAY TO PARTICIPANTS' TRUST

I rapidly discovered that going beyond this perceived barrier between 'me' and 'them' is necessary to gain participants' respect and trust and requires self-disclosure on my part. I felt the urge to replace my professional identity as a researcher with a more personal identity, an identity as a 'fellow imperfect human being', to get closer to my audience. Desperate about gaining professional legitimacy, being personally and emotionally involved appeared to me as a way to gain participants' trust and empathy and to get closer to them. I decided to use jokes and humour with masculine journalists, while sharing my difficulties of being a woman – an especially a mother – in a male dominated setting (Bell, 1999) with female, but also male – often young fathers – journalists. While I first had the feeling journalists had every reason to reject me, I had finally found something in common with most of my research participants: not only my particularly offbeat humour, but more pragmatically, parenthood and all the struggles that go with it. Subsequently, motherhood and the sharing of my experience of it have helped me get to the know research participants: HR and journalists, men and women. My status as a mother seemed to many to take precedence over my status as a researcher. Even if my baby was not physically there, motherhood itself seemed to be unanimous when it came to understanding (e.g. from young fathers) and empathy (especially from fellow mothers), as illustrated in the following extract from my fieldnotes.

> Talking about working conditions during the interview, Nathalie shares the difficulties she met as a young journalist when she was pregnant. When having to leave the office a bit earlier for an appointment with her obstetrician e.g., her manager would compare it with a hairdresser appointment. She tells me that journalists would generally fear the moment they announce they will become a parent. I share with her my sleepless night when I found out I was pregnant, wondering how the news would be received, which impact it would have on my academic career. I notice that after this exchange, she talks about 'us' as a 'us, mothers' (including me in it) rather than the 'us, journalists' that clearly identified me as an outsider. (Fieldnotes, 29 October 2021)

This kind of interaction made me feel both comfortable with the research participants at the time and optimistic and more peaceful regarding the future of my fieldwork. While motherhood was not central in my life – not to say that I had integrated it as something unprofessional in the workplace – it became fully part of my identity in the field. Similarly, I also revealed my spontaneous – and sometimes offbeat – nature to research participants, to gain their sympathy and trust. This way, the 'authentic' personal identity that characterized me in my student years and that I repressed during my professional beginnings at university, resurfaced and became part of my professional identity, at least in the field. While I cannot share all the difficulties and discomfort participants experience with regard to the new organizational model I am studying because I have not experienced it myself, I can unveil my own vulnerability to gain their empathy and trust getting 'closer together as fellow imperfect human beings' (Tracy, 2004, p. 459). This display of my vulnerability did, quite paradoxically, make me experience the fieldwork more serenely. I then moved from defensive emotions to rather grateful ones.

IMPLICATIONS FOR ETHNOGRAPHY

As a young female PhD student in management, my experience of doing research with mainly male journalists has proven to bring about a different dynamic than with other previously encountered populations such as HR employees or managers. Facing journalists' critical and analytical stance and their divergent vision about inquiry and knowledge creation made my vulnerability all the more obvious. It did make me feel uncomfortable and lacking the necessary legitimacy to study this field. Reflections on my experience as an ethnographer show how vulnerability and putting the personal into the professional are necessary conditions for ethnographic proximity. Indeed, I (partly) overcame my lack of legitimacy feeling towards my research participants through an attempt to show myself as a 'fellow imperfect human being', which appears to be a prerequisite for human connection. This proximity to the research field not only permitted a more peaceful field experience but also called for reflexivity about my position in relation to what and who I was studying, as well as the effects my position may have had on the research process and results, adding to the debate on the way our understanding of relationality and intersubjectivity can inform organizational ethnography (Cunliffe, 2003; Gilmore & Kenny, 2015).

My experience presented here above sheds light on the difficulties and the 'feelings of confusion, ambiguity, exclusion and insecurity' (Gilmore & Kenny, 2015, p. 71) ethnographers may experience when having to ensure socialization both at university and in the studied organization. Trying one's best to develop good ties with the field, meeting the difficulties that are described in this chapter, and integrating the field's norms and practices, on the one hand, while remaining a member of the university with its own norms and practices, on the other hand, may lead to what I sometimes experienced as a schizophrenic situation that needs to be acknowledged. Indeed, while conversations at university often imply debates with deeply constructed and reasoned opinions about a certain (mostly public) topic, conversations in the studied organization are diverse and with no taboos. Individual private life, emotions, and feelings are not hidden behind the façade of the analysis of an external phenomenon. The form of these exchanges is another important element of differentiation. Whereas at university, both oral and written expression often sounds pompous, punctuated by academic concepts, discussions within the studied organization are conducted in everyday language, albeit punctuated by corporate language. Being aware of and accepting this double socialization also led to increased identity work to develop a coherent self-identity while constantly shifting between two contexts and roles (Järventie-Thesleff, Logemann, Piekkari, & Tienari, 2016). This identity allows reconciling the necessary personal involvement in the field and the required professional and critical distance (Anteby, 2013). The writing of this chapter is both part and the result of this identity work.

The specificity of the identity work I present here does not especially deal with occupational and organizational identity, as one could expect when constantly shifting between two roles and organizations (being a critical researcher in management at university versus being an HR colleague without taking part in activities in Mediabel), it rather regards the personal side of the identity as a researcher. In doing so, I become an insider in the relationships I build with participants within the organization. However, I remain an outsider to the organization's activity and to its members' work. Hence, although the impact of my integration within the organization on the interpretation of the collected data requires increased reflexivity, the question of the impact on the actors' work is less salient. In particular, my story confirms Anteby's claim that 'there is no reason to assume that personal involvement cannot coexist with professional distance' (2013, p. 1278). The result of this identity work in the field – (partly) leaving my identity as a researcher in management to become a fellow imperfect human being, a mother struggling with parenthood, a person with offbeat humour … –, does not keep me from the set of mental activities that must help me to detach from the field in order to analyze it with the necessary professional distance. This happens partly by reflecting on my positioning in the field and on my experience of it in my writing and my communication with academic colleagues but also by using this very knowledge as a way to inform the data analysis.

The reflection offered here also provides new insights into power relations in ethnography, when the researcher – often presumed to be in a position of power towards research participants – gets a sense of powerlessness in the field. Indeed, while most ethnographers include this reflexivity in their work, there remains a tendency to start from the assumption of an 'ethnographic authority' (see e.g. Van Maanen, 1995). One could hypothesize that this ethnographic authority can only exist in the situation where the researcher – paradoxically – keeps a distance from the field. This distance is induced by the purpose of the work, the researcher being the one who gives meaning to what he or she observes. However, the inverse relationship between the field and the researcher, as a way of rebalancing this relationship of authority, is still understudied. Few authors talk about the difficulties an ethnographer may face when trying to become immersed in social settings he or she is not familiar with or he or she feels excluded from. With this chapter, I wish to answer the call for taking the emotional engagement that appears in the researcher-researched relationship into account, including the researcher's own emotions

(Gilmore & Kenny, 2015; Rhodes & Carlsen, 2018) and the way it contributes to identity work.

REFERENCES

Alvesson, M., & Sveningsson, S. (2011). Identity work in consultancy projects: Ambiguity and distribution of credit and blame. *Discourses of Deficit*, 159–174. https://doi.org/10.1057/9780230299023_9

Alvesson, M., & Willmott, H. (2002). Identity regulation as organizational control: Producing the appropriate individual. *Journal of Management Studies*, *39*(5), 619–644. https://doi.org/10.1111/1467-6486.00305

Anteby, M. (2013). Relaxing the taboo on telling our own stories: Upholding professional distance and personal involvement. *Organization Science*, *24*(4), 1277–1290. https://doi.org/10.1287/orsc.1120.0777

Barros, M. (2018). Digitally crafting a resistant professional identity: The case of Brazilian 'dirty' bloggers. *Organization*, *25*(6), 755–783. https://doi.org/10.1177/1350508418759185

Bell, E. (1999). The negotiation of a working role in organizational ethnography. *International Journal of Social Research Methodology*, *2*(1), 17–37. https://doi.org/10.1080/136455799295168

Coffey, A. (1999). *The ethnographic self. The ethnographic self.* London: SAGE Publications. https://doi.org/10.4135/9780857020048

Deuze, M. (2005). What is journalism? *Journalism*, *6*(4), 442–464. https://doi.org/10.1177/1464884905056815

Gilmore, S., & Kenny, K. (2015). Work-worlds colliding: Self-reflexivity, power and emotion in organizational ethnography. *Human Relations*, *68*(1), 55–78. https://doi.org/10.1177/0018726714531998

Järventie-Thesleff, R., Logemann, M., Piekkari, R., & Tienari, J. (2016). Roles and identity work in "at-home" ethnography. *Journal of Organizational Ethnography*, *5*(3), 235–257. https://doi.org/10.1108/JOE-07-2016-0015/full/pdf

Le Cam, F., Libert, M., & Ménalque, L. (2021). *Être femme et journaliste. Enquête sociologique dans un monde au masculin.* Brussels: Éditions de l'Université de Bruxelles.

Rhodes, C., & Carlsen, A. (2018). The teaching of the other: Ethical vulnerability and generous reciprocity in the research process. *Human Relations*, *71*(10), 1295–1318. https://doi.org/10.1177/0018726717741530

Van Maanen, J. (1995). Style as theory. *Organization Science*, *6*(1), 133–143. https://doi.org/10.1287/orsc.6.1.133

CHAPTER 10

BEYOND THE COMPANY LINE: STUDYING WORKPLACE INEQUALITIES ETHNOGRAPHICALLY

Lauren A. Rivera

Kellogg School of Management, Northwestern University, Evanston, IL, USA

ABSTRACT

While scholars have demonstrated persistent demographic inequalities in hiring, performance evaluations, and compensation decisions, many of the mechanisms driving these effects remain less clear. Qualitative research methods, including ethnographic approaches, are uniquely poised to fill this gap because they can illuminate how workplace inequalities are produced and reproduced on the ground. But studying workplace inequalities qualitatively also poses specific methodological challenges and considerations. In this essay, I discuss common issues researchers face when studying workplace inequalities ethnographically, including barriers in gaining access to sensitive organizational processes, building sufficient trust and rapport to move beyond official narratives of organizational practice ('the company line'), and managing the emotional and psychological burden of discovering what lies beyond that line. I discuss potential strategies for navigating these challenges.

Keywords: Qualitative methods; workplace inequalities; ethnography; discrimination; organizations; sensitive research topics

Ethnographies of Work
Research in the Sociology of Work, Volume 35, 183–195

Published under exclusive licence by Emerald Publishing Limited
ISSN: 0277-2833/doi:10.1108/S0277-283320230000035010

There is a rich sociological literature on workplace inequalities. Scholars have demonstrated persistent gaps in hiring, performance evaluations, and compensation decisions by gender, race, social class, sexual orientation, disability status, and other status characteristics. The bulk of this literature examines quantitative analysis of firm personnel records, employer surveys, publicly available data, laboratory experiments, or field ('audit') experiments (e.g. Baert, 2016; Castilla, 2008; Correll, Benard, & Paik, 2007; Fernandez & Fernandez-Mateo, 2006; Pager, 2003; Pedulla, 2018; Quadlin, 2018; Rivera & Tilcsik, 2016). While this scholarship documents unequal outcomes with ever-increasing precision, many of the mechanisms driving these effects remain less clear (Castilla, 2011; Reskin, 2003; Rivera, 2020).

Qualitative research methods, including ethnographic approaches, are uniquely poised to fill this gap because they can illuminate how workplace inequalities are produced and reproduced on the ground (Reskin, 2000; Rivera, 2015). But studying workplace inequalities qualitatively also poses specific methodological challenges and considerations. A core obstacle is getting beyond official narratives of how organization policies and procedures work in theory – what I call 'the company line' – to observe how opportunities and rewards are allocated in practice. In this essay, I draw from existing work on ethnography as well as my own experiences in the field to discuss common issues researchers face when studying workplace inequalities ethnographically. These include (1) gaining access to sensitive moments of stratification; (2) building sufficient trust and rapport to facilitate disclosure of unflattering aspects of evaluative and distributive processes; and (3) managing the emotional and psychological burden of discovering what lies beyond the company line. I discuss each issue in detail and outline potential strategies researchers can draw from when navigating these challenges.

GETTING IN AND GETTING INSIDE

While gaining access to field sites is a defining challenge of ethnography as a method (Harrington, 2003), it is especially difficult when researchers attempt to study workplace inequalities (see Smith, 2001). Analyzing factors that produce and reproduce categorical inequalities at work requires observing an organization's most sensitive – and often most sacred – gatekeeping routines and rituals, such as how organizations identify, select, and reward talent and decide whom to include and exclude from prized opportunities. These interactions often fall under the scope of laws surrounding workplace discrimination and harassment. Researchers studying workplace inequalities ethnographically may very well observe activities during their fieldwork that would damage the reputations of individuals or organizations or are downright illegal. As a result, this type of research has high stakes for organizations, and gatekeepers are often hesitant to allow outsiders in.

Historically, some scholars have dealt with such obstacles through covert or semi-covert ethnography, such as procuring employment in an organization without official approval to use what one observes on the job for research purposes (for contemporary examples, see Ho, 2009; Pierce, 1996). There are, however, ongoing debates about the ethics of obtaining access in such a manner as well as issues of concealment and disclosure in ethnography more broadly (see Fine, 1993; Lugosi, 2006 for discussions). In addition, in the United States, some academic professional associations strongly discourage covert methods (see Smith, 2001 for discussion), and university institutional review boards often prefer – or require – researchers to obtain explicit permission from an organization before observing.

Given the extremely sensitive nature of this type of research, one of the most common questions I am asked when presenting my ethnographic work on discrimination to academic audiences is how I gained access to the organizations I have studied. The simple answer is that I typically do not approach an organization cold. While cold contacting can be fruitful in recruiting research participants for one-off interactions, such as completing an interview or a survey, it is unlikely that an employer will allow a stranger to live at their workplace for months or years, observing processes that could potentially get them sued. Research suggests that familiarity is a major source of trust and liking (see Bornstein, 1989; Reis et al., 2011). Consequently, when in the initial stages of a research project, I reach out to people I know via personal and professional networks who inhabit the types of organizations I would like to study. My goal is to get their perspective on how the phenomenon I am interested in (e.g. hiring) works in their organization and to find out if there are potential allies within the organization who might want to partner with me for research. As opportunistic as it sounds, I am often on the lookout at social events, industry and academic conferences, and panels for people who could serve as organizational informants and liaisons in the future. When formally approaching an organization to talk about a potential research collaboration, I try to get a well-placed sponsor – someone in the organization who shares an interest in and may directly benefit from the research – on board first and solicit their help in making the case to relevant gatekeepers. This sponsor can help translate the importance of the research to decision makers in ways that resonate locally, can vouch for my trustworthiness and credibility, and otherwise help persuade them that I am the right person to conduct the study.

Along with familiarity, perceived similarity can induce trust and liking (Byrne, 1971; Montoya, Horton, & Kirchner, 2008). Access may be easier to obtain when the researcher is perceived as being an industry or organizational insider. While there is ongoing debate about the benefits of insider versus outsider status in qualitative methods broadly (see Lareau, 2021, for a discussion), when studying highly sensitive organizational processes, being perceived as similar to an organization's members can help decrease suspicion and facilitate entry. An especially valuable type of insider status is having prior or current work experience in the organization or industry a researcher is studying. For example, many recent ethnographies of work investigating sensitive organizational processes were conducted by scholars with direct work experience or training in the fields they were studying (e.g. Anteby, 2013; Besbris, 2020; Harrington, 2017; Mears, 2011). In my own experience, having previously worked at an elite professional service firm facilitated research access to one such firm (Rivera, 2015). When presenting my research proposal to gatekeepers at the company, which I refer to by the pseudonym of Holt Halliday, my organizational sponsor began with a discussion of my work experience in the industry as evidence that I was trustworthy. This shared history also provided a sense of comfort while I was in the field. Employees commonly said things to me such as, 'You get it' or 'You're one of us'. Likewise, my professional background was vital in obtaining access for my study of university hiring committees (Rivera, 2017). I had originally wanted to conduct an ethnographic study of academic – rather than elite corporate – hiring for my doctoral dissertation. Back then, my graduate school advisor reached out to members of her academic networks at a variety of universities to help source potential leads but struck out. The feedback she received from her contacts was that I was not the right status to observe such sensitive moments; faculty would feel on guard having a doctoral student in the room while they spoke about junior faculty candidates. Nearly a decade later, I did successfully gain access to junior faculty search committees. My experience as a tenure-track faculty member was crucial in persuading relevant gatekeepers at the university I studied to sign off on the research. Likewise, my insider status helped decrease obtrusiveness during observation.

Overall, gaining access to field sites for research on workplace inequalities is challenging. But when thinking of potential field sites, it is important to think connectedly – in terms of the universe of relevant organizations that a researcher is already connected to – and expansively. Even when approached by a trusted and familiar source, organizations frequently decline access of this sort, so cultivating multiple leads simultaneously can help save time and increase the chance of successful entry.

FRAMING A REQUEST

In addition, how researchers frame requests for access matters. Practitioners are rarely concerned with the details of academic debates. Framing the overall purpose of the research in terms of its broader implications for organizational life or policy can help gatekeepers more easily understand the importance of a given study. In her recent book on qualitative methods, sociologist Annette Lareau (2021) also writes about how it can be beneficial to frame the purpose of a qualitative study in a 'vague but accurate' way.[1] I find this to be especially helpful for studying workplace inequalities. For example, when studying hiring, I present the goal of research as understanding how hiring works, with the aim of developing best practices rather than delving into the details about which types of inequalities I believe may be salient in a given setting.

Organizations may also be more motivated to participate in a research agreement when there is something in it for them. In the past, I have offered to provide a free service that an organization would have otherwise paid for in exchange for access for research purposes. For example, at Holt, I worked as an unpaid intern helping to plan and execute company recruiting events. Because the firm was originally looking to pay an intern for this role, they received a service they valued and saved money by granting me access versus hiring someone for the job. In my study of doormen at an elite nightclub (Rivera, 2010), I likewise worked for free in various club roles (e.g. coat check and cigarette girl) and could substitute for club employees who called out on a given night, which provided valuable staffing security for the club's management. While the literature on ethnographic methods often assumes that researchers have nothing of value to offer participants (Van Maanen, 1991), social scientists do have two things human resources departments and executives charged with managing workplace personnel issues tend to value: analytical training and bandwidth to perform analyses. Sometimes organizations are amenable to exchanging research access for related analysis. In my study of academic hiring committees, I provided the university I studied with a customized report detailing how to improve equity in hiring based on my observations and current research. This is a service that the university would have otherwise paid a consultant a substantial fee to produce. Including a researcher in a project may be more appealing to a potential field site if organizational gatekeepers derive something valuable to them (e.g. labour, analysis, consulting advice) for free. However, it is crucial to spell out the terms of these reciprocal agreements up front so that both the organization and the researcher have a clear and common understanding of the terms of access and exchange. Such agreements can also reduce the potential for exploitative relationships.

CONFIDENTIALITY AND PUBLISHING CONTROL

While some scholars have advocated naming rather than concealing the identities of research subjects and field sites (see Jerolmack & Murphy, 2017; Reyes, 2018), this practice gets tricky when studying sensitive organizational processes that have the potential to uncover illegal activities. Depending on the specific topic studied and the profile of the organization, there is a very real risk that a researcher or their field notes could be subpoenaed. For these reasons, along with general concerns about reputational risks, confidentiality has been a precondition for access to the organizations I have studied. Offering confidentiality can help researchers get in the door and decrease obtrusiveness and defensiveness once in the field. Research shows that when people believe that they can be held personally accountable for their actions, they are less likely to engage in biased or unethical behaviour (Lerner & Tetlock, 1999). In my research, participants have often asked me in a somewhat joking tone before confessing or doing something that is not aboveboard, 'My name's not on this, right?' Providing confidentiality can, therefore, be an important tool that helps researchers observe typical rather than best behaviour. Confidentiality can be achieved through carefully masking the identity of an organization and key informants and involves considering not only names but also factors including the size, location, and type of organization studied. Wehner and Gilmartin (2022) provide systematic guidelines for organizational masking. They suggest thinking carefully about what is necessary to disclose about an organization, developing a list of peer organizations that are similar along these dimensions and describing the organization in a way that makes it indistinguishable from its peers.

True confidentiality, however, requires more than just removing potentially identifiable information about employees, employers, clients, and customers in final reports and research articles. It also entails removing this type of information from field notes and analytic memos and being careful about what is communicated via email, given that these records may become the subject of public or legal interest. Personally, I do not record potentially identifiable information in my field notes or memos. When taking notes in a group meeting, for example, I create a key of pseudonyms or short-hand markers and use those to indicate speakers. I keep the hard copy under lock and key in a secure location.

Finally, when working through the details of access within a potential field site, researchers must specify in writing that they are free to publish their findings without the review or approval of the host organization, adhering to any confidentiality agreements that have been made. These types of studies will often uncover unflattering or even illegal information. If an organization retains right of review of results, it may try to kill a project or stop publication if it does not like the findings. A good friend of mine from graduate school conducted an ethnography of a Fortune 500 company, spent over a year in the field, and completed a draft of the dissertation based on these observations. However, the host organization retained the right to approve reports produced from the research prior to submission. Gatekeepers at the firm read the dissertation draft and thought the findings would portray the firm in a negative light; they prevented the student from submitting the dissertation. Very late in their graduate program, the student had to start over from scratch with a new dissertation topic and field site. Successfully completing workplace ethnography, therefore, requires permission both to observe and publish, no matter what is found. Thinking carefully about the terms of research agreements in advance can help facilitate both goals.

GETTING IN VERSUS GETTING INSIDE

Getting in an organization, in terms of obtaining official permission to be there, does not always guarantee *getting inside* to observe the sensitive, behind-the-scenes moments of stratification that are at the heart of ethnographic work on workplace inequalities. Once a researcher enters the field, organizational gatekeepers may attempt to *curate access,* in which they selectively restrict what a researcher can and cannot observe to limit their observations to the company line and portray the organization in the best possible light.

I experienced this first hand during fieldwork at a large technology company. I had been approached by a personal ('warm') contact to observe the company's selection of new executive level hires. I was thrilled by the request. I had been working on an interview-based project on executive searches, and directly observing selection procedures would provide vital insights into how inequalities are reproduced or challenged on the ground. And, frankly, after having worked hard to secure access in prior projects, the idea of a company going out of its way to open its doors to me sounded like a dream. I was so excited by the prospect of participating that I hopped on a plane without a clear research agreement in place.

When I arrived at the company's headquarters, I discovered that the company's public relations team oversaw both the selection process and my access. Perhaps unsurprisingly given their role, they had curated access and limited my participation in the selection process to moments that were low stakes and presented the organization in a positive light. For example, they allowed me to interview a handpicked roster of individuals who had varying involvement in the process and observe group-based discussions of evaluative criteria and processes. However, they barred me from observing moments of stratification where evaluations and decisions such as candidate interviews and post-interview deliberation meetings actually took place; they even refused to disclose any details about the people who were being interviewed or given offers. Accordingly, my observations were limited to official, company-sanctioned narratives about how executives *should be* chosen rather than how selection works in practice. Given that I was not able to get beyond the company line, I exited the field after a few months. This experience, although frustrating, underscored the importance of obtaining explicit agreements about the conditions of access that spell out what the researcher will be allowed to observe once in the organization.

BLENDING IN AND ROLLING WITH

Getting in and getting inside are crucial steps in analyzing workplace inequalities ethnographically. To move beyond the company line, research participants also need to feel comfortable enough in an ethnographer's presence to go about their work life in a typical way. Cultivating comfort involves general friendliness, politeness, and agreeableness in interactions with research participants. It also involves blending in. In an ideal world, research participants view the researcher as another organizational member, a fly on the wall, or even a piece of décor.

Dressing similarly to other employees is one way to blend in. While we often coach qualitative researchers to look professional, what this entails may vary drastically between organizations and departments. For example, if someone is observing a technology firm where the dress code is bright socks and hooded sweatshirts, a crisp Oxford shirt and pressed pants would stand out sorely, whereas the same attire might blend in perfectly in an accounting firm. A good rule of thumb is that researchers should look the part for the world – and the role – they are studying. Things that call substantial attention to a researcher's presence are tangible reminders that someone is watching and to be on alert.

In addition to dress, note-taking methods have the potential to help researchers blend in or make them stand out. In some situations, it is possible to take notes in real time without seeming out of place. During group meetings, for instance, I have found that taking notes by hand allows me to blend in more than does typing notes on a laptop. First, a laptop screen serves as a physical partition between the researcher and the world being studied. Second, the clickety clack of a laptop keyboard – no matter how stealthily one believes one types – serves as a continuing reminder of a researcher's presence and can disrupt the flow of a meeting. It also serves as an auditory cue that something noteworthy is happening and can draw people out of the moment. Finally, having physical rather than electronic notes can enable more control over data for privacy and confidentiality purposes. Of course, there are times when taking notes by hand would stand out. Part of my job duties at Holt involved taking down official written debriefs between two interviewers of a particular job candidate, and all other employees who performed this task did so via laptop. To blend in, I did the same. In informal interactions, such as a conversation in the hallway or at dinner, it would be jarring for participants to see a researcher take notes in real time. For this reason, I carry a pocket-sized notebook to jot down notes in a bathroom stall, and I also keep a file for quick jottings on my mobile phone. The timing and medium of notetaking matter for a researcher's overall obtrusiveness in the field and the degree to which people feel relaxed and comfortable in their presence.

ROLLING WITH IT

Fieldwork can be unpredictable. Organization theorist John Van Maanen (2011, p. 2) famously summarized of ethnography:

> Fieldworkers, it seems, learn to move among strangers while holding themselves in readiness for episodes of embarrassment, affection, misfortune, partial or vague revelation, deceit, confusion, isolation, warmth, adventure, fear, concealment, pleasure, surprise, insult, and always possible deportation. Accident and happenstance shapes fieldworkers' studies as much as planning or foresight; numbing routine as much as living theatre.

Likewise, fieldwork on workplace inequalities may uncover information that is sensitive, uncomfortable, offensive, or illegal. Learning to respond to curve balls with grace and composure is crucial for maintaining comfort and preserving the flow of interaction. Researchers may observe actions or hear statements they find distasteful or wrong. Because these moments can be deeply uncomfortable, they may feel an urge to stop or interrupt them. But these are precisely the times where it is essential to stay to get beyond the company line.

How can fieldworkers respond in such unsettling moments in a way that allows the scene to carry on? Improvisational comedy provides a useful clue. There are important parallels between ethnography and improv. In both, there is no set script to follow, and actors need to respond to whatever situation or line is given to them, no matter how absurd, in a way that enables the scene to progress. Indeed, several scholars have described qualitative research as a form of improvisation (Harrington, 2003; Lareau, 2021).

A golden rule of improvisational comedy, popularized by the Chicago troupe Second City, is known as 'Yes, and …' When a participant in a scene gives other a line or a bid, their partner must acknowledge it as real and build from there. For example, if an actor presents their improv partner with an orange and tells them it is an antique globe, even if the partner personally thinks the idea is ridiculous, they have to accept this statement and build on it; maybe they give the orb a whirl or point out Santa's house. By contrast, the number one way of killing a scene is to reject a partner's bid by denying (e.g. 'That's not a globe!'), denigrating (e.g. 'That's silly'), ignoring the idea, or changing the topic. These types of responses can feel to participants and audiences like a needle scratching a record to a halt; they interrupt the shared reality that was being produced.

Likewise, when I encounter sensitive or upsetting information in the field, I do my best to 'Yes, and …' Given that my research focus is typically discrimination, I frequently hear research participants articulate biased perceptions of specific social groups. Even though I may be tempted to call out these perceptions as wrong or offensive, it is precisely in these moments that it is important to stay with the subject to understand their world. When this type of information is disclosed to me in a research interview or hallway conversation, 'Yes, and …' often looks like keeping a calm face, nodding, maintaining eye contact, and accepting this bid by asking in a friendly voice, 'That's interesting, tell me more'. When presented with this type of situation in the field, 'Yes, and …' may look different. In my study of faculty hiring, I was at a meeting where search committee members insisted that they needed to know the marital status of a particular female job candidate. They began Googling and searching social media for any type of indicator that this woman was married.

I was pretty surprised that they did this in front of me, given that using marital status in hiring decisions is against their university's policy and is illegal in their state. But my actions during this time were crucial for how this scene unfolded. Had I verbally protested, told the meeting participants that these actions were in danger of violating their state's law, rolled my eyes, or given verbal or nonverbal cues of disapproval, this could have interrupted what they considered to be a legitimate and necessary act. Had I walked out, they could have continued to go down this path, just without a researcher there to document precisely how far they went down it – pulling up marriage and divorce records online, private messaging faculty and former students, even searching *New York Times* wedding announcements and various wedding registry aggregator sites for any evidence of marital status. I would have missed the opportunity to see if there was any internal pushback to these activities (there was), by whom (one male committee member), and what the response was (to dismiss his concern and assert that marital status is necessary to understand if women are 'moveable'). Instead, I kept a calm demeanour, took physical notes, smiled when the group laughed or joked about what they found, and let the scene unfold. The goal of fieldwork on workplace inequalities is to understand how things work – not in theory – but in practice. Sometimes that means putting aside personal beliefs, entering a role, and rolling with it.

There are, of course, situations when a researcher cannot – and should not – roll. For example, researchers may be asked to participate directly in illegal activities. In the example above, the search committee asked me to use my personal networks to find out private information about this job candidate, which I knew was a legal grey zone. Had I said yes, I would have potentially violated state law. So, I declined but did so in a way that did not convey judgement or disproval. Instead, I provided a rationale I knew would resonate with them: at the time, I was untenured and told them I did not want to do anything to rock the boat in my field. I was able to maintain this boundary, but in a way that preserved trust and rapport. There may be other times when rolling with it would put the researcher in physical danger. In my nightclub study, a newer doorman whom I barely knew invited me to travel with him to his parents' house in rural New England for Christmas so that he could introduce me to them. This request felt odd because I had only spoken to him once or twice. Accepting would have entailed being in a car alone with a stranger without an exit. I politely declined. Later that week, he called me on my phone, letting me know he was outside my door (I had never told him where I lived). The behaviour was sufficiently concerning that I ended up exiting my field site earlier than expected because of safety concerns. While in the field, building comfort, allowing scenes to unfold, and rolling with it are important tools for observing typically hidden aspects of organizational life, but there are limits. Researchers perform a delicate balance of gathering data and looking out for their own safety.

EMOTIONAL LABOUR

Studying workplace inequalities qualitatively can be emotionally taxing for researchers. Scholars have discussed the increased emotional labour experienced by fieldworkers studying sensitive research topics (Blix & Wettergren, 2015; Rager, 2005). This burden is especially pronounced for researchers from historically under-represented or marginalized groups studying the continuing under-representation or marginalization of others. It requires strategic impression management, 'face work' (Goffman, 1959), and 'surface acting' (Hochshield, 1983) to remain calm and agreeable while politely listening to negative stereotypes of one's ingroup rather than standing up, setting the record straight, or simply screaming. Fieldwork, in general, can be exhausting – dealing with sexism, racism, ableism, and the like on top of it can take a mental and emotional toll that lingers well after observation hours are done for the day. In addition, as the experience I had researching nightclubs highlights, women and members of marginalized groups are more likely to experience harassment while pursuing fieldwork (for a discussion, see Hanson & Richards, 2017). The cognitive and emotional load of watching out for physical safety while also trying to fully participate in a world can be very heavy.

Another complication arises when coping strategies that are often suggested for fieldwork on sensitive topics – such as building a support network of trusted family, friends, and colleagues to debrief with (Dickson-Smith et al., 2007) or journaling (Goodrum & Keys, 2007) – may be limited when researching workplace inequalities. When researchers disclose details, they may inadvertently reveal the identity of the organization and open other researchers or their contacts to subpoena.

But there are strategies that can be used to help cope with the emotional labour that this type of work can entail. Scheduled self-care, in the form of exercise, long walks, or comfort activities, can help release stress. While I often cannot talk to others about what I've observed in the field, as silly as it sounds, I have found surprising relief in talking to myself in the car or the shower. But what I have found most useful is a strategy commonly used in cognitive behavioural therapy: cognitive reframing.

The idea behind reframing is that negative events exert psychological and physiological tolls not only because of the events themselves but also because of the stories people tell themselves about the events (Beck, 2019). Therefore, people can decrease the negative psychological impact of an event by crafting a narrative that reduces negative attributions and arousal (Clark, 2013). The story I tell myself about hearing biased or discriminatory sentiments that are counter to my own personal values and not speaking up in the moment is that by remaining in my role and rolling with it, I am privy to organizational scenes and scenarios I would never otherwise be able to observe. By being able to write about these events in my research, I can shine a light on processes that typically remain hidden with the potential goal of diversifying opportunity and increasing equity. In these moments, I repeat to myself the adage, 'Sunlight is the best disinfectant'.

CONCLUSION

Ethnographic fieldwork can be an extremely useful tool to understand workplace inequalities. Seeing how opportunities are actually distributed within an organization can challenge existing narratives of how workplaces operate and call attention to new, hidden, or counterintuitive mechanisms of stratification. This type of research can be challenging in terms of getting in and getting inside, building sufficient rapport to get beyond the company line, and coping with what one discovers behind that line. Yet, unearthing organizational realities is crucial for developing more accurate theoretical and empirical models of how workplace stratification occurs and, ultimately, increasing diversity and equity in organizations.

NOTE

1. Fine (1993) refers to this type of framing as *shallow cover*.

REFERENCES

Anteby, M. (2013). *Manufacturing morals: The values of silence in business school education*. Chicago, IL: University of Chicago Press.

Baert, S. (2016). Wage subsidies and hiring chances for the disabled: Some causal evidence. *European Journal of Health Economics*, *17*, 71–86.

Beck, A. (2019). A 60-year evolution of cognitive theory and therapy. *Perspectives on Psychological Science*, *14*(1). 16–20.

Besbris, M. (2020). *Upsold: Real estate agents, prices, and neighborhood inequality*. Chicago, IL: University of Chicago Press.

Blix, S. B., & Wettergren, Å. (2015). The emotional labour of gaining and maintaining access to the field. *Qualitative Research*, *15*(6), 688–704.

Bornstein, R. F. (1989). Exposure and affect: Overview and meta-analysis of research, 1968–1987. *Psychological Bulletin*, *106*(2), 265–289.

Byrne, D. E. (1971). *The attraction paradigm*. Cambridge, MA: Academic Press.

Castilla, E. J. (2008). Gender, race, and meritocracy in organizational careers. *American Journal of Sociology*, *113*(6), 1479–1526.

Castilla, E. J. (2011). Bringing managers back in: Managerial influences on workplace inequality. *American Sociological Review*, *76*, 667–694.

Clark, D. (2013). Cognitive restructuring. In S. Hoffman (Ed.), *Wiley handbook of cognitive behavioral therapy* (pp. 23–44). London: Wiley Blackwell.

Correll, S. J., Benard, S., & Paik, I. (2007). Getting a job: Is there a motherhood penalty? *American Journal of Sociology*, *112*(5), 1297–1339.

Dickson-Smith, V. James, E. L., Kippen, S., & Liamputtong, P. (2007). Doing sensitive research: what challenges do qualitative researchers face? *Qualitative Research*, *7*(3), 327–353.

Fernandez, R., & Fernandez-Mateo, I. (2006). Networks, race, and hiring. *American Sociological Review*, *71*, 42–71.

Fine, G. A. (1993). Ten lies of ethnography: Moral dilemmas of field research. *Journal of Contemporary Ethnography*, *22*, 267–294.

Goffman, E. (1959). *The presentation of self in everyday life*. London: Doubleday.

Goodrum, S., & Keys, J. L. (2007). Reflections on two studies of emotionally sensitive topics: Bereavement from murder and abortion. *International Journal of Social Research Methodology*, *10*(4), 249–258.

Hanson, R., & Richards, P. (2017). Sexual harassment and the construction of ethnographic knowledge. *Sociological Forum*, *32*(3), 587–609.

Harrington, B. (2003). The social psychology of access in ethnographic research. *Journal of Contemporary Ethnography*, *32*(5), 592–625.

Harrington, B. (2017). *Capital without borders: Wealth management and the one percent*. Cambridge, MA: Harvard University Press.

Ho, K. (2009). Liquidated: An ethnography of wall street. Durham, NC: Duke University Press.

Hochschild, A. (1983). *The managed heart*. Berkeley, CA: University of California Press.

Jerolmack, C., & Murphy, A. (2017). The ethical dilemmas and social scientific trade-offs of masking in ethnography. *Sociological Methods & Research*, *18*(4), 801–827.

Lareau, A. (2021). *Listening to people: A practical guide to interviewing, participant observation, data analysis, and writing it all up*. Chicago, IL: University of Chicago Press.

Lerner, J. S., & Tetlock, P. E. (1999). Accounting for the effects of accountability. *Psychological Bulletin*, *125*(2), 255–275.

Lugosi, P. (2006). Between overt and covert research concealment and disclosure in an ethnographic study of commercial hospitality. *Qualitative Inquiry*, *12*(3), 541–561.

Mears, A. (2011). *Pricing beauty: The making of a fashion model*. Berkeley, CA: University of California Press.

Montoya, M., Horton, R., & Kirchner, J. (2008). Is actual similarity necessary for attraction? A meta-analysis of actual and perceived similarity. *Journal of Social and Personal Relationships*, *25*, 899–922.

Pager, D. (2003). The mark of criminal record. American Journal of Sociology, *108*, 937–975.

Pedulla, D. S. (2018). How race and unemployment shape labor market opportunities: Additive, amplified, or muted effects? *Social Forces*, *96*(4), 1477–1506.

Pierce, J. L. (1996). *Gender trials: Emotional lives in contemporary law firms*. Berkeley, CA: University of California Press.

Quadlin, N. (2018). The mark of a woman's record: Gender and academic performance in hiring. *American Sociological Review*, *83*(2), 331–360.

Rager, K. (2005). Self-care and the qualitative researcher: When collecting data can break your heart. *Educational Researcher*, *34*(4), 23–27.

Reis, H., Maniaci, M., Caprariello, P., Eastwick, P., & Finkel, E. (2011). Familiarity does indeed promote attraction in live interaction. *Journal of Personality and Social Psychology*, *101*(3), 557–570.

Reskin, B. (2000). The proximate causes of employment discrimination. *Contemporary Sociology*, *29*, 319–328.

Reskin, B. (2003). Presidential address: Including mechanisms in our models of ascriptive inequality. *American Sociological Review*, *68*, 1–21.

Reyes, V. (2018). Three models of transparency in ethnographic research: Naming places, naming people, and sharing data. *Ethnography*, *19*(2), 204–226.

Rivera, L. A. (2010). Status distinctions in interaction: Social selection and exclusion at an elite nightclub. *Qualitative Sociology*, *33*, 229–55.

Rivera, L. A. (2015). *Pedigree: How elite students get elite jobs*. Princeton, NJ: Princeton University Press.

Rivera, L. A. (2017). When two bodies are (not) a problem: Gender and relationship status discrimination in academic hiring. *American Sociological Review*, *82*, 1111–1138.

Rivera, L. A. (2020). Employer decision making. *Annual Review of Sociology*, *46*(1), 215–232.

Rivera, L. A., & Tilcsik, A. (2016). Class advantage, commitment penalty: the interplay of social class and gender in an elite labor market. *American Sociological Review*, *81*, 1097–1131.

Smith, V. (2001). Ethnographies of work and the work of ethnographers. In P. Atkinson, A. Coffey, S. Delamont, L. Lofland, & J. Lofland (Eds.), *Handbook on ethnography* (pp. 220–233). London: Sage Publishing.

Van Maanen, J. (1991). Playing back the tape: Early days in the field. In W. Shaffirand & R. Stebbins (Eds.), *Experiencing fieldwork: An inside view of qualitative research* (pp. 31–42). London: Sage Publishing.

Van Maanen, J. (2011). *Tales from the field: On writing ethnography* (2nd ed.). Chicago, IL: University of Chicago Press.

Wehner, J., & Gilmartin, S. (2022). A systematic approach to site anonymization in case study research. Paper presented at the American sociological association annual meeting, August 7, Los Angeles, CA.

INDEX

Printed and bound by CPI Group (UK) Ltd, Croydon, CR0 4YY

12/12/2023

08206422-0001